004

WILL WE SEE TOMORROW?

WILL WE SEE TOMORROW?

A German Cavalryman at War, 1939-1942

Max Kuhnert

LEO COOPER

LONDON

First published in 1993 by
LEO COOPER
an imprint of
Pen & Sword Books Ltd
47 Church Street, Barnsley, South Yorkshire S70 2AS

Copyright © The Estate of the Late Max Kuhnert 1993

ISBN 0 85052 290 0

A CIP catalogue record for this book is available
from the British Library

Typeset by Yorkshire Web, Barnsley, South Yorkshire
in Plantin 10 point
Printed by
Redwood Books,
Trowbridge, Wiltshire

CONTENTS

PUBLISHER'S NOTE

It is unusual—and possibly undesirable—for a publisher to provide the introduction to a book. The justification, in this case, is the author's untimely death, which inevitably left a number of questions unanswered.

Max Kuhnert died from leukaemia, quite suddenly, in the summer of 1990, not long after he had heard that *Will We See Tomorrow?* had been accepted for publication. He was a month past his seventy-third birthday. There died with him not only, as the Epilogue states, his record of what happened to him between the end of this narrative and his capture by the Americans in September 1944, but also the answers to some of those questions. Most of these are relatively minor—spellings of names of people and places, the subsequent fates of characters briefly mentioned, some technical military terms (especially those relating to German cavalry units, which in Kuhnert's war seem to have been untypically flexible), and so on. To some of these questions answers, now, can simply no longer be found, while patient detective work, and the help of the author's family and his agent, have answered many others. The occasional remaining gaps in no way detract from the interest of the account.

Where possible, 'modern' spellings of Russian place-names have been used. But at various times after the war, and now, after the break-up of the former Soviet Union, some names may have been changed yet again (it is worth remembering that what was founded as St Petersburg was first renamed Petrograd, then Leningrad, and has now reverted to St Petersburg. And that is a big city, the centre of all the revolutionary movements from 1825 to 1917, and a famous battleground). In addition, some of the places in Russia where Max Kuhnert served have vanished: hard fighting, and the scorched-earth policies adopted by both sides, saw whole hamlets, and even villages, wiped off the face of the earth. Even some French villages have suffered name-changes since 1940.

Max Kuhnert did not talk of his war. It was only when his family read the typescript of this book that they came to know of what had befallen him between 1939 and 1942. He seems to have written it alone, in spare moments, and without help from a native English-speaker. His English must have been excellent, but his original text does at times read as though he had translated it himself from diaries he had written in his first language, German. In particular, he will sometimes employ English words but with a German idiom. In the finished text, some of these phrases and sentences have been altered where it was felt that clarity was affected; otherwise, however, the narrative is substantially as the author set it down. As a result, one of its particular merits is a freshness of writing coupled with a strong feeling of how the man himself thought and spoke.

For all the brilliance of its leadership and organisation, and the advanced state of its technology, the German Army of 1939-1945 was largely horse-drawn. This reliance on animals tended to increase as the war progressed, rather than the reverse; Germany's lack of natural resources (primarily oil and rubber); and intensified Allied bombing of oil and engineering targets, coupled with her growing isolation, kept her army short of wheeled and tracked vehicles, while their replacement became increasingly difficult. Images of German horsed transport are common enough, but the Wehrmacht's cavalry units have largely escaped much attention, in English-speaking countries, at least. *Will We See Tomorrow?* therefore forms a small but significant part of the Second World War's history: a personal narrative by a man who served with cavalry employed very much in one of its traditional roles—reconnaissance—which even by 1939 had generally become the preserve of motorcycles and cars, light armour, and aircraft.

The German Army that went to war in 1939 was unquestionably one of the finest field armies the world has ever seen. It is not, perhaps, surprising, therefore, that the last thirty years or so have seen the emergence, in some British and American books and films, at least, of the 'good German soldier'; that is, one who is not merely a good soldier, but also a moral and honourable man. This concept is at once an admiring and a generous one; it is also possibly an attempt by writers to deal comfortably with the stark fact that, until quite late in the war, German troops were generally more than a match for anything the Allies could range against them. But it also ignores another reality—that many, perhaps most, successful German soldiers of the period were Nazis, and often deeply committed ones, at that. For all his later disillusionment, Rommel, regarded by many as the epitome of the decent German soldier, joined the Nazi Party in 1933.

Max Kuhnert was not a Nazi. Like many of his comrades, he probably regarded them as diseased children, unable to see the truly awesome evil they in fact embodied. He was clearly a good soldier, brave and enduring, and a fine horse-master; he was also a moral and honourable man. When at last he laid down his arms, he was to become a model citizen in the land of his former enemies—though, to him, his adversaries were not enemies but, like himself, soldiers doing their duty. He reserved his enmity for those who killed his friends by what he considered dirty means. The German Army of the Second World War must have contained many thousands, perhaps even hundreds of thousands, of such soldiers. If it is true that by their unquestioning obedience they made Nazism possible, and then, by their soldierly qualities, made the Allies' primary task—the extermination of Nazism—a great deal more costly and arduous, it is also true that they must frequently have acted as a restraining influence upon the worst excesses of the Nazis among them.

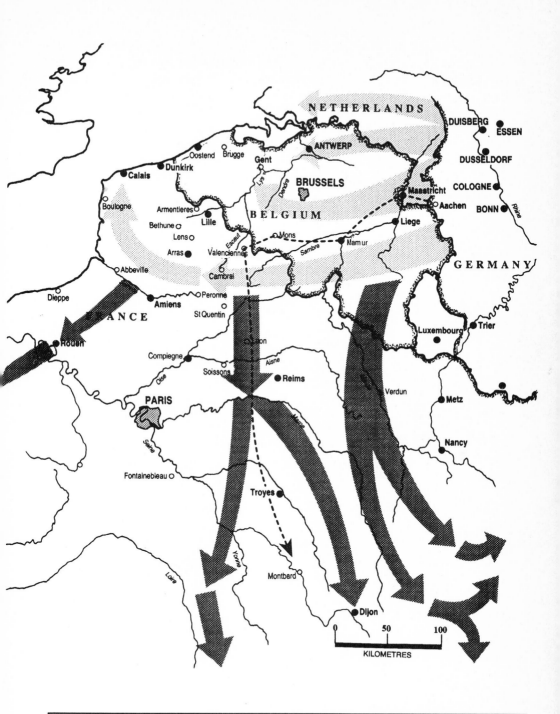

THE GERMAN CONQUEST OF FRANCE
MAY—JUNE 1940, SHOWING THE ROUTE OF
MAX KUHNERT'S UNIT

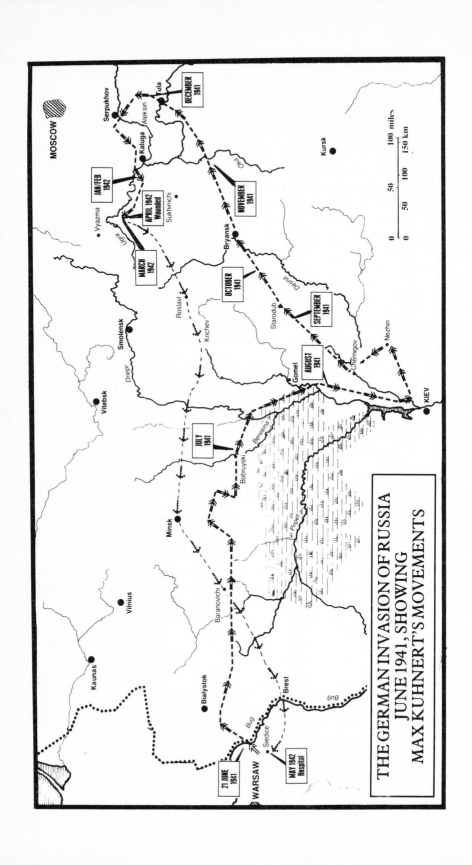

MOSCOW

DECEMBER 1941

Serpukhov
Aleksin
Tula
Kaluga

Kursk

100 miles
150 km
100
100
50
50
0
0

JAN/FEB 1942

APRIL 1942 Wounded
Sukhinichi
Vyazma
NOVEMBER 1941

Oka

MARCH 1942
Ugra
Bryansk

OCTOBER 1941
Desna
SEPTEMBER 1941
Starodub

Roslavl
Krichev
Nezhin

Smolensk
Dnepr
Chernigov
Gomel
AUGUST 1941
KIEV

Vitebsk

JULY 1941
Beresina
Bobruysk

Minsk
Pripet

Baranovichi

Vilnius

Siedice
MAY 1942 Hospital

Brest
Bug

Kaunas

Bialystok
Bug

21 JUNE 1941
WARSAW

THE GERMAN INVASION OF RUSSIA
JUNE 1941, SHOWING
MAX KUHNERT'S MOVEMENTS

INTRODUCTION

The air was full of bullets, shell splinters, grenade fragments and a whole assortment of lethal missiles the majority of which seemed to be aimed at me personally. It was September 1944 and the Americans were driving further and further into Normandy on the flank of the British and Canadian forces. My unit had been broken up and dispersed and I was very much out on my own.

My left leg was out of action with a knee-cap wound. I could only move in a series of hops using a machine-rifle as a sort of crutch. An ambulance a short way from me was suddenly hit by tank fire and burst into flames. As the screams started from inside, I instinctively hopped towards it with some vague idea of at least opening the doors so the wounded men could try to escape.

But I never made it—nor did they. A burst of machine-gun fire came my direction. I was hit below my right knee. An increase in the already furious rate of firing sent a fresh surge of energy through me and I dragged myself across the road by my arms, looking for shelter in a semi-ruined house. I need not have bothered. The cellar was almost full of water and a shellburst set the top part of the building on fire just as I got to it.

The frightening roar of the flames drove me painfully away and I crept behind a small wall. My riding breeches were soaked with blood; I had long since given my first-aid kit to another soldier. I could not walk, and all my comrades were scattered. It was the end of my military career.

Slowly I fumbled the bolt of my machine-pistol out and threw it away. My bayonet whirled across the grass and I began to grope for my stick grenades to get rid of them as well. It was difficult work undoing the stiff clips on my belt and I was rapidly losing interest in the whole affair. A noise differing from the roar of gunfire caught my attention and I looked up to the top of the wall.

American steel helmets capped the heads of two of the blackest men I had ever seen and, for a moment, I forgot all my troubles as I gazed, fascinated, at the first Negro soldiers I had come across. The pair regarded me silently for a moment and then one of them spoke.

'Wounded?' he asked. I guessed at the word but it was close enough to the German *Verwundet* to make it a reasonable guess.

'Yes,' I replied, using one of the very few English words I knew.

1

'OK,' came the reply and then the two men jumped down beside me, removed my grenades and carried me to a field dressing station.

I was a prisoner of war, badly wounded. My comrades were either dead or in the same condition as me. My beloved horses had vanished for ever, but I hardly cared. Hovering on the verge of fainting, my mind drifted back to when it all started.

I was born in 1917 in Dresden, Germany. Dresden is a city divided by the River Elbe; in the south is the old city, and in the north the new one. Dresden was a city of art, museums, beautiful gardens and music.

I left my home town when I was only thirteen to learn my trade as a saddler and upholsterer in the east of Germany. At the age of eighteen I moved to a small town between Hanover and Bremen, right in the heart of the Lüneberg. Two years later, in 1937, I was called up for my compulsory service, to be mustered into the cavalry at Lüneburg. First, however, I served for six months in the *Arbeitsdienst* (labour force), which was also compulsory. This I actually enjoyed. We helped the farmers on the land, cleaned river banks, planted trees and had plenty of sport and fresh air. Most of all, we had comradeship and learned discipline.

In the Army, discipline was very strict, more military. For the first six months it was almost unbearable; we felt that we had lost our identity as slowly but surely we were moulded into soldiers. Politics never entered into it—in fact, no one in the Army was allowed to vote.

So we, the fit young men, become grown-up young men. When war broke out our regiment was dissolved into rider troops to serve in infantry regiments as reconnaissance units. We were incorporated into a mighty war machine, and to a *certain* extent I even enjoyed it. But like millions of other young men all over the world, I was caught up in a war I did not want, and when the shooting started and we saw the first dead soldiers lying on the roadside, then it was too late to turn back. It was then that for the first time, I experienced a new fear, a fear of dying like them, down there in the mud, pale, bloody, the flies crawling all over you. It was only for a second, but it was there, this terrible thought that made me shiver, with its great big question mark looming: 'It could be me...?'

No doubt many young men in those horrible days were also thinking, *Will we see tomorrow?*

1

Who Knows How Soon...

Barracks, Lüneburg, early autumn 1939.
There we were, our energy unlimited, longing for excitement, and filled
with a foolish desire to do something great, especially now that the time had
come to prove oneself. We could all feel it deep down; something big was
going to happen and we—our generation—were privileged. We were told
not by our elders but by our supervisors to be a part of it. It was a kind of
outlet for the energy we had too much of; the smart uniform, the tinkling
of spurs and sabre, all this helped us to walk taller, made us feel more
important, made us put on a get-out-of-the-way demeanour. And, of course,
we were part of a military machine; as my brother Willy said in one of his
letters to me, 'Even a tiny screw is important.' (Not that I felt like a tiny
screw—far from it.) The big wheels were the officers and senior ranks, while
I, at the bottom of the ladder (to change metaphors), was a plain private, or
as it was called in our Cavalry, 'rider'.

Yes, I was Rider Kuhnert of 3 Squadron, Cavalry Regiment 13. Our
barracks were right opposite those of 4 Squadron; they had the tradition of
the Hussars, ours was the Blue Dragoons. We had in our barracks, which
were brand-new and highly modern, a sort of 'Hall of Fame'. On the ground
floor, it had big glass cases containing lifesize dummies wearing the
respective uniforms, standing in the corners. The 'Hall of Fame' was also a
place to assemble the entire squadron, about 180 men, when there was an
announcement of some importance to be made, such as: 'War has been
declared', and 'It is up to us to bring honour to the uniform of our squadron'.
I could not help musing over the enshrined objects, feeling a bit sorry for
those things behind the glass. At least I could move about.

Moving about was indeed what we were doing. The barracks was like an
enormous beehive, all hustle and bustle, Reservists kept coming—manpower
was being brought up to field service strength—and the number of horses
was ever on the increase. Emergency stables were erected in our large riding
school; saddles, bridles, etc., had to be issued to the queues that were
everywhere.

One of the new sergeants in 4 Squadron, Sergeant Dopke, was in charge

3

of a newly formed unit—'Infantry Rider Troop'. Every infantry regiment had a rider troop to make use of in operations; our squadron had been split up into troops of 35 riders, consisting of one officer, one staff sergeant, and three sergeants, each in charge of a unit of ten men. In the way of equipment, each sergeant had one machine-pistol, a sabre and a P38. Each man had a carbine, a sabre and a bayonet. Other equipment included a steel helmet, a tent sheet—which was triangular in shape, for the dual purpose of raincoat, and tent, when three men buttoned their tent sheets together—and a gas mask, which was an infernal nuisance the way it flapped about your back, especially when trotting on horseback. The sabre was carried on the right of the saddle; the carbine was stuck on the left in a carbine shoe and fastened with a stud strap to your belt. We were also each of us responsible for his horse and its equipment.

Of course, we had had these things for quite some time, especially our horses. A comradeship or understanding developed between horse and rider in time, and parting with them was not something we always agreed with very easily. However, those were the orders! 'You will leave all your equipment including your horses etc, and assemble in front of the riding school of 3 Squadron at 11.30 sharp.' So here we were, feeling rather stripped and a bit lost. Officers appeared, orders were shouted, names were called and, in the end, there I was, part of a new unit, the 'Infantry Rider Troop'.

Sergeant Dopke was in front speaking to three other sergeants. One of them we had never seen before, looking also very new in his uniform. His name was Lutze. Another was Sergeant Ruch, a small fellow with brilliant black hair, a barber by trade, who plaited the manes of the squadron horses when there was the need. He came from my own squadron. I never did like him—to me he was always too oily—but he had been in 2 Squadron before the war broke out and I had not had much to do with him. Sergeant Dopke, however, was a different character, taller, with dark short hair, of a slim build, he was a very good horseman. He had kind eyes—the first thing one looks for in a superior—and he was straight to the point: 'Gather round and listen,' he shouted. Then he explained the situation to us in an almost civilian manner after introducing himself. He made it clear that we were shortly to move away from Lüneburg and then left us guessing as to where, why and how, as is always the case in the army. Secret stuff!

Our third sergeant was Sergeant Mauve, a polished blond, soft-spoken, and a walking notebook, whose civilian occupation was accountancy and who became sergeant when at the regimental office during his two years' conscription service.

That night we were to sleep about our stables, leaving our rooms to the Reservists, who had not yet arrived. We had to take all our belongings, while anything that was not on the list had to be sent to our home address.

Tomorrow we were to meet our new Commanding Officer, a lieutenant, and, the most important item, The New Horse. So our quarters from now on were the stables, discipline was considerably lessened, new faces were everywhere, and we were left practically to our own devices, so long as we did what we were told in such matters as packing. Leave for the town was granted and our whole life began to look up. Adventure was at its beginning and we felt great.

My personal belongings, so far as clothing was concerned, I sent home to Dresden. My dress sabre I left with a friend in Lüneburg. Goodness only knows what happened to it. On one side of the blade was engraved my name and unit, on the other there was a saying from Frederick the Great: 'Last Sie Herzen, Lachen, Küssen, wer weiss wie bald Sie Sterben Müssen' ('Let them embrace, laugh and kiss, who knows how soon they will have to die'). Somehow, it was all rather sad, but who cared? A very dull person indeed if nineteen, listed A1, and with nothing to worry about but himself.

Horses were everywhere; we even had some from Sudetenland (Czechoslovakia), many of which were like zebras, with very short or upstanding manes, and biters and kickers—dreadful creatures. We stayed well away from them and hoped that we would not be unlucky enough to get one. But not to worry. After a snatched breakfast, in one of the mess halls, we lined up to meet our new CO. Ours was a Lieutenant Becker. In civilian life, he was a newspaper proprietor in a small town near Lüneburg. My first impression of him was not promising, but on further acquaintance he was not too bad. He looked very smart; of medium height, he had everything just so: highly polished boots, plaited whip, his cap slightly cocked; he also had a sense of humour, mixed with strictness when he spoke to us. It was us he was interested in at the moment. He was canny, only the best was good enough for him and we were, each and every one of the thirty-three of us, to stand in front of him and virtually tell him our life story. There he was, fondling the top button of one or poking his whip at another... he behaved like a father to us and intended to take care of everything. He did not say so, but that is how he made us feel.

Eventually we got our horses. Lieutenant Becker had his specially brought from home. Sergeant Dopke was allowed to keep his old one, Halla, because he had taught her advanced dressage, which he also planned to teach us. So the rest of us, very excited and unsettled, were looking for something special. 'One man, four horses, the rest line up,' Lieutenant Becker shouted. At a given order, everyone was to take the nearest horse and mount. There were no saddles, no bridles, only stable head-collars with ropes. Pandemonium was the only word for it. The ground in front of our riding school was all flying sand in the scramble.

Some of the horses had short manes, most of them were Hanoverian, with a few Trakehners in between. Lovely horses, Lieutenant Becker had seen to that all right. He was half killing himself with laughter, smoking one of his special brand of cigarette in a holder. 'Loosen up your horse,' he spluttered, 'and stop in front of me when I call you.'

This was even more fun, because he did not know our names yet. 'You with the funny ears, come here'—nobody wanted to. In the end it was Old Fatty, as we already called him, a farmer's boy of enormous size. Bing Crosby had nothing on him in terms of his ears. 'Hmm, how do you like him?' He indicated a black Hanoverian gelding. 'Fine, Herr Leutnant.' 'Good, keep him.' '*Jawohl*, Herr Leutnant,' replied Müller (Fatty).

This went on for some time, and eventually I too had a new horse, a lovely little mare, about 15.3 hands high, six years old; her name was Quinta, and we took to each other like old friends. Saddle fittings took a little longer. I also had, from now on, two curb chains in my pocket, one for my own horse and one for Sergeant Dopke's (for I was given the honour of taking care of his horse as well as mine). To keep your curb chain in your pocket served two purposes—it did not get stolen, and it burnished itself.

Halla, the Sergeant's horse, also a mare, was about a year or two older than Quinta, a lighter brown in comparison to Quinta's almost black brown. Both horses were of good character, with no vices, as far as I could see. If anything, I liked Halla better; she was a strong, eager horse with a well-balanced gait, while Quinta, although willing enough, needed a great deal of schooling. Both horses were excellent jumpers, with big hearts, as we found during our first exercise as a new unit the next day.

Lüneburg is situated in the middle of heathland, great for riding, with endless stretches of sandy terrain and plenty of natural obstacles such as ditches, fallen trees, embankments. Wooded areas were plentiful too—in fact, it was the perfect place for horse and rider, which is probably why our regiment moved there from Hanover in the first place. Lieutenant Becker, we saw on that first exercise, was not a bad horseman. His horse was a bay mare about seven years old and 15.3 hands high. Her name was Püppchen ('Little Doll') which suited her personality to the ground. She seemed to me rather too lively a creature, not bad looking but she walked stiffly as if she had high-heeled shoes on; maybe it was his fault, because he kept on turning her round, inspecting his newly acquired outfit from every angle, shouting corrections here and approvals there and, in general, making everybody rather nervous, as naturally nobody wanted to look a fool on the first day out.

Sergeant Dopke smiled sideways at me—I was next to him as his horse holder—saying nothing but meaning a great deal, for, if anybody knew anything about horse handling it was him. I felt very secure, and greatly appreciated his confidential gesture; interchange of this nature furthered a mutual understanding and was to prove of great value later on.

Time was getting short and as we were a 'green unit' an awful lot of work had to be done to turn us into a fighting-fit troop. We had to get to know each other, finding out abilities and learning one another's characters, to start with. And we had to forget a lot of our previous training, as our job as an infantry rider troop to the Regiment would be entirely different from what we were used to. For one thing, our regiment was now infantry, not cavalry, the 35-strong rider troop being under direct orders from the HQ of the newly formed regiment. Already speculation was buzzing, all sorts of false information kept coming to our ears, and we were, understandably, only too eager to go as far as possible from here as it became more and more unbearable with the arrival of Reservists. We got to know one another gradually, with some ups and downs in the way of likes and dislikes, and came to know one another's capabilities. We found out, for instance, that Sergeant Mauve was not too good at riding. In fact I believe he was actually scared of horses.

On the whole, it was a pretty good outfit. Most of the others were farmers' boys, who received plenty of food parcels from home, but seldom gave anything away, except in return for a service . I was fortunate in my trade as a saddler, for although the regiment had an official saddler, I found plenty of jobs of that sort and most of them paid well. One of those was to fit the tops of the riding boots properly—for payment in advance, of course. If payment was not forthcoming, as in the case of Sergeant Freund of the rider troop next door, I simply removed the small transparent or rawhide strip of leather which was at the back seam of the boots to hold them up, and then finished the job, stitching everything together, minus the strip. Poor old Sergeant Freund, no sooner had he walked off in his boots, admiring the lovely fit, than the boots started to slip down and down, like corkscrews; and he could not come back and complain, because he had never paid, and it was strictly forbidden to make any alterations to equipment without authority: this served as a warning to others.

Somebody once said to me, 'Life is like a swing—one moment you are up and the next you are down', and I was certainly down after we had our sabres sharpened at the blacksmith's; we had never had them sharpened before. Later that day we had sabre practice, which involved cantering with a drawn sabre at a dummy on a post, which in my case was to my right as I approached. You could please yourself which thrust you employed; there was a choice of three—a downward hacking motion, a stab as with a lance, or, as I did (stupidly), you could pull your sabre back over your left shoulder and swipe it to the right, hitting the dummy over its right shoulder. My Quinta was not happy. In fact she shied, giving a startled look at the dummy, snorting and throwing her quarters to the left. My sabre came down and hit her right ear. I could have sunk into the ground in shame and fright when

Quinta shook her head and there was blood everywhere. The names I was called are unmentionable. The vet was very understanding, Sergeant Dopke looked at the ground, Lieutenant Becker tapped his whip thoughtfully on his boots, as if he were seriously considering sending me to the bicycle brigade or something, and the rest grinned or looked sympathetically in my direction. To someone like me, who loved his horse, it was a disaster.

However, I got over it and so did Quinta, minus a bit of her right ear. For days I darkened the bandage around her right ear with coal so that it would not be too conspicuous, and gradually the leg-pulling—such as 'You'd better do this properly or we will cut your ears off'—ebbed away.

At the end of September 1939 things really began to move. It was announced that we were to march to the station Sunday next. (Come to think of it, almost every time we moved it was on a Sunday—very annoying as Sunday was the day you saw your girlfriend, sweetheart or whatever you had.) This left us two days to get everything fixed, packed, collected, to kiss or say *Auf Wiedersehen*. Even our lieutenant got excited and worried—after all, he had the responsibility and from now on he was on his own; he had to make do with what he had in the way of men, equipment and horses, and there was no easy way of getting replacements after we left this place of plenty.

I wrote a letter home, telling my mother not to worry and that I would take care of myself in my own fashion. I told her how much I enjoyed it and how at last we were to see the world. I felt rather brave, like a knight in shining armour off to slay the dragon, leaving the damsel behind. That's a laugh, to start with—I didn't have a damsel, at least not any more, as I am afraid, I had rather neglected Irmgard, my girlfriend, and we had fallen out. I did send her a postcard later on, but never got a reply. Maybe she had found someone else. And we no longer had a proper address, just name, rank and a field/post number which we had to memorise. During the war years those numbers changed as often as we changed units. To reach my brother, for instance, one addressed a letter simply: 'Sgt W. Kuhnert, FPN 15836-B', my number was FPN 39462. How the post found its way to the correct destination, goodness only knows. It was a very complex system, but very efficient.

So, on that Sunday morning we moved in earnest, with full honours—even a band was playing. It was not only us who moved or marched to the station, there were several other units, including rider troops from my old squadron. At last we had found out where we were going. Our end station by train was to be Aachen, on the border of Belgium and Holland.

Quite a few civilians were at the station, mostly relatives of officers. They must have been the only ones to know our departure time. In any case, we were far too busy getting our horses loaded. This we had practised quite often with the squadron when there was a manoeuvre or sharp-shooting exercise away from Lüneburg. There were eight horses per wagon, four on each side, facing each other, with reins stretched across both doors so that the horses could not move forward. Bales of hay were opened to satisfy their appetite, and we took their bits out. One could sit at the centre of the wagon or settle wherever there was room in one of the other carriages; some were reserved for officers, others for equipment.

It was now early afternoon and only small groups of people were at the platform, mostly officers with their wives, sweethearts or friends. I noticed one of the sergeants, Sergeant Lange, standing with his parents and Lieutenant Becker in a small group together. Lieutenant Becker knew that Sergeant Lange, who only became sergeant at the time I was called up, was aiming to become an officer, and we heard later that they were actually distantly related. In any case, Lange was a fine chap, and we all wished him the best of luck.

We arrived early on the next day after stopping several times to get water for the horses, for which a good deal of running to and fro was required, as we used nosebags as carriers. We were dog-tired after little sleep and all the excitement. We unloaded at a small place just outside Geilenkirchen, about 25 kilometres north of Aachen, because there was a ramp, needed for unloading the horses and baggage carts. There were a great many new faces on board, men who had joined us from Hamburg, mainly staff from the newly formed infantry regiment of which we were now a part—from 13 Company, with small field-howitzers, 14 Company (anti-tank), and the Staff Company, consisting of officers directly attached to Regimental HQ, along with saddler, bootmaker, tailor, blacksmith, cooks and so on, and of course the regiment's CO, Colonel von Tchudy.

Our unit, the Rider Troop, was something special as we found out later: in the CO's own words, 'we were a proud asset to the Regiment'.

Beggendorf—a very small village about 25 kilometres north-east of Aachen—was our destination. When we arrived in the late afternoon, everybody was disappointed, practically insulted. It was just not good enough. We, 'the élite on horseback', to be humbled like this. To start with, there were only two inns. The larger was to be the HQ for the regiment and that left us with the tiny one, hardly big enough to hold fifteen people, let alone a whole company. Obviously, nobody wanted to go into the pub where all the officers were. The next disappointments were the sleeping and stabling arrangements. Everyone had been given a card with an address—in my case two cards, one for Sergeant Dopke and one for myself—but there were simply too many soldiers in a small place, and already we were hoping that we would move to a more suitable place near Aachen. However, we had to make the best of it and maybe it was not too bad after all. This was a new experience for us.

So, armed with two cards and two horses, and unshaven, because we simply had had no chance to shave, I walked down to the village, leading Halla on my right and Quinta on my left, staring now and then at my card and at the houses. I eventually reached the bottom of the road where, before a right-hand bend, I came upon several people standing about, as it was a Monday night and still early. They had never seen soldiers so close before and it must have caused quite a stir in that small secluded place to be swamped with such a field unit, and horses as well. For us, too, it was strange; coming as we were to a different part of the country, everything seemed to us almost foreign. Maybe it was because we were tired and hungry after this most strenuous journey from Lüneburg, and also we had been expecting a larger place, somewhere of more importance than just a small village. Things began to sort themselves out quite quickly, however, and after some waiting around here and there and a short wash and brush-up in our quarters, we assembled in front of the only pub we could see. Even the weather improved; the miserable drizzle had stopped. And by and by we recovered from the shock of being sent to practically a Siberian outpost. Here we were, in our first wartime quarters.

I stayed with a family called Dreesen—a small farmer, his wife, and two daughters, of fifteen and seventeen; in short, a nice family, very old-fashioned, Catholic like most people in that area. I was invited into the family circle. Sitting at their table was like a holiday compared to barrack life. I only wish I had used my head better and showed more appreciation, especially later. I did not even write a card and I still feel bad about it. My room with its small single bed was upstairs and like all the bedrooms very creaky. It also had the farmhouse tang. I know I never really appreciated the whole situation, otherwise I would have returned, if only to say 'thank you' for their hospitality.

Quartered in Beggendorf besides us of the Rider Troop, were the whole regimental staff—officers, starting with the Colonel and his adjutant, ordnance officers, veterinarians, communications officers and so forth; a very important unit, the field kitchen, with two cooks and their helpers, all horsedrawn; and the motorised unit consisting of two motorcyclists with BMWs, and the official staff car for Colonel von Tchudy and the adjutant.

As I have already mentioned, there were two inns in the village, one occupied by the officers' HQ, which had to be guarded night and day, and the other, on the other side of the village, which had only two rooms and was far too small, for the rest of us. A complete washout, we felt, especially as we were not allowed to leave the village; what were we going to do?

For fourteen days we had nothing but inspections of quarters, horses and equipment, and many exercises to get to know the surrounds of Beggendorf. These things took care of our time, day and night. Not only were we fed up with the reduced freedom, we were also very tired. At least twice a week we had night alert practice and had to take everything with us—every single item we possessed had to be shown when we were notified of an alert, which was not always in good time. The gate of the farm where I had my quarters was well and truly locked at night. So when the despatch rider arrived on his motorbike, he could not get in the yard and had to stand in the road, throwing stones at my window and shouting until I eventually woke up. Our procedure was as follows: first, get dressed; then grab your personal equipment, like your rifle; stuff everything else inside the saddle bags; then thunder down the corridor and stairs, yawn, wake everybody in the house, wake yourself up by bumping your head on the doorpost, which is too low, stagger towards the stable on the other side of yard. Then undo the old-fashioned catch on the stable door and find your way to the horses (remember I had two, Halla and Quinta); there was a light there, but only very dim and one could hardly see anything—in any case, too much light was not allowed: after all, it was an 'alert'. Thank goodness, I had myself well organised—bridles, saddles and everything else were well laid out and it took very little time to get the horses ready. Then I led them out into the yard, leaving them, their reins looped over the old-fashioned trough, got the enormous key for the front gate—this hung inside on the doorpost, the one I always knocked my head on—got out into the road, four houses down the front gate, first right, then left, turning round the house, first window and make an enormous racket (that was the order).

Always when Sergeant Dopke saw my face, he would say, 'Yes, what is it?' as if he did not know. I would shout, 'Alert—I come with the horses in a second.' Back I would run leaving the gate wide open, and mount Quinta, take Halla on my right, and off I would go to meet Sergeant Dopke. By this time he would be ready—after all, he only had himself to think about. Off we would go down the road, and assemble, as always, in front of the HQ. It turned into a race between the units as to which would be the first to arrive. It took another 20-25 minutes before the whole outfit was ready to march.

Everybody would be there—as well as the Rider Troop, the whole regimental staff was there, including communications people (we called them 'wire pullers'), 13 Company with their howitzers, all the officers, including Colonel von Tchudy, Captain Mauve, Lieutenant Becker; and the *tross*, the baggage-train—cooks, kitchen personnel, saddler, tailor, bootmaker, etc.

At the pub, there would be a spot check of possessions—as I said, we had to take everything, including such things as dripping washing off the clothes line. It was bad luck on anyone found to have left something behind: a points system still existed, and it meant extra guard duty, usually on a Sunday. Officers' NCOs were not exactly in a very good mood—after all, alerts were almost always at about two or three in the morning, and by the time we got back to our quarters, it was nearly time to get up for a day's duty. So one could not expect a lot of mercy from them if things went wrong. I must say, I was very highly favoured by Sergeant Dopke; in fact, I could hardly do anything wrong. It did not make me slack; on the contrary, it spurred me on to do even better. It became embarrassing, though, when I was pointed out as a good example... too bad the whole thing went wrong.

Army life means a busy life—in other words, an idle soldier is only half a soldier—that is the policy in any army. So plenty of extra work was invented and the results then inspected—such as stable and equipment cleaning. In my case it was not too difficult, since unlike the others, who were in small groups of five or six I was on my own in Mr Dreesen's barn. I had plenty of room for initiative. First I swept the barn floor, then I got a pair of ladders, placed them on two bales of straw and put all the tack neatly on top. Then I pulled the horses out into the yard, groomed them thoroughly, gave my rifle a final wiping over, then I cleaned myself up and by the time the inspection committee arrived, everything was in splendid order.

The committee consisted of all the sergeants and, to my surprise, Lieutenant Becker. My little construction seemed to impress everybody—I could see Sergeant Dopke grinning—in fact, he gave me a wink, which meant 'You'll do all right'. Twenty minutes later, after they had left, a despatch rider on motorbike arrived and told me to report at once to HQ. I got to the officers' inn to find the whole Rider Troop assembled there, and I was told to lead the lot to my place and show them what a neat arrangement of equipment should look like. I was a bit shaky, since it was my first time to command a large troop. You had to march beside them and shout orders correctly, and maintain the correct distance. I was, as they say, over the moon.

Well, everything went smoothly, turn left, platoon hold, right turn, straighten out, and then I reported to Lieutenant Becker. 'Order carried out, Rider Troop present at Rider Kuhnert's quarters.' Lieutenant Becker told Sergeant Dopke to take over, make a little speech and explain why they were there. Then, disaster— when I opened the door of the barn, there were no ladders, no equipment and no clean barn floor. Mr Dreesen, assuming that the inspection was over, had pulled everything into one corner, and put the ladders up to get hay from the loft. Dust was everywhere, everything was a mess. I could have sunk into the ground, and so I am sure, could Sergeant Dopke. The others grinned, Lieutenant Becker laughed; explanations did nothing to help, it was a black day for me. The worst thing was that I could not blame anyone, not even myself.

2

At Frau Schroten's

Alsdorf was our next destination, a lovely town, only ten miles along the road to Aachen. It started as one of the much-practised alerts, and that's all we thought it was—but this time we actually marched off, to arrive at Alsdorf at about 4.30 a.m. I remember that it was on a Sunday morning. If there was one thing that the regiment staff were good at, it was keeping things secret from us, so *Sunday* again ... oh well, we felt, it was no good getting mad.

Most of us left our wet washing behind. Transport was practically non-existent, except the odd borrowed bicycle. However, it was not very important, because now started a period of marvellous events, to which I often like to look back. It was the end of October, where frosty nights were no exception. Frau Schroten—a lovely woman, petite and rather plump—her husband, a semi-invalid (he had miner's disease—dust in the lungs), and little Willy, six years old, were to become my new family: I was privileged to be welcomed into it. Our stable, in what used to be a coal merchant's, was only 200 metres away, and had room for about six horses. In the same yard was the Rider Troop office. Regimental HQ was a mile towards the other side of town— in fact Alsdorf stretched the length of one road about three miles long. We were based at the east end of it.

Downstairs at Mrs Schroten's was Lucy, a lovely girl of eighteen, working in her mother's hairdressing salon. The first time we met was the very day I arrived. I was tired from all the hustle and bustle of trying to get organised. She was standing at the bottom of the stairs watching what was going on, and as I went past her, instead of taking one step at a time, I took two and promptly fell flat on my face. (Mind you, I had my equipment including saddlebags, over my arm.) She was in hysterics of laughter, and I eventually joined in, sitting rather bewildered at the bottom of the stairs.

Frau Schroten rescued me, picking up some of my stuff, and asked, 'Are you hurt, my boy?' which only made the laughter worse for Lucy. Her mother then came on to the scene, a very attractive platinum blonde, and told Lucy off for being so unladylike, so that made us even for the time being.

Frau Schroten was marvellous, a mother to me; it was just like another world for me, very homely. She treated me as if I had just returned from the war, and helped me to take my boots off—I looked like a kid in those days. It was very late that night before I got into bed.

The problem with horses is that they need looking after, so a rider's time is only half his own. The next morning we assembled early in front of our office where there was a nice convenient square. Many things had to be sorted out in respect of future alerts and exercises. Sergeant Dopke's quarters were half a mile along the high street, upstairs in an inn called Die Traube, or, in English, The Bunch of Grapes; his horse Halla was with my Quinta next door to the office. Regimental HQ was at a large restaurant called, ironically, Friedenshof (Court of Peace), half a mile further on from the Traube. Alsdorf was a paradise for any pubcrawler.

Next door to our office was a large room suitable for the issuing of instructions and *Waffenappell* (arms inspection). So there was no escape from the stringent rules of army life. Nevertheless, the cosy quarters compensated for it well. Even when we had our first alert in Alsdorf it was child's play because Frau Schroten insisted on helping me get ready for it, repeating over and over again, 'You poor boy, in the middle of the night—I have a good mind to go and give them something to remember,' and insisting that I have a cup of coffee first, before I charged the half-mile up the road to let Sergeant Dopke know what was at hand, and then ran all the way back, trying to catch up with the others who had nobody to think of but themselves. (Well, there was Berens who also had to look after two horses, his own and Sergeant Lange's, but he was in a different stable.) By the time I had arrived home from our masquerade, Frau Schroten was sitting in the kitchen waiting for me, as if I were a lost sheep.

'I kept your bed warm with a hot-water bottle,' she said. It was one of those stone ones, very handy indeed. What more could one ask? I helped her as much as I could in the house, fetching coal from the cellar, getting the washing in, turning the wringer, doing the washing up, and so on. She seemed only too pleased to have me around. One way she had of keeping me in the house in the evening was to invite Lucy from downstairs—we all had the most marvellous games together. Mind you, nothing out of place, but nevertheless, it formed the basis of a deeper friendship, especially with Lucy. It was great fun when we played 'matchboxes'. You had to take the top of the box and place it on your nose, then transfer it on to the nose of your partner without dropping it; putting it on to Lucy's nose took a long time, as you can imagine.

Saturday night was bath night. For me too, because Frau Schroten insisted, so out came the bath from behind the curtain in the hall, a great zinc bath. It was filled up with hot and cold water—'and it's all yours,' she said. Believing myself to be all on my own, I really enjoyed it, till I

15

could hear the whispers and giggles from behind the kitchen door. The two devils had been looking through the keyhole for quite some time. Then I put a flannel over it—but it was all in good fun; I shall never forget it.

We in the Rider Troop never discussed war or politics in our quarters, and neither were these topics ever mentioned at Frau Schroten's. We would hear now and then on the radio that skirmishes had taken place in the west, near Kaiserslautern or thereabouts, and that was all. We once had a long patrol with the whole troop along the Dutch border, and not wishing to have any contact with the Dutch, we went along very carefully so as not to stray over the border. I had never met a Dutch soldier in all my life and bore no grudges against anyone. I remember our squadron's CO had an English wife, and when England declared war on Germany on 3 September 1939, and we were all assembled in the 'Hall of Fame' we all thought how awful the major must be feeling about it. Now, since we had moved down here, nearer the border, I personally was not keen any more to cross the border, telling myself how silly it all was.

The whole regiment, except for a few on guard duty, went to the large cinema in Alsdorf and watched the film, *Rose Marie*. It was of course in German, and we were told that despite England's declaration of war on Germany, America was still friendly with us.

The French I did not like, but only because of my class teacher, Herr Bösenberg, who told us all sorts of stories about what had happened in the First World War. But we were nowhere near France at the moment, in fact we were nice and snug in the corner of Holland, Belgium and Germany, living it up in Alsdorf.

Fourteen days went by before I could muster up the courage to ask Lucy for the evening out. It was the first snow and it really came down, so she took her toboggan along and showed me the more pastoral side of Alsdorf. I found out what a lovely person she was. It was late when we returned this evening, exhausted but happy. Frau Schroten gave me a long questioning look with concern in it—I think even some jealousy was involved. A cup of cocoa, however, made us all happy friends again.

The following day it was pouring with rain and there was mush everywhere after the snow. Exercising our horses was no fun at all. Everything got wet and dirty, and we spent hours cleaning and drying our equipment. Night exercise had been forecast for a long time and no one was looking forward to it. It came on 15 December—as an alert, of course. What a mess, and to make matters worse, the frost had returned and the place was like a skating rink. Sixteen studs had to be screwed into the shoes of Quinta and Halla. The terrain was completely unknown to us and we were only allowed to whisper. We were not even sure if it was an exercise or the real thing, but Sergeant Dopke murmured to me, 'Not this time'; in fact, had it been the real thing we would have been given live ammunition for our rifles. So far we had only been issued with blanks.

The Sergeant kept addressing me as Corporal Kuhnert and I was surprised, thinking surely he could not make this mistake so often; then he told me, in confidence mind you, that I was indeed promoted to corporal, and it would be announced when we got back from the exercise in the morning. Just as he'd said, on our return, Rider Berens and I were told to step forward. It was indeed a great day, to have it announced in front of everybody, 'Promoted to Corporal.' 'Get your stripes sewn on at once,' was the order, 'and report back to the office.' 'Oh, blast it' I thought, as I also had to get two horses back to the stable and clean them up, etc. I sewed the stripes on myself as I was faster than Frau Schroten. She was in tears and repeated over and over again, 'I knew you would, you are such a good boy.' I just hugged her and gave her a great big smacker. Now, I was Corporal Kuhnert and I felt ten feet tall. The cold shower came with the order, 'You are in charge of the guard at the Regiment's HQ.' Just for a night and a day. As corporal, I had to report and detail the rest of the men right through the day and night and just after a night exercise. Thank goodness we were fit in those days. At about 2200 hours, who should appear at the entrance to the HQ but Frau Schroten—with a pot of hot soup. 'I thought you could do with it,' she said. 'It is such a cold night and you didn't have any sleep last night, Max—somebody has got to look after you. And Lucy sends her love. Willy is practising with his clock.' I had cut a clock face from cardboard with all the numerals on it, and two hands on the front held by a cork on the back, to teach the little boy to tell the time. 'Herbert hopes you are all right.' (Herbert was her husband.)

Well, what was I to do? I just thanked her and took it into the office and we, all eight of us, had a feast and were very grateful for it. Dear Frau Schroten, what a heart of gold she had. She was still waiting outside hoping to keep me company, but of course it was improper for a soldier especially on guard duty. It was impossible to make Frau Schroten understand this, bless her.

Now the snow was very deep—mind you, nothing like I had to experience in Russia later on, but enough to make life very difficult. We had to exercise the horses—one man to four horses—and no gloves were allowed. 'Put your gloves in your pockets, you are too soft. Besides, how will you handle your guns if you muffle yourselves up like girls?' Yet the officers had their hands in their pockets when they were shouting their silly orders.

One horse on the left, two on the right and hope for the best. Right across the ploughed or open terrains, some got stuck in the ditches that were full to the brim with drifting snow. A few horses returned without their riders. How marvellous it was when it was time to go home.

I very seldom ate in the field kitchens as Frau Schroten insisted that I ate with them, and she refused any help from me in the way of food. One morning I really put my foot in it with Quinta. It was my custom to save some bread and give it to her when I got into the stable first thing in the morning. This particular morning I only had a sandwich with some sausage meat and I offered it to her. I was very lucky to get out from between the beams—she really went for me, her hoofs up, snarling and trying to bite me; I did not know what hit me. All day long I just could not get near her—thank goodness there was nothing on that day. She simmered down eventually, but we never were really good friends again as before. I used to hold a piece of sugar between my lips and very carefully she would take it from me, but not any more, as if the trust had gone from between us; very sad. I had other horses during the war — in fact I lost four—and I was careful never to try sausage sandwich on them.

I never was one for going to the pub, and as there was nothing much to do in the evenings, I usually went out with Lucy and her toboggan. Sometimes we met other soldiers from our troop or staff, and plenty of nice girls too. Ilse, a short, very attractive brunette, also had a toboggan. So we all took it in turns to go up and down, as there were plenty of hills, not too big, but big enough to have fun on. I took Ilse home the first evening. She lived with her parents a mile and half on the other side of town. Lucy did not mind as she lived around the corner. In the daytime, Ilse was employed as a manageress in a grocery store, near to where I was staying. So the following evening I collected her there to take her home and it developed into a routine unless something came in between. Her parents were very nice, though unfortunately her father was deaf and we had to shout if he wanted to know what we were saying. Quite often I had supper there.

We had the regimental dance on a Saturday a week before Christmas and a day before I was to go on leave to Dresden to see my mother and sister. I looked forward to it so much. The dance was a happy affair. Our old Colonel von Tchudy was swinging his legs on the dance floor and we were entertained by well-known singers and dancers. We were ordered to take our spurs off as it was getting too dangerous on the dance floor and stockings were expensive in those days. Ilse was there with her parents at the same table as Lieutenant Becker. We were encouraged to invite girlfriends. Lieutenant Becker had two of course, and little did I know what a headache I was going to get from them later on.

It was a great day for me, 22 December 1939. For the first time wearing a greatcoat and a corporal, only a small bag, no need for a sabre, only a side-arm as our sabres were far too hefty to carry on your side. It was a very long journey to Dresden from Aachen; the sandwiches and cake from Frau Schroten helped a great deal.

It was so lovely to be back home in Dresden; what a beautiful city it was. Pity it was cruelly destroyed later on in the war. My mother lived on her own, as my parents had separated when I was fourteen. Willy, my brother, the one I looked up to, was not there—he was with his regiment in Landshut in Bavaria, having returned there after the Polish campaign. Kurt, my eldest brother, was somewhere about in the town as he was still a civilian, and my sister was happily married and also living in Dresden. I went to see her the day after I arrived. One week's leave went only too fast, and saying goodbye is never very easy, especially in those uncertain days. I felt some sense of foreboding about my home town; somehow I felt much older suddenly and I was only twenty-two. I did not see Dresden again until about thirty years later.

My sister Lotte gave me for my journey a large piece of 'Dresdener Christollen', a cake loaf, baked with currants, almonds, and so on, very famous, still today.

Train journeys gave one plenty of time to think and it was a long day, changing twice before I was in Aachen. From then on it was only a bus ride to Alsdorf and back into the old routine. I thanked God I had a nice place to come back to.

3

A Man of Many Needs

It came as a shock to all of us in the regiment to learn that yet again we were to move. Only about seven miles, to Wurselen which was nearer to Aachen. Wurselen was a small place, smaller than Alsdorf, and not very interesting.

The day we moved out of Alsdorf, most of the population were standing at the roadside to see us off, and we saw many moist eyes; we were very much liked there and had made many friends. Poor Frau Schroten was heartbroken, but I promised to come and see her often as possible. Lucy was in tears—'You can just about walk it—or get a bike. But come you must.' And as for Ilse, she really was down. I'm afraid she had been far too serious about me. The weather did not help raise anybody's spirits. It was practically a blizzard all the way, and nothing was really organised.

Only the Rider Troop and a few from the regimental staff were to stay in Wurselen, where I was billeted with Rider Leiner. The rest marched into Aachen, only three miles further west.

I was to take charge of Lieutenant Becker's horse besides mine. Halla was now with Sergeant Dopke and Rider Gerlich was to look after her. 'After all, you are now a corporal,' I was told. Every day I had to saddle Lieutenant Becker's horse and mine and we rode out together; when he was not there I had to ride his horse myself, leading mine and his dog Morris, a boxer, very beautiful and obedient. There was only one snag with Morris—his poor paws could not stand up to the frost and snow; they became very sore indeed, and so every morning, before setting out for our morning ride, I rubbed plenty of Nivea cream into his pads, and again when we returned. Our stable, which was separate from that of the rest of the rider troop, housed Püppchen, Quinta, and Lieutenant Becker's second horse, Paladin, a four-year-old gelding. He was a splendid-looking bay, but very naughty sometimes, as I found out when we had our horse inspection. There had been a thaw the day before and the ground was very messy; the inspection took place on a large square, 50 x 50 metres, which was black with masses of coal dust intermingled with sleet, and puddles everywhere. I had to get all three horses ready, which was no easy task, and there was only a short time allowed for this. The Veterinary Officer, Lieutenant Becker and all the sergeants were lined up, and one by one the horses were led in front of them for inspection. Name and rank, then the name of the horse had to be called out. I was still in the stable waiting for my turn. Paladin in his head collar, was standing in his place, and I thought how smart he looked. Then he dropped a pile of dung. Well, I have just time, I thought, to clear it away. I took a sponge, and, not wanting to make my boots dirty, I stood away from Paladin and lifted his tail to clean his dock. Then a hoof hit me like a sledgehammer, right on the left side of my chest. I flew back, and landed half-sitting on a bale of straw, gasping for air. It seemed like half an hour before I could breathe again and I was holding my chest in pain. Someone called my name, so I limped over and led Paladin out in front of the vet.

Lieutenant Becker pointed with his whip at my chest. 'What is that?' There was a nice big hoof-print on my nice clean white drill coat. Not thinking I said, 'He just kicked me when I wanted to clean his dock.' 'Did he now?' As he said so, he touched Paladin on his quarters rather hard. Paladin took off and I held on for dear life, round and round we went. The more they shouted advice, which I could not hear anyway, the faster he went. Eventually he slowed down. What a sight I was, and what a mess, black from top to bottom; and my chest was aching. The horse was filthy too. It just was not my day. Later on I went to see the doctor, but he said I had nothing broken, just badly bruised. Nevertheless, it was very painful. As for Paladin, I had learned my lesson there. Talk gently, approach slightly from the side and lean on his quarters when you lift the tail to clean.

Frost had returned and snow was again in the air. We had several exercises, but alerts did not come about. Maybe it was because most of the regiment were in Aachen. On the following Saturday I decided to risk it and borrow a bike—after all, it was only about seven miles to Frau Schroten's.

Oh, what a welcome. Lucy came upstairs and it was questions all round. Have you got everything? Nothing short? Are you sure?

Another unit had moved into Alsdorf, infantry. An older chap, a Reservist, now slept in my old bedroom. They made it plain it was not the same. The evening went by very fast, nobody had noticed that snow was coming down in buckets. What was I to do? They had only the one bedroom, a little box room for Willy, and my old room, in which the other soldier was.

Frau Schroten had the answer. At first I was embarrassed, but Herbert her husband said, 'It is quite all right, my boy, not to worry, you can sleep on my left and Emma on my right.'

I laughed, it was the first time I had heard her first name. 'Very funny,' she said and kicked me. Thank goodness, I thought, it was Sunday the next morning and I could more or less take my time. Maybe even the snow will disappear by then. Nothing happened in the night, except a lot of snoring on my right. No lights were switched on, so as not to embarrass anyone or make anyone laugh.

Next morning I was by myself in bed. Frau Schroten and Herbert had crept out silently some time before to see to breakfast. The snow was very deep indeed, so it was a seven-mile march for me, pushing the bike through it. Promising to come again soon, I cheerfully set off for Wurselen. Inside though I was far from cheerful. It was the last time I ever saw Alsdorf or anyone from there. But forget them I never shall. Kindness, hospitality, and friendship could not be better anywhere. I wrote now and then, and once got a very nice letter from Frau Schroten, telling me all about her family and the goings on in and around Alsdorf.

I arrived in better spirits, before lunchtime. I had not been missed, thank goodness. Rider Leiner had known where I was and had been prepared to cover for me should someone have asked about me. I would have done the same for him. And he had fed and watered my three charges.

The weather really settled in and it snowed practically every day. We had great fun riding in the ups and downs of Wurselen, a new kind of manoeuvring. Everything was white, so one could not only see further, but it was also easier to be spotted, especially by other horses. Did you know that a horse can see objects about seven times further than any humans? Also a horse has a homing instinct, so if you got lost, the horse could take you home quite easily. Those qualities saved me many times later on, when I was a scout in Russia.

Weekends were always quite peaceful, mainly because the officers had quarters and friends in Aachen town. We had, of course, an office with a guard post and a sergeant on duty. I had to report one Saturday afternoon to Lieutenant Becker, who was sitting in the office in a large armchair, as always, with his plaited whip beating his boots. 'Ah, Kuhnert,' he said, 'you are just the man. Colonel von Tchudy, myself and several other officers are invited tonight to a good friend's house. So, would you like to attend?' That 'would you like' meant of course 'you will'. I did not mind, it was a challenge, in fact it was quite a compliment. After all, private parties of this kind needed someone who knew what he was doing and I had been for several weeks an attendant in Lüneburg Officers' Casino. The friend's house was on the outskirts of Aachen, an enormous bungalow situated in parkland. Besides myself there were four other attendants from different units. A clean uniform, well polished boots and of course perserverance in serving all the goodies was all one needed. I had to prepare a large punchbowl with white wine, spirits and herbs and also plenty of ice. The only setback was the

Max Kuhnert, in his uniform as a scout in the German cavalry, exercising Colonel von Tchudy's horse, Nachbar, in 1940.

With his beloved Siegfried, the horse he rode during much of his time in Russia. He was distraught when Siegfried, standing right by him, was hit by a Russian mortar bomb and died almost in his arms. 'I had always relied on him in a thousand and one situations. I had cried on his shoulder when I was in despair, and he had even made me laugh at some of his antics . . . he had been my best friend.'

highly polished parquet floor. It was like an ice rink, and it was not easy to balance ten glasses on a tray and serve them in turn according to rank, running to and fro. Several ladies were present, but most of them were older and respectable.

Later I heard that this good friend was a Dutch businessman—but it was not the business of a small fish like me.

We—the other attendants and myself—enjoyed ourselves very much, and how I got home that night through the snow, with two bottles of the best outside and quite enough inside, I shall never know. I went straight over the fields, to cut not only the distance, but to keep away from anyone military. It would not have looked too good, to say the least.

A week later, at two o'clock on a Sunday morning, I was rudely called to the office, where, wiping the sleep out of my eyes, I listened to Sergeant Stache: 'Corporal Kuhnert, get four horses ready and report to the Sun.' (The Sun was a more refined public house, with a dance floor.) He explained that Lieutenant Becker had telephoned. 'Take Püppchen, Quinta and two from troop one, quieter horses.' This lieutenant of ours was getting out of hand. Thank goodness it was not icy, but quite deep snow. It saved me from having to screw studs into the horses' shoes. Eventually I arrived, still fuming at the cheek. What a difference from last Saturday. Lieutenant Becker came out with two lady friends, and I was startled by one of the ladies, who had been at the private party of the week before and recognised me, saying, 'Ah, there's the handsome little boy from last week. Will you help me up? I have not been riding since I was very little.' She had an evening dress on and at first I could not find her leg to give her a lift. There was some shrieking going on, because the other one also was no expert. What a show-off Lieutenant Becker was, with a cigarette in his long holder, and his faithful whip. I still remember his particular brand of cigarettes—Gold Dollar. He had them specially sent from home.

We proceeded in the direction of Aachen and arrived at, of all places, the International Tournier Ground. It is still used today. But before we got there, we stopped at a small inn and he, without dismounting, knocked at the window and got us all a drink. Amazing man. Several practice jumps were always set up at the Tournier Ground, even in the snow. Maybe someone had left them outside by mistake. Crazy Lieutenant Becker, he led the charge. Well, I did not mind, it was quite light in the snow, but how about the two dolls in evening dress? Quite a sight, they followed him, though how they managed it, I really do not know. They got down—one could not really call it dismounting — and Lieutenant Becker told me to return home without hurrying. 'If you encounter any patrols just tell them you are returning from an exercise from the regiment.' Oh well, that is the lot of a soldier.

23

The ladies' home was nearby, just the other side of the mountain, and presumably they got home safely. I felt, however, that 'one load of manure' for Lieutenant Becker's two ladies was the last straw. Just because I was the only one who knew where they lived, in the middle of the week I had to sit with Lorenz the baggage-cart driver on his cart with a load of the juiciest and smelliest horse manure. To make it more official looking, we were to drive through the middle of Aachen to collect a few items from the army store after we had delivered the stuff to the front garden of the ladies. It was not as simple as it sounds; the garden was at the back and we had to carry everything in baskets through the side entrance. I think we stank more of manure than the manure itself.

'Thank you, fellows,' said one of the ladies, 'and here is something for the journey home,' and she handed us a bottle of three-star cognac. No sooner had we mounted our cart than the top of the bottle came off. It was, we felt, well earned. In town, we pulled ourselves together—after all, we could very easily have been arrested by the MPs because of our dirty appearance, and smelly, half-drunken state.

It was the first time I actually saw Aachen city centre. It is a very old city indeed, and I believe, the home of the Hohenzollern monarchs who ruled the German empire from 1871 to 1918. Many Holy Roman emperors were crowned in the city cathedral. The city is very nicely situated between two mountains and is bordering on Holland and Belgium.

By the time we neared Wurselen on our way home after getting one or two items from the army depots, we were well and truly stoned. A whole bottle of cognac—it had quite a kick.

We moved off at the end of January, going right through the town to reach our next destination. We did not know then that it was to be in the middle of the forest, south of Aachen, very close to the Wolfsberg. Beautiful no doubt in the summer, but not so comfortable in the winter. Lieutenant Becker was promoted to 1st Lieutenant and spent more and more time away from our rider unit. Sergeant Lange was promoted to Staff Sergeant and became acting leader of our unit as he was working his way up to becoming an officer. I was actually the only one in touch with Lieutenant Becker every day. He had quarters in a very exclusive area in Burtschied, the southern part of Aachen, and every day I had to travel into town by tram, or sometimes on horseback, to collect him from his hotel. As soldiers, we had all public transport free, so that was no problem. Sometimes I had to get the Lieutenant out of bed because he had had a late night. He ordered that, if I thought that he was over-sleeping I should make a racket on the small staircase to his door; nine times out of ten he ignored it and I had to take more drastic measures to get him out. Sometimes he was very generous and let me have tickets to a comedy or a concert. The only problem was that the last tram left town at about 10 p.m., and it could mean a seven-mile walk for me through the woods. Since there were also other units stationed in the woods—air force, observers and one or two posts from some infantry units—that was very dangerous: one could easily be mistaken for a Belgian or Dutch, as the border was only about half a mile away.

Our forest quarters were very nice, but, as I said, it was the wrong time to be there. We had a lovely wooden stable built to accommodate all thirty-three horses plus Lieutenant Becker's two. We had two long houses, one for sleeping quarters and one for kitchen and stores, etc.; our toilets and washroom were 50 metres into the woods. Water was laid on specially, so we had no problem with our horses. The routine was quite cruel after we had been spoiled at Alsdorf. Alerts became more frequent, but although no lights were allowed at night, we became so practised and highly organised that it took us almost no time to get ready for marching. Our breeches and boots were always in the right place for us to jump into when there was an alert, and everyone knew exactly what to do. I was the one who warned the troop. As I had to go into town to see Lieutenant Becker or collect the post in the regimental office, and I had many friends there, if there was anything like an imminent alert, I was to get the message back. Lieutenant Becker was all in favour of these arrangements—after all, it was still his unit. Colonel von Tchudy called us his very special troop, and naturally if we were all on time it was satisfaction all round. In our view the only silly thing was that alerts were almost always at the weekends—so that we did not interrupt the city life too much was the excuse.

Lieutenant Becker was a man of many needs; it would not have been too bad if he had left other people alone. He also had the gift of bringing the impossible out of them. When he asked me to make him a small holster for his pistol, he handed me a piece of brown leather. I was not surprised, it was just the sort of thing he would ask. Well, I had to go to the saddler and get all the necessary materials to make him one—needles, thread, some brown studs, and so on—but I managed it. What was impossible was when he wanted me to get the horses right to his doorstep in the morning. His quarters were in the select area of Burtschied, in the middle of Aachen, about five miles outside our area, where our barracks and stables were.

'All right,' I said. 'No problem, sir,' without thinking what it entailed. The horses would be no problem to ride through the town, but I also had to bring Morris his dog along. In the open country, it would not have mattered but I could not let Morris run loose in the town. So I had to put my thinking cap on. A long lead was just no good; although Morris was quite obedient, it was too risky. I decided to try giving Morris a ride on Püppchen. But she didn't want to know, so I decided to put him on Quinta;

she did not mind. Of course, I had to practise first before venturing into the town, with the trams and all the noise. I got both horses ready, then I put Quinta on my right and put one bale of straw next to her and said to Morris, clapping my hand on the saddle, 'Jump, boy,' and he did. I had to laugh, he really looked funny. 'Do you want to hold the reins in your paws?' I asked. He looked quite at home there. Now for the more difficult part: I went round the front and mounted Püppchen ... so far so good. Giving Morris a pat on the head, I said, 'Sit tight, boy, here we go.' I held his collar lightly in case he slipped, but he had a marvellous balance: we rode several times round our quarters and the stables, and he actually seemed to enjoy it. Quinta did not mind a bit.

The excitement mounted. The next morning, the day for the great occasion—actually taking Morris into town—the rest of the rider troop all stood by, wishing me luck and making some fitting remarks. What I would do if a cat ran by, I just did not dare to think. The venture was a great success, though, except for when we arrived at the hotel: Morris knew right away where we were and jumped off, startling Quinta, and ran straight upstairs, barking loudly, which was not allowed in this establishment, wanting to tell his master what a clever boy he was. Lieutenant Becker came downstairs, ready for once. I helped him into his saddle and off we went. Morris was now his responsibility; he swore several times at him, telling him to stay at heel. Eventually he asked, 'How the devil did you manage to get him here?'

'He rode Quinta,' I replied as if it was nothing, he half turned and gave me a sideways look, not quite sure of himself for a change.

'Yes, really,' I said. 'He liked it.'

'Kuhnert, if you are pulling my leg you will regret it.'

So I explained how we did it. He could really laugh, this lieutenant of ours. 'Full marks,' he cried. 'Let's hope he does not get saddle sore.'

I did this three times and then Lieutenant Becker told me to stop, some spoilsport had reported it to regimental HQ and they had ordered that I should stop this 'unmilitary masquerade'—what a pity.

It was now approaching March 1940, and we were having many night exercises as well as alerts. My Quinta let me down. She just did not like to be on her own, away from the troop. Whenever I got an assignment, everybody knew exactly where I was in the forest, because she would neigh ever so loudly. I tried holding her nose, but to no avail. One of the reasons for night exercises was the important one of perfecting complete silence. Any clattering of equipment, as from a sabre or carbine bouncing on a gas mask, could be heard for miles in the still of the forest, at night especially. A neighing horse was nearly as bad. We once saw a patrol, Dutch I think, on horseback, only about fifty feet in front of us; they made an about-turn when they saw us. There were only three of us on this, my first encounter with the 'other side'—but we were not at war with the Dutch, only with the British who were in Holland.

Very suddenly we had orders to move, this time to the other side of Aachen, the west side, not too far from the Schneeberg (Snow Hill), to a disused farm, which we found very primitive; cowsheds were converted into stables by hanging beams in between horses. At least, the snow had all but disappeared, remaining only in some parts as a slush. There was one farmhouse, still occupied by the owner's sister, an elderly spinster who was very nice and offered to do our washing. Our food we had to collect from a nearby nunnery. The sisters were very kind but expressed quite openly their disagreement with soldiering or war. It all seemed rather odd to me because, from what I knew about Hitler, he was a Roman Catholic himself. Many a time I thought about those things, but always gave up in the end. I considered politics and religion none of my business. I was brought up a Lutheran, and that only because of my family, especially my mother. Deeper thoughts never came to me in those days, not until later on when the war began in earnest for me. At that moment we had far too many duties to perform up and down the line. And for all that rumours were circulating all the time about what was going to happen, our immediate preoccupations were more basic. Our clothing, for one thing, was beginning to wear thin, and it was not easy to get replacements. Besides, once you had a nice pair of fitted riding boots, you did not like to change them; I got soles for mine and did the stitching myself—I still carried tools with me, some of which I had bought off Lehman, the saddler.

And, of course, we had our riding. There was a lovely meadow right behind our farm, just right for elementary dressage. We had missed that in the forest. Sergeant Dopke really put us through our paces. We all considered him the best rider in the troop—even Lieutenant Becker took notice of him. How pleased I was when he offered me some extra lessons because since I was away most of the day, sometimes without horses, I missed out on all other activities during the day. I had a longer way to travel to Burtschied, with Lieutenant Becker's horse on a leading rein, where I had to meet the Lieutenant every other day; and then we went off together to the outskirts. Thank goodness, from now on he had Morris in his quarters, otherwise it would have been chaos.

4

A Bit of Bad Luck

It was promotion time again and everyone was whispering, 'Who is going to be lucky?' Since I had access to the regimental office and brought the post home every night, I was continually being asked questions, and I decided to get my own back on Full Corporal Fischer. He was a Reservist and was just about the oldest member of our outfit. He was also a proper nana—I could tell him anything and he would believe it. The devil got in me and I said in a very important whisper when I got back that night, 8 May, that he was on the promotion list. Well, after all, he was a full corporal, and also the oldest, so it was time he became a sergeant. 'You may as well start to celebrate,' I said.

'Don't be silly,' he replied. 'You can always call me Herbert.' He was beside himself. I was already having second thoughts and debated with myself whether to tell him of the big mistake I had made. Too late, he was already away with one of his squad fellows to get some 'celebration fluid'—beer—and, considering our number, he needed plenty of it. I told all the sergeants about it too—they were only separated from the rest of the troop by some sacking hanging from the ceiling and had heard everything. 'After all, what can we lose?' they said. 'Let's have a drink, especially as it is free.' They all knew of course that I had only made up the story about his promotion. But when he returned no one had the heart to tell him and we felt that he might as well be happy for a little while. Fischer called all the sergeants by their first name, they all grinned and drank his beer to his very good health. I myself had a bitter taste in my mouth; what about the cruel awakening?

An alert came at 2 a.m. that night. You can well imagine how we all felt about this one after our celebrations. We left a great many things behind, and it was just as well that we returned in the morning after marching for some time straight along the Dutch border. After only a few hours' sleep I had to be off again into the town. I was trying to figure out an excuse for poor Herbert. All I could say to him was 'Don't be so impatient; those things take some time to get through.'

It was 10 p.m. on 9 May when the next alert came. Still tired from the night before, we were not pleased about it as you can imagine. We were called together by Sergeant Dopke, who said, 'Boys, this time it is different, I am waiting for Lieutenant Lange to arrive.' Did he say *Lieutenant* Lange? Yes, he had been promoted to 2nd Lieutenant. When Lange arrived, he introduced himself and we all congratulated him and meant it. Corporal Fischer looked at me, as if to say, 'I wonder when I'll get told about *my* promotion.' Lieutenant Lange told us that this time we were not coming back and we were to be issued with 60 rounds of rifle ammunition, to be carried 30 on each side in our belt.

Goodness only knows what we left behind in all the excitement. I for one left my pullover, an alarm clock and some underwear in my quarters. Even our horses were excited and there was a great deal of coming and going. We took the same route as a few days before, after contacting the rest of the regiment units. It must have been about midnight when we crossed the border into Holland, not that we knew exactly at which point we crossed because the terrain was wooded and there were no white lines. We marched northwards and on reaching Kerkenrade, turned westwards to Maastricht.

On our way to Kerkenrade, we could see our Luftwaffe—bombers accompanied by fighter planes which next to the heavy bombers looked like flies. There must have been several squadrons, it looked like an endless stream, and in the brilliant sunshine it made an awe-inspiring sight; and the droning noise disturbed even our horses. By 10 o'clock in the morning of 10 May, Maastricht was occupied by German troops. It all happened very fast and we had a job to keep up on horseback. We seemed to march in and out of Holland till we reached Kerkenrade, where we made a halt to catch our breath, then we stayed in Holland.

On the next day, 11 May, we saw our first dead soldier on the roadside, a Dutchman. It gave me funny thoughts; the first that struck me when I looked down at him was that he too had a mother and family. And it was his country that we were in. He was very young, wearing a greenish uniform—maybe he came from a special unit.

We set up camp in a dip where there was a small brook with several fruit trees grouped together, to which we tied our horses; we let them graze and were allowed to take off the saddles. Then we stripped to have a good wash in the brook. A substantial meal from our field kitchen, which had caught up with us, was very welcome. Most meals came out of one pot—they had no time for better presentation—and usually contained beans or peas or lentils etc., but after marching through the night, we could not have cared less. After our comparatively luxurious life in Aachen, we were still shocked. It really dawned on me as I rolled myself up in my blanket, with the tent sheet underneath, that this was no manoeuvre, this was the beginning. And goodbye to all the little things one takes for granted—shaving with hot water, toilets in general (we were told to dig a small hole every time and fill up afterwards), lavatory paper was not provided (grass had to do) and so on—we did indeed miss home now. Of course, the horses always came first, too; only after them was it your turn—if, that is, you were lucky enough not to be selected to stand guard right away.

Whitsun, 12 May, and we were again on our way. The heat was really fierce. Before noon, Royal Air Force planes started attacking our advance route and we had to take cover very quickly. One aircraft was shot down by our fighter planes and one by flak. Our feet were beginning to burn as we had to lead our horses most of the time to keep them fit in case we had an assignment.

As we were marching towards the River Maas, near Maastricht, we had our first gas alert. It was soon over, thank goodness, but we still had to get the canvas nosebags for the horses out of our saddlebags, collect hay from the supply cart, dampen it, and fill the nosebags with it, and then get our gas masks ready. In the heat we were experiencing it was no fun whatsoever as breathing became all the more difficult. This was the only time in all the war years that we actually had to take the gas masks out of their containers—round drums that banged on our backs constantly. I know I speak for all the others who had to carry that thing around when I say that it was an instrument of torture, especially on horseback.

Everything went smoothly crossing the River Maas over a pontoon bridge, very shaky, but safe enough. Now we were in Belgium. We were surrounded by gruesome sights from the battles; corpses were everywhere, and I could not stop myself looking at the nearest ones if I had time. Willy, my brother, might, I knew, be on the same route; I knew he was in the west and that quite a few of the fallen soldiers were from our side. The stench was everywhere and filled our nostrils with a sickening odour. Our horses did not like it either and were constantly shying away from it. We were still in a built-up area before moving into the countryside, roughly along the river that we had just crossed, when suddenly we received heavy rifle and machine-gun fire from our right flank. Luckily an embankment provided some shelter and we pulled one man and four horses into cover. The rest of us had to attack in line, covering one another and jumping from sparse cover to sparse cover. The fire came from a small building, a cottage perhaps, in a cluster of trees behind a large hedge. This was our baptism of fire, so to speak. The bullets were whistling and splattering into the ground between or right in front of us, some over our heads. I really began to sweat, we were in a stupid position and one in which no one could help. I wished myself a thousand miles away, my nose was right in the ground in between the new sprouts of the cornfield and yet I had to get up and jump again and again; I did not care how much dirt I had on my uniform, the ground was my best friend at that moment.

Friedensberger, one of my squad, was next to me. He asked me to write to his mum, *if*... We had received no casualties so far, I was shaking, but quite calm. 'Don't be silly,' I said, trying to be brave. 'It will all be over soon,' wishing that it was three or four hours later in the day when it would be dark. Sergeant Ruch was on my right, a bit further forward, and he, like us, could see the hopeless position, for we were pinned down on open terrain. The machine-gun started to hammer again and I automatically pressed myself deeper into the ground. Blast it all, we were not equipped for this kind of attack—not like the infantry, for example, who had spades with which to dig themselves in. Ruch, the only sergeant around, shouted to us to move to the left where there was better cover. 2 Squadron were going ahead to the left and 3 to the right, which left us in the middle. Apparently, none of them was gaining ground quickly enough to relieve us of our position. Fortunately, however, our predicament had been spotted and reported to Captain Krone, the Commanding Officer of 13 Company, which had two field-howitzers. Very soon he put an end to the onslaught on us by firing a few shells into the tree next to the cottage, after which all became very quiet. By the time we were under cover next to our horses, it was all over.

We mounted and approached the cottage, 300 metres away. Rider Knechter and Sergeant Lutze were already there, but I am afraid they had arrived too soon, maybe they wanted to be brave; in any case they must have run straight into the line of machine-gun fire—they were an awful mess.

Lieutenant Lange was lying on his back and, fearing the worst, I rushed to him; there was blood on his chest. But it was nothing but a nasty nosebleed, thank goodness, and Knechter and Lutze were our only casualties. Very depressed, we tried to be grown-up men, but one could not help a tear: poor devils, only half an hour ago they were running just like us. They must have been hit just before our shells went into the cottage and trees. They were lying side by side. I still remember the freshly dug garden on the other side of the damaged cottage, with a small bench nearby; I thought then, what a peaceful place—if it wasn't for this silly war.

We all helped to dig neat graves and bury Sergeant Lutze and Rider Knechter. Corporal Müller made two crosses and placed their helmets on top. It was not easy to put their names, ranks and other details on them; we tried first with coloured pencils, but finally had to burn them on. We were all thoroughly shaken as we marched in the direction of Namur, the last few hours weighing heavily on our minds. As we were often in the way of our own tanks and supply vehicles, we tried the terrain off from the road, but it really was not suitable for horses, with ditches, fences, wires. The road was the only place in the end.

On the 15th, we stopped near Namur as a great deal of fighting was still going on there. We had to take cover many times, our horses were kept well apart because of artillery fire.

The next day, 16 May, was a very black day for all of us. We set off at about 9 a.m. for the front line. Fischer, as always, had too much to say and was in a happy mood. 'At last we are going to front!' he shouted, as if to say he was looking forward to it. Just over the bridge leading into the town, we found in front of us many dead soldiers lying about at the sides of the road. What a waste, I could not help thinking and I felt very silly suddenly. One of our soldiers, a full corporal of the infantry, was lying there still clutching his rifle. I noticed that he had gloves on; the attack must have happened during the night. We made a halt in the town and were allowed to help ourselves from the shops—there was plenty of food everywhere. Of course, the town had been deserted by the population.

On we went, not knowing what was in store for us. It must have been late afternoon, about 5.30, when Lieutenant Lange got a despatch from a motorcyclist. He explained briefly that we were to report to the regiment's HQ at once; 'Most likely an assignment,' he said, and without explanation, swung into a minor road on the right and ordered, *'Fliegermarschtief,'* (meaning that all squads should ride well spaced out in case of plane attacks). Air attacks became more and more frequent. We were passing a few lonely houses on the left, the road was quite narrow and we were chatting about this and that as we rode along. Sergeant Dopke was on my right, Lieutenant Lange in front of him, and Rider Berens, who took care of Lieutenant Lange's horse, was in front of me. The first squad followed us, then the second and the third, and so on. Very suddenly heavy fire came from the house on the left, hand grenades exploded on the road, and voices from the back were shouting, 'Tanks from the rear!' There was no time for us to turn round, so we tried to gallop through. I can still see now Lieutenant Lange's right arm and shoulder being torn off. My Quinta got hit in the croup. My waterbottle was torn from my belt. Sergeant Dopke slipped off Halla. I think all the horses were screaming, my eyes were burning and I was half blinded. I jumped off, and as soon as I did Quinta was on the ground, kicking wildly and screaming in pain. I will never forget how she looked at me, her back practically torn away. I was shouting and crying at the same time, helpless, not knowing the right thing to do. I took my rifle off my shoulder, tearing open the stud fasteners on my belt. Standing in the middle of the road in a daze, I shot her just above the left eye. Then I allowed myself to fall to the ground; I could not have cared less what was going on around me any more. I could not get my poor horse out of my mind. Sergeant Dopke was lying very still behind Quinta, blood was everywhere and someone was calling for help, the firing had stopped and I could also hear shouts from the house on my left. The shouts were in a foreign language, probably Arabic.

How long I had been lying there I could not say; it became very quiet, except for the crying of wounded horses. I turned to where Sergeant Dopke was lying; he was dead, his left cheek was torn away. I cradled his head in my lap, closed his eyes and stared at the scene in horrified disbelief. Lieutenant Lange was lying about twenty feet away on the same side of the road, also very still. Then I heard the roar of a heavy motorbike. The regiment's despatch rider was looking for us. He was fired on from out of the houses before he reached us, when he swerved round; his footrests hit the cobblestones, making the sparks fly, but he made it. Five minutes later our howitzers were firing into the very houses, and I was running, crouching and dodging, trying to reach a small ditch a little further along the road. I then lay very low and hoped for the best. It was nearly dark and I prayed that I would be able to get out of this mess. A scout car arrived—it was ours, thank goodness—and an ambulance as well, which took some of our fellows away, a few of them really badly hurt. Apparently both squads behind us had turned and run right into the firing line of the Belgians' small tank. Lieutenant Lange, Sergeant Dopke, Riders Bremer and Holzer, dead. Sergeant Buck, Betram, Berger, Riedel, and Bruckmann were wounded and were taken to the field hospital. We lost nineteen horses. Now we only had Sergeant Stacke left, and we were incorporated into 13 Company (the Howitzer Company) for the time being.

We assembled as well as we could and took our orders from Captain Krone, until we got our new positions and fresh horses. 'Get yourself some transport, those who have lost horses, and also get equipment' (such as saddlebags, sabres, horse blankets, bridles, etc.). It was a grim task. The dead were already rolled up in their tent sheets and were to be buried early in the morning. We moved into an empty barn, sleeping in between hay and straw. I had terrible nightmares and woke up shivering several times until I eventually fell into a deep sleep.

The next day, 17 May, everyone from the regiment tried to make it easy for us, and graves had already been dug by someone. The dead were buried at the side of the road whenever possible so that they could later be transferred to a communal grave. I was dry-eyed, still unable to grasp it completely. I was lost and kept wondering why I was still there, by rights I should have been dead like the others next to me. A bullet that grazed my forehead in between my eyes had burned my eyelids (later on I was told that my tears helped a great deal), and a bullet had gone into the heel of my left boot. Quinta had taken the brunt of it; I remembered how she had looked at me so pleadingly as I shot her. For the first time in this stupid war, I prayed very hard.

When we marched off that morning, I could not help but look around much as I wanted to get away from this place of disaster. I had helped to drag the horses to the side of the road and into the ditch. They already smelt—it was very hot in May of 1940. Halla, Sergeant Dopke's horse, had several bullet holes in her stomach, how clearly they could be seen. The flies were also busy. Again those of us who had lost their horses and had not got an assignment were told to get ourselves some transport—anything would do, a bicycle if possible—and to report back. Rider Hanau, who was in the same position as myself, and did not like walking either, and I set off and we soon found a bike, a good one too. After a long search we eventually found our own troop: there were so many of our troops all over the place and changing direction continually. Reporting back to the Company Sergeant-Major of 13 Company, we were blasted at. 'Where the blazes have you been all this time? Go for a picnic or something? Clean yourselves up, you are filthy. Report back in ten minutes.' That shook us back into reality, we were not used to such rough treatment. We looked at each other and had to agree that we were looking rather dirty. So off we went on our two-wheeled mount in search of water, plenty of it if possible. Bloodstains were everywhere on our clothing and I will never forget the afternoon at the small brook we found, absolutely starkers, scrubbing and scraping at our clothes and underwear. We also had a shave with French shaving cream. I was careful not to use toothpaste instead as I had the last time—one looked much like the other, and for me, reading French was impossible. It made me feel so stupid, but we were learning fast, especially in the food line.

(Food was something we never had to worry about—there was actually plenty everywhere, and people were helpful in an apprehensive manner, not quite knowing how to behave. We were still very cautious—after all, we were the invaders, and to make matters worse we could not speak French. I remember the first time I asked for some water, entering a very large kitchen in a farmhouse. There were quite a few people present. I asked for water please in German, gesturing at the same time, and it went like clockwork. I asked the woman of the house to make sure it wasn't poisoned. Later I had to smile—after all, it had come straight from the pump, which was in the kitchen. 'Mercy bokoo' was my first attempt at French, accompanied by a shy smile. I meant no harm and I could see no anger in their eyes. I only wondered what they were thinking. One thing I never did, though, was to let go of my rifle.)

Scrubbed and shaved, we rejoined our unit to be ordered to go to Frameries, a town about ten kilometres ahead, to look for suitable quarters for 13 Company, and their howitzers. Since the guns were used all the time, it was important to find them shelter. A barn preferably, so that they could not be spotted by the French planes. Rider Hanau and I enjoyed a nice afternoon's ride along the very lonely road—it was off the route of most of the front-bound traffic—which had little life beyond a lonely house here and there. We arrived at about six in the early evening and looked around for people, but there was no one about. It was completely deserted, so we took a good look at the nearest farm building, went into the yard, and sized up the situation. I wandered into the barn, barns were usually well stacked with plenty of straw—and rats. This barn had an upstairs: there was a pair of ladders standing there, and I took the invitation and had a look up top. It hit me like a wet towel. There, unbelievably unconcerned, snoring and in apparent bliss, were goodness knows how many English soldiers. Of course I didn't realise this at first—I was thinking more of French or Belgian—then I saw the helmets over their faces, the rifles and machine-guns standing or lying about everywhere. I froze, then quickly tip-toed down again, and, indicating to Hanau, who had come looking for me, to shut up, I explained the situation to him. What a situation! 'We'll go up there very slowly and carefully, grab all their guns and throw them downstairs, and then we'll shout *"Hande-Hoch!"*,' I decided. Hanau asked what that was in English.

'I don't know, but *"Hande-Hoch"* will do. I can shout it and you can show them what I mean.' So that is what we did, but before I shouted I had a dreadful thought, what about the side-arms some of the ranks must be carrying? We will just have to bluff them, I said to Hanau who was getting more and more nervous.

We need not have worried, the poor chaps were absolutely worn out. Apparently they had been marching for the last three days and nights trying to get to the coast, but had been cut off from their units and had decided to rest in this lonely place. That was why we did not see anybody in the village—the people had just run away, they had been too frightened to get involved, they were only farm folk.

To my relief our unit arrived as I was wondering what to do next with them. They all climbed down; I felt rather sorry for them, after all their marching and then to become prisoners. Well, that was war.

Sergeant-Major Knobler of 13 Company shouted at them, trying to line them up in the yard, then turned to me. 'You, Corporal. Look after them.' He then went off and returned after a few moments with Captain Krone, who said to me, 'You've done a good job here.' I had to tell him what happened and he said, 'Take them back to Ath', a town about twenty kilometres north. He explained the route very carefully to me. I was beginning to like him; he was the one who had fired several rounds in the house when I had been lying in the road with Quinta. I got six men, all on bikes, to help me. The English were rather surprised, maybe they were expecting hard treatment from us.

I placed two men in front, two at the rear and one on either side, and, feeling rather proud of the trust put in me by Captain Krone, I pedalled, going up and down by the column. The only thing that worried me was the darkness, it was bound to come very soon.

We had forty-seven English prisoners altogether, but strangely enough no officers, only four NCOs. They became quite cheerful on the march and I talked with a few of them. One was a confectioner from Birmingham and another a watchmaker, also from the Midlands. I lost the addresses they gave me and I still regret not having taken greater care not to lose them. I went ahead several times to ask the people for sandwiches for them and something to drink. When we halted for sandwich breaks, one of the sergeants who could speak a little German and I agreed that it would be silly for anyone to try and run off as we had orders to shoot and my men were very nervous.

We arrived about midnight on 18 May, and halted outside Ath. I then set off to find the camp for the prisoners of war.

The compound was enormous and already full up, but I was assured by a sergeant that I didn't have anything to worry about—I was just to hand them over and they would take care of them. Most of the other prisoners of war in the camp were French, Belgian and Moroccans of the French army. My prisoners were the first English ones and everybody had a good look at them.

Well, that was the end of my stardom. I waved to my English acquaintances and we promised to write when better days came again. Maybe they are still about. We stayed until daybreak, having found a good place to stay in town: there were very few civilians left, but plenty of empty houses.

It looked like being another hot day as we set off at dawn to find our unit. We didn't hurry back, in fact we made a detour over the countryside so that we could have a meal here and there.

When we eventually found our unit, it was nearly dark. There was a new rule now: instead of marching in the daytime we were to march at night as there had been much more resistance of late from French forces, and also a great deal more activity from spotter planes, which usually led to artillery fire, from which we had some casualties.

One thing we found out was that when, every time we approached a small town or village, we got heavy fire from the French batteries, it was not always because of the spotter planes, but because people in the bell-towers of the local churches sent signals to one another. This we learnt when Captain Krone put an end to the ringing by firing a few shells from his howitzer into a church tower—the result was surprising; no more artillery fire from the French.

We marched the night through in the direction of Valenciennes, a town still only half taken. It was never really dark, especially when the eyes got used to it, but we were moving very slowly—in fact, it was more stop than go. We had a surprise visitor on one of our long halts at the roadside—

Lieutenant Becker. He came to see me, and we had a long conversation. I told him all about our disaster—he wanted to know every detail, and was very sympathetic, and particularly saddened by the death of Lieutenant Lange, who, as I mentioned earlier was a distant relative of his. Then he dropped his bombshell: 'Corporal Kuhnert,' he said, 'report tomorrow at the Château So-and-So.' (I have forgotten its name; it was about four miles back on some side track.) 'Make yourself smart and report to Colonel von Tchudy.' The reason was for me to take over two horses, one for the Colonel and one for myself.

'What happened to the other fellow who was in charge?' I asked.

'Oh, he got the push. So don't be late, Kuhnert. I hate being let down, besides the Colonel knows you—I told him all about you and your bit of bad luck.'

Bit of bad luck! I could have kicked him for that remark; maybe I still had a lot to learn.

The next morning, slightly apprehensive, I set off. I had polished my boots, had shaved carefully, and had even cleaned my nails, the lot.

I was ushered straight into the office, where I saluted smartly and reported. The Colonel was a great deal more cheerful than I had imagined. He told me that, from now on, I was to be responsible for his four-legged transport.

'Don't ever let them go,' he said before he dismissed me to my new position.

Later I found out what had happened: when there had been a French air attack along the road the corporal in charge had taken cover in the ditch when he should have stayed with the horses.

5

Willy

From now, I was a member of the regimental horse staff, whose charges included, besides the Colonel's horses, the horses of the adjutant, veterinary surgeon and the rest of the staff officers—about twelve horses in all. Since I had the Colonel's horses, I was also the top notch, so to speak, and always got the best quarters for them, if there were any. On the whole, a pretty cushy job if you knew what to do.

The Colonel rode very seldom; most of the time he was being driven in his staff Mercedes. An old friend was there as well—yes, you might have guessed it—Püppchen, Lieutenant Becker being a staff officer. He grinned when he saw me the next day. 'Everything all right?' he shouted across the road. 'Look after Püppchen for me; you know what she is like.'

The two horses I was to take care of were excellent; the one the Colonel rode was called Nachbar (Neighbour), a Hanoverian gelding, dark bay, very versatile, good-natured, and—typical Hanoverian—compact yet elegant in movement. The other, a gelding of 16.2 hands, seven or eight years old, was called Ire (Irish), and was in fact Irish or of Irish descent. He was very well schooled, but quite a handful—always full of life, he would race over a plain and jump over whatever was in the way, while Nacky (Nachbar) was well-behaved, but still shied away from certain obstacles. The two horses got on very well together and I never had any problems with catching them: I just whistled through my fingers and along they came, always together. All those things I found out on our first rest day. Oh, what a marvellous feeling— I was again with horses. They depended on me and I on them in a strange way; once you understood them, somehow they understood you, the rest came by itself; they were your comrades and even if you felt annoyed with them sometimes, you took care of them just the same.

The town, Valenciennes, was a battlefield at the moment. We were exhausted from the seven- or eight-mile march to this area, but the French were in no mood to give up easily and everyone from our side was needed to take the town. There was a river nearby, which seemed to be a stumbling block for our troops, and we were required to fight with only a skeleton troop behind. The horses we put out to graze; happily they always stayed near the wagons.

In town was the usual stench of warfare, bodies lay everywhere, and artillery fire from the French harassed us at regular intervals. There was mortar fire, too, forcing us under cover. We were near the market-place and got our orders to take better positions. As I was also trained in the use of heavy machine-guns, I had to take the gun and two men, to use as No. 1 and No. 2; we skipped No. 3 (ammunition carrier) as there was plenty of ammunition around us.

It was just like old times on Lüneburg Heath. Here I was, lying on my stomach, field-glasses (which I had taken off poor Sergeant Dopke) to my face, with No. 1 behind the gun, and No. 2 feeding the ammunition belt into the gun. So far, we had nothing to fire at; we were almost in a defensive position just behind the town fountain.

'Work your way towards the bridge,' came the order. So off we went, running bent over double, expecting sniper bullets, which never came. I was really in my element—or at least I was not pinned down as I was five days before. Then the regular barrage of shells started, but luckily they all fell just behind us in a fruit orchard, behind the houses of the market-place.

A bridgehead was already established on the other side of the river, I think at Saint-Quentin; I'm not sure—at such times one does not really care about names. A motorbike despatch rider came from the direction of the river, shouting for a volunteer to hurry over the bridge with a message and supplies of ammunition immediately. We had been drinking some champagne, which was plentiful in the French army depot just 200 metres north, and who should volunteer but our dear friend Corporal Fischer. 'Where do you think you are going?' I shouted to him. 'To the front, to the front,' he answered, it was just as if he had come from a wedding party. So off he went with two of our cases of 300 rounds each towards the officer at our end of the bridge to collect the message for the bridgehead, before crossing the river. The bridge was under heavy machine-gun fire from the French positions, and I would not have given tuppence for his chances of getting to the other side. In the meantime, heavy artillery fire came uncomfortably near to where we were lying so we decided to jump into one of the houses on our right and take positions in the basement windows, from where we could spray practically the whole of the market square, and also observe our friend, Fischer. He was singing at the top of his voice, rocking from side to side from the weight of the ammunition boxes he carried, one in each hand. He just walked on and on until he vanished—for ever, we thought. But then he reappeared, exactly the same, minus the boxes of course, and all we could do was shake our heads in disbelief. Well, he did it; how, I will never know. He slept most of the afternoon, a satisfied smile on his face, next to us between boxes of false teeth—the house must have been a dentist's.

I needed to go to the lavatory, but the shellfire was not exactly helpful. So, I went up the stairs to the back door leading to the back garden; first I waited till the French had fired their regular half-circle, and as soon as they passed us I ran like hell into the garden, breeches down, prepared for the worst. I only made it back just in time. It was worse than in my first army days, at least then you were allowed five minutes.

Then we heard tanks rumbling along the cobblestones and we knew that the resistance had been broken. We were able to take what we could carry from the army depot; there was everything there from a box of matches to enormous wheels of Swiss cheese, and of course plenty of clothing. We also took some champagne with us, feeling rather satisfied with ourselves as well, of course, as relieved.

This episode gave me a good opportunity to get better acquainted with my new unit. The regimental horse staff's Corporal Schutte, a Reservist from Hamburg, married, with a two-year-old daughter, was a very nice fellow; he was in charge of the Adjutant's horse. Then there was Buschmann, the Colonel's batman, who also looked after the many needs of the staff officers, such as breakfast, dinner, drinks and smokes. Photography was one of his hobbies and he took many pictures of me and my horse; I still have one of me with the Colonel before we rode out. Then there was Wedel, a sturdy farm boy, in charge of the vet's horses. Altogether there were about six of us, and we each had two horses to look after except Buschmann, who always got a lift in the baggage cart with Lorenz—the very cart in which I delivered the horse manure in Aachen.

Off we went again, passing by areas where so many battles had been fought in the First World War. One could not help becoming thoughtful in this terrain; maybe my father had been here in 1915, or one of my uncles—maybe some were still here. We marched in the daytime again, and only now and then had we any trouble from the French artillery. I think the French were holding their fire because so many civilians were heading south-west. The horses hated the dreadful noise.

Many troops were marching on foot; I was one of the fortunate ones, having the use of two horses, the Colonel's and mine. I rode them in turn and saved my legs. As the roads were crowded we would, when possible, ride across the fields or along the grass verge on the side of the road.

Something most wonderful happened to me then. From the marching column, a voice called out my name. I knew it at once—it was my brother Willy. 'Hey you,' he called, 'on your high horse.' I was overjoyed and so was he. I jumped down at once and pulled my horses behind me to get close to him. He came over and I helped him up on the Colonel's horse so that we could ride together. 'You know,' he said, 'this is the first time in my life that I have sat on a horse—and what a horse.' Willy was a sergeant in the infantry of our neighbouring division. 'Always look out for a yellow triangle,' he said; that was his divisional insignia, ours was a blue square with a white line. I told him that I knew he was in the area but that it was still a marvellous surprise to see him. We talked and talked about so many things, my eyes were wet. He gave me a 9mm pistol, Czechoslovakian, and a full magazine to go with it. He had got it in Poland but as he also had a P38 he said, 'You have it. You've only got the carbine and a sabre, which is nowhere near good enough if you get into a built-up area.' I promised to look after it, it was like a new toy for me, or a present I had always wanted.

We were still in touch with his unit, but I was losing sight of mine, so Willy said, 'You'd better get going to catch them up at the next fork; we should be making a longer halt there.' The sun was very high and everyone was sweating, especially those on foot. I said, 'I will wait for you there,' and off I went. I never saw him again; we journeyed south and they went in a straight line to Paris. I was so proud of him and he looked well; we had not seen each other for two years and then only briefly. I was still hoping to see him again later, but it was not on the cards, as they say. Every time he had leave, I didn't, and vice-versa.

From then on we marched like mad, very short rests and off again, until we eventually arrived in a large open space next to a château. The horses were very pleased. I let them loose in a very large fenced meadow where there was no worry of them running away. There was plenty of water about for both men and horses, we had a good meal, and then, looking up at the sky, we fell asleep; it was simply heaven.

The next day, 25 May, was my twenty-third birthday—Willy had reminded me of it the previous day by saying that he was now only three years older than myself (he was born in January).

In the afternoon I wandered off on my own, my 'treasure', the pistol Willy gave me, on my belt. I simply had to try it out, but I had to go some distance away so as not to cause any false alarm with the sound of shots. I went a long way, stopping only when I was fairly sure not to be heard. Taking the gun out of the holster was practically a ceremony. It was in an oiled cloth to keep it clean and free from rust and moisture. There was a bullet already in the chamber, which I removed, then, making sure there was no obstruction in the barrel, I reloaded, feeling very safe having a gun of this kind in my possession. I aimed at a tree trunk a short distance away and fired, it made a loud crack as I had expected. Pushing back the safety catch, I carefully replaced the gun in my holster and thanked Willy again, vowing to myself to take care of it as I had promised. No one could have given me a better birthday present.

★

I was sometimes frightened, not for myself but for Willy. The nearer one was to Paris—where he had gone—the more intense the fighting. Our route was in between Soissons and Reims, crossing over the River Aisne at Bourg-et-Comin, then south through Fismes. The sound of artillery fire halted our march forward many times and the picture around us was not very nice at all. There were dead cows everywhere, for we were in a farming country, and live ones literally crying out to be milked. Luckily we had farm boys with us and they were kept busy milking them, although the milk could not be used.

Quite often we found ourselves travelling alongside French people, mostly women, children or old folk, with all their belongings. It was a puzzle to us why they were going south: why on earth didn't they stay in their own place instead of risking their lives through the artillery fire and air attacks? We were not going to do them any harm. And in fact many of them accepted our offer of food from our field kitchens. I don't think there is anything better than a plate of soup from our field kitchen, a most ingenious service, self-contained in many ways. The soup was a mixture of vegetables and herbs with a hint of vinegar, all stirred well and cooked slowly. It was quite delicious, the best ingredient of course being hunger. With beans and lentils, it was just the same. It was not always soup; often we had cutlets or as a special treat liver with potato mash. Everything was cooked on a wood fire. It was just magic—not to forget the knowhow of our two cooks.

Not everything went smoothly, however. We had many mishaps and setbacks, and once had to help out a French family and sort out a quarrel between them and the others. It was because their big cart (and those French carts were big), left the road and fell into a ditch. Their horse was just not strong enough to pull them out and they wanted to borrow a bigger one. But, oh no, none of the others were prepared to oblige. So we requisitioned a horse and did the job for them—it was unbelievable, everyone for themselves, voices screaming, tears from children and women. But we managed it eventually; and they were ever so surprised when we returned their horse to them afterwards. Funny people, I could not help thinking; yet many were friendly, and we also had many laughs because of the language difficulties. Slowly but surely my French improved.

Then came a French counter-attack, about six miles away. First we were told it was cavalry, then we realised it wasn't horses, but tanks. Panic broke out all round, and to make it more difficult, darkness was setting in. We pulled off the road at once and scattered to get better cover—for what were we, with horses and carbines, against tanks?

6

The Booby Trap

The worst thing for a soldier is always the waiting. I maintain that, during the whole war, at least one third of my time I spent standing, sitting or lying around waiting for something to happen. It was nearly morning when we heard that the counter-attack was over—just like that. In fact what happened was that virtually a whole division of the French tank unit had surrendered without any great resistance, which was why we didn't hear any gunfire near us.

For several days we marched on in a southerly direction, only now and then stopping to get some rest. Nothing particular happened, though some funny things happened to me—things I think could happen to anyone in a strange country. One day, determined to get some eggs, I left the road and rode into a farmyard. Seeing a woman in the doorway, I dismounted and approached her. She hurried back into the house, but then came slowly out again. I asked her for some eggs—she said, *'Ne comprend pas.'* So I opened my arms, and bent my knees to indicate the laying of eggs. Her face lit up and—*'Oui, monsieur'*—she motioned me to follow. I left my horses near the house and, filled with anticipation, followed her into a small building. She pointed to the floor; it was concrete with a small hole in the middle, two footprints in the cement. Then it dawned on me, this little building was not a hen house as I hoped, but a privy.

I did get my eggs from her, though, and we parted the best of friends; she had a marvellous laugh. I expect if she is still alive she probably remembers the occasion too. She even helped me to get on my horse and put the eggs in a large cloth so I could carry them without crushing them. I had the impression that most French people were afraid of us to begin with, but soon found out that we did not eat little children, as some had been told.

Something was in the wind; I could feel it. Sure enough, we marched on but this time we swung to our right, more to the west. For the first time our CO was looking at us and the horses. Lieutenant Becker and most of the other staff officers were also standing at the roadside, and Lieutenant Becker even raised his whip towards me in recognition; I sat up even straighter, knowing we were being scrutinised. The march came abruptly to a halt. Everybody off the road came the order, and there we waited and waited in the blazing heat.

Eventually we were told that we were to be engaged for the first time since Valenciennes. There was excitement all round—but what about me? What was I to do—I had the Colonel's horses! I soon found out when Lieutenant Becker came again on the scene. 'Kuhnert, get your horses under cover, the Colonel won't need them at the present.' Schutte, Wedel, Burgert, and one or two others, all Reservists, were to stay behind to take care of the horses and equipment. The rest of us (about thirty men) were to take only carbines and small arms, to comb through all houses along the advance route. We had to inspect them and declare them free from any French soldiers, mines and booby traps. I did not like it at all and felt rather lost. The sergeant in charge of this clearing party was a very crude fellow. 'Please your bloody self what you do. It's up to you to get blown up, if you are bloody well stupid enough,' he said. Instead of getting advice from him we had to get on with it. Oh, how I missed Sergeant Dopke—he would have told us exactly what to do in his marvellous way.

He was standing at the top of the stairs. I had not looked up before, foolishly, because I had been busy examining the floor, looking for an opening or trapdoor to the cellar, which most buildings had. I was petrified and dropped down on one knee, brought up my carbine and fired blindly in his direction, then jumped to the left, rolling over at the same time. I reloaded and fired again, and lay still. Nothing happened, not even a groan, but one of the chaps came racing into the doorway looking for me. I shouted, 'Get down! They are upstairs.' He gave a yell and disappeared.

I gradually recovered from my shock, and edged my way very slowly round the banister and looked up the stairs, and there he was, still standing, leaning to one side, as if to mock me. I brought my pistol out of its holster, thanking Willy for it, but as I was taking careful aim it dawned on me that the man was not alive, but was supported by some sort of tallboy and leaning against the doorpost. I still kept my pistol aimed at him, though, as I edged my way upstairs. He was a big fellow, black, probably Senegalese. His eyes were half open, staring down at me. He was stone dead.

From the yard, I heard the voice of my compatriot shouting to me to take care, as he was going to throw a grenade through the top window as he could not find the back door. I just swore at him not to be so bloody daft, but too late, the thing came crashing through the window as I plunged back down the stairs. Talk about being killed twice.

Outside, there were many dead about, from both sides, and I was afraid that I might find Willy among them. God, it was hot, and no water anywhere.

'Go carefully in the cellars,' came the first sensible advice. 'Don't open any doors or drawers in the houses and take your heart in your hand.' I went into the next house. Emil, a Reservist corporal from the kitchen staff, a very nice fellow, much older than I, attached himself to me. 'Watch the top of the stairs whilst I look down here,' I said. I could have sworn I heard his knees knocking—or were they mine? I just got on with it, continually grumbling to myself to keep my courage up, 'Damned stupid job;' we were not trained for this lark, one never knew what was around the corner.

This cellar, like most of them, was stocked with wine and other drink. We were parched. 'Emil,' I shouted. 'When we've finished upstairs, we'll get back down here and live it up.' Silence. 'Did you hear me?' I bellowed. Then there was an almighty explosion, a scream and a groan. I jumped for the short wooden steps, took a deep breath and shouted again, 'Are you all right?' Just a groan was the answer. I got upstairs, to see him sitting, or crouching, holding his stomach. 'What's the matter, Emil?' His face was ghastly, blood was everywhere, the lower part of his body was dripping through his fingers. He was desperately trying to hold his intestines together. Why the blazes didn't he wait, instead of going upstairs by himself, blast it all?

I ran outside and shouted loudly for a stretcher bearer, and searched for the sergeant, but he was too busy with something else. Herbert Kleiner, our Paymaster clerk, came over; he knew Emil very well. By the time we got there poor Emil was gone. 'I told him to wait and watch, but he was a plucky little fellow, just not cautious enough,' I explained to Kleiner. Then I was sick. The heat was unbearable, I hated the whole bloody business. We had been warned about booby traps and it had to happen where I was. I kicked a heap of French rifle rounds, all dum-dums; to use those bullets was strictly against the Geneva Convention. I kicked them again, more out of frustration than anything else.

We were then told to withdraw as the French were about to launch another counter-attack. I hoped it would not come to anything—I was tired and besides I had had a good drink of wine in one of the cellars and had washed my face in wine, so I smelled rather of it. I don't think anyone noticed, though—most of them had done exactly the same.

What we really needed was food, and, since we were about twelve miles from our unit, we tried to find some in one of the shops in town. I still think what a lousy town it was, without remembering the name of it. Then there was more artillery fire and we got out of town altogether; maybe, we thought, we could find a farmyard or something, somewhere where we might at least get water. All the sewage pipes in the town were in pieces and the smell was revolting. There were no more French people to be seen; the actual front line was only four or five miles to the west, if there was such a thing as a clear-cut front. We did get to some houses with some water and it was sheer ecstasy to strip, if only briefly, and splash oneself all over. We were spotted by some French fighter planes, but no harm came to any of us.

On our return to our unit, I had a nice surprise: the post had arrived. How they found us still remains a puzzle to me. I got a small parcel and two letters. I put them in my coat and first collected some of our much loved and, in my view, well-earned pea soup. It was just delicious. Putting my field tin on the ground, I opened the first letter. It was from Frau Schroten—she was very anxious about my well-being, they in Alsdorf had heard about our disaster in Mons. I was actually reported dead at first, but later they heard the truth—what rejoicing there was among those I had come to love in Alsdorf. There was also great sorrow for the men who had been killed or wounded.

The second letter was from Ilse, also very much relieved that I was still about. As usual she swore me everlasting love and told me all sorts of things, what to do and what not; she even sent kisses from her mother, which immediately sent a kind of danger signal to my brain—poor Ilse, I really liked her but, as I have said, I felt I was too young to be promised for good.

The small parcel had come a long way, from my home town of Dresden. A pretty girl, I knew there, called Dorle, had sent me some sugar for my horse and also all my mother's love—apparently Dorle had been visiting and got my address from her. I still remember the lovely times we had together on my last leave there, we went out together and I took her home, her parents had long gone upstairs, asleep, and we spent some time together downstairs.... A letter suddenly from her was somewhat worrying at first but everything was all right. I did take some stupid chances in those days, but, thank goodness, always managed to get away with it.

We had two days' rest after our little adventure, if you could call it that. At first we were ordered to get ready to march, then we marched, then we stopped, then we marched again. Eventually we kept on marching—this was just routine now, we even marched in circles sometimes.

On the third day, we pulled off the southern advance route and entered what I thought to be a most beautiful parkland. The château in the middle was already occupied by our regimental staff. Nearby were a large pond and a beautiful meadow in which I let the horses run loose, making sure they would not run away; they knew where we were and usually I only had to whistle and both came cantering. The pond below the château soon became the centre of our attention: while watching the surface. admiring the water lilies, we discovered there were fish in it, not goldfish, but carp, and carp meant food—in Germany we sometimes had carp for Christmas dinner. But how to get them out of the pond?

Lieutenant Becker, smoking as always, had the answer. 'Hand me over

46

one of those grenades and get out of the way,' he said. The devil, I thought, we only wanted one or two not half the pond, but that is what we got. In an instant countless numbers of fish floated up to the surface. After a while Heckert, one of our office corporals, took off his clothes and waded in to start retrieving them. They tasted a bit muddy but otherwise made a good meal.

Something nasty was in store for me for just after our fish meal. I heard a commotion and someone shouting for me and pointing to the meadow. I ran like hell when I saw Nacky on the ground and Ire standing nearby, still grazing as if it had nothing to do with him.

Nacky was thrashing his legs wildly, but lay still when I approached and spoke to him. Now I could see the trouble. His hind legs had become entangled with telephone wire which was, or had been, laid across the meadow. Wire cutters were the only answer, and I shouted for a pair as loudly as I could, at the same time practically sitting on top of Nacky, trying to get him to lie still—but you try it when a horse panics. His fetlocks were already burnt from the friction, and he got more and more tangled up as he went on thrashing his legs. I was furious for not having seen the wire or the laying of it, blaming all sorts of people for it including myself.

Eventually I got the wire cutters. Now it became very tricky as the moment Nacky was free of me he tried to get up, and it was almost impossible for me to get anywhere near the wire on his legs. So I decided to cut the wire anywhere I could, and everywhere I saw the wire, I cut and cut. Nacky was now standing, shaking all over.

I was not much better, but I was relieved. I led Nacky away towards some trees, carefully looking out for more wire. What a nightmare—what could I do? I definitely could not ask for the vet as the Colonel would then have to be told. I had only had his horse about three weeks, and I had promised to look after him. Lorenz, who had brought the wire cutters, led my horse Ire towards where I was among the trees. He looked at me, and I saw that he had guessed what I was going to do with Nacky's fetlocks. 'Hold his front firmly and push his quarters towards the tree trunk,' I said. I was ready then and unbuttoned my fly and urinated straight at the horse's legs, spraying all the burnt parts of it (urine has disinfectant and healing properties).

'Have you got any cream anywhere?' I asked Lorenz, who said that he didn't think so, but promised to get some from somewhere without giving the game away. For all his simpleness, old Lorenz was a true friend, and he was always there—besides, we would not forget our manure tour of Aachen in a hurry!

The communications people, who had laid the wire in the first place, were none too pleased and swore about 'those damned horses' of ours, as they had to mend what I had cut so neatly in so many places. I only hoped the affair would not reach the Colonel's ears. Fortunately, we stayed for nearly a week there and that gave Nacky's fetlocks time to heal.

The month of June had arrived; the sun continued to blaze down every day. I felt I could stay here for ever; we had very little to do except routine jobs like grooming the horses. I simply loved grooming mine, especially when I could give them a good wash first and make sure they could not roll in the mud afterwards, which they liked doing.

One day I was summoned to the office in the château and my heart sank for I expected that the wire affair had slipped out, and I would get a grilling—but I was not to worry, it was only that the staff doctor wanted to examine my eyes and foot. 'Just give it time,' he said. He was a nice chap, not like the one we had in Lüneburg when I was a recruit—there you had to have two heads and four arms before he would look at you.

We had plenty of time to ourselves, which gave me the opportunity to scribble home and also to get to know everybody in the regimental staff company. One of the Reservists, Ruhmann, especially, was an outstanding character. He was the regimental carpenter, a very nice man, who when he spoke did so very slowly and deliberately. As it happened we were all—that is, the riders, shoemakers, cooks, saddler, etc.—sitting on the grass when we heard that Italy had entered the war, on our side—in fact it was on the very day, 10 June.

Well, there was a subject for discussion. Politically uninterested, I was never up with all the events and was rather amused by Ruhmann's elaborate explanations of things past and things to come. Everybody around him listened fascinated, and then Stolze of the kitchen staff (who had replaced poor Emil who was killed) had to spoil it all by saying, 'Well, if you are so bloody clever tell me why did England declare war on Germany?'

We could not believe our ears; everyone could answer that, or could they? So Ruhmann blew himself up to a better position and, after giving little Stolze a dirty look, explained that Germany had declared war on Poland, and because England had a pact with Poland, it had no alternative but to stand by Poland and declare war on us! So there. But stupid Stolze was not silenced. 'Why didn't England declare war on Russia when Russia attacked Poland early on?' Now there was deep silence from the rest of us.

'Well, Ruhmann?' chirped Stolze (it was like a tennis match—we turned our heads from one to the other), but for once our Prof. Ruhmann had no answer. I still haven't a satisfactory one to this question myself!

Some more news came that our troops were only about twenty-five or thirty kilometres from Paris. I was very pleased about this and I asked myself that night, lying in my little lean-to tent, why war at all? I for one didn't like it, and as soon as it was over the better for everybody. 'Be honest,' I said to myself. 'You are still really frightened.' But maybe we were not needed any more on the front—what a marvellous thought.

7

Ceasefire in France

Rain, rain, rain, it just pelted down in buckets—and after we'd been spoiled with long periods of dry, hot weather. What is more, we had left most of the equipment lying about in the open. My little tent shelter was no shelter at all, the rain just laughed at it and I got soaked. To make matters worse it was pitch dark. My thoughts were with my horses; having had enough problems with Nacky's fetlocks, I didn't want any more. Luckily, though, his fetlocks had healed very nicely; Lorenz had provided some antiseptic cream which I rubbed in daily, and so far everything had gone very well. But now where were my horses? It was two in the morning and, with the rain clouds it would be at least three hours before it got light. The rain was relief in one way, because everybody was fed up with the heat, but being soaked in the pitch dark was no fun either. So I tried to join the cooks underneath their wagons where they always slept. However, there wasn't much room for a soaked invader like myself and I decided to find shelter under Lorenz's wagon. As he was in 13 Company and I was now regimental staff, it was a little way away—not far, but I never found him, it was too dark. I crept into a summerhouse near the château, but then, worrying about all my equipment—saddles, blankets, etc.—covered only with my tent sheet, off I went to collect them. Oh, how I hated this war; not even on a wet night was there any peace. Later in Russia I only wished I had the luxury I had been enjoying at that moment.

Then came the order to get ready. It was 4.30 a.m. and everyone was swearing—what idiot had the right to give such an order? Two hours wouldn't have made any difference.

This really showed how spoiled we had become in the last ten days or so. Even the officers didn't like it, they had enjoyed even more luxury than us. It was nearly light, thank goodness, otherwise finding our horses, all running about, would have been impossible. I just whistled and there they were, Nacky as always in front and Ire following up. It made me feel really proud of them. 'Come on, we've got to go,' I said; I always talked to my horses, it made me feel less lonely, I suppose. I'm sure they understood every word I said to them. I only had to put the bits in—the bridles stayed on always, except for cleaning; that was the order. The blankets were wet only on one side so in no time I was ready.

The order to march, I heard later, was given because of the rain—we would have nothing to fear from enemy planes. It became clearer to us why we marched in a circular or up-and-down pattern: we—our unit—were the left part of a pincer movement, and since the pincers were closing with all the French troops inside, we had sometimes to go back and forth to reinforce the pincers and help to prevent break-outs. So off we marched, leaving our lovely place of rest behind us. I'm quite sure the horses felt as regretful as we did.

It rained all day; there was water simply everywhere after the very long spell of hot weather. We did not stop once all day and were exhausted by nightfall, when we made a halt at some village. I had just had time to get my horses ready for the night when I was ordered to report at once to Staff Sergeant Weber. He happened also to be in charge of communications— his men had laid the wire across the meadow where Nacky had got entangled. 'You've got the first watch,' he snapped. Well, I thought, he's got it in for me after all. I had never had to stand watch since I had been put in charge of the Colonel's horses, and besides, I was not a member of his company. I decided to keep quiet about it and complain in the morning to my Regimental Sergeant-Major Glück—he would put things right for me because he liked horses, and very often came over to me when I was grooming mine.

After two hours of wandering about in all the stinking puddles, listening to the snoring of the troops beneath the barn's overhangs where there were great heaps of straw, I was relieved of my watch by a corporal of the communications company. Being too tired to do anything else, I just dropped where I was in the next straw patch and must have fallen asleep right away. The next thing I knew was the sensation of something dragging across my lips—the whole place was alive with rats, it must have been a rat tail. I wanted to be sick but I had not eaten since lunchtime so I wandered about spitting and rubbing at my lips, and looking for water, in the dark of course. The corporal who had relieved me was sympathetic and helped me to look for a pump or something. We dared not go near the house because the officers were in there, but we eventually found a brook near a meadow behind the barn. I lay underneath a wagon for the rest of the night. Everybody was scratching themselves in the morning—apparently there was not only a plague of rats in the barn, because of the rain, but also several regiments of fleas—and could they bite: they definitely did not like Germans; or they liked them very much, whichever way you look at it.

Full of sympathy, one of the cooks gave me the first mug of coffee. I played with my initial sips as if to wash my very thoughts away. Sergeant-Major Glück arrived on the scene to see how the officers' coffee was coming along and said to me, 'You look awful and tired. What is the matter with you?' So I told him, first about the rat tail and then about having to stand guard as well as looking after the horses. He was furious, not so much about my having to stand guard, but that this yellow-bellied creep from the wire-pullers had the nerve to order any of *his* men about. There was clearly a showdown on the cards, and I for one stayed out of the way, feeling responsible for it, though at the same time mentally rubbing my hands—after all, Staff Sergeant Weber had no right whatsoever to order me about. I promised myself, too, that when Staff Sergeant Weber was next slogging along on foot and I was riding high, I would give him one of my dirty looks; I definitely would not give him a lift, no matter what.

Air activity increased this morning as the weather was clearing; it was just the weather for surprise attacks, aeroplanes could slip out of the clouds and then slip back into them after delivering whatever they were shooting or dropping. We knew we were nearer the front because of the comings and goings at HQ, and we could also hear the rumblings of the guns. Very loud humming overhead made us take cover at first, until we realised it was our own planes, Stukas, always in groups of twelve, coming and going once they had delivered their load. We could tell the dive bombers were not too far away because of the howling noise of their sirens. It must have been very demoralising for those on the receiving end.

I lost count of the time and was surprised to find that it was already 14 June 1940. Marching became routine again, night and day, and we also became more involved in fighting. One day Colonel von Tchudy asked for his horse. I was pleased that both mounts were in good shape. What, I wondered, was the reason for the Colonel's sudden need of a horse? I asked him as he and I were riding along. He was due to visit one of the battery HQs, I learned, but just before he was to set off his staff car had run over a mine and been blown up, in fact it had somersaulted. Only the driver was in it at the time, poor devil; it had happened while he was taking a short cut instead of sticking to the route he had been given. The Colonel was immediately provided with another staff car but preferred to ride, rather than take any old car. He spoke very little, maybe he was still thinking about his driver who got blown up or perhaps he was concentrating on our route as it was still very dangerous.

Why didn't we take an escort? I asked him. 'My dear boy,' he said, 'the fewer we are, the less we will be noticed.' Well, there was something in that, I agreed, making sure my rifle was handy and sharpening my senses, remembering the observation I was trained for.

I felt intensely proud when, while we halted for a while, he leaned over and showed me the map criss-crossed with blue, red and black pencil marks. We discussed the terrain and decided on the route.

It was not too difficult but it could have been nasty if we had lost our way. A number of French units had broken through, so strengthening of front lines was ordered and also cutting off the smaller units that had somehow filtered through. Very relieved to see our company posts en route, we asked for the HQ and a chap actually offered to run in front and show us the way. It was in the middle of a large wooded area, and suddenly there was a lot of activity around us. We caused quite a stir, the Colonel being CO of the Regiment, and we even got a mug of coffee and some brandy.

Everybody made a fuss of the horses. They all seemed to be in a very good mood, practically celebrating indeed: German troops occupied Paris, they told us, which explained the smiling faces.

The pincers had closed—hence the break-outs of smaller French units—and now arrangements were being made for huge masses of prisoners of war. Nothing like my little bunch of POWs back in Belgium: I heard the number was at least twenty thousand.

It would not be too long now before the war in France would be over. On the way back the Colonel was a great deal more talkative, whether because of the good news or the brandy it was hard to say, but I told myself to be doubly alert for I did not like the wooded terrain and the prospect of being ambushed by stray troops from the French units made me very uneasy.

'Cheer up, my boy, it won't be long now. Tomorrow we march south and then, who knows, we should be home in Germany.'

The fifteenth of June 1940. We marched south, but in a greater hurry than I thought necessary. The reason was—I heard later on from Buschmann, the Colonel's batman, who sometimes knew more of what was going on than all the rest of the officers—so as not to get caught up with the POWs.

We marched on for the next couple of days, and it became routine again, stopping only to feed the horses and ourselves. I actually developed the art of sleeping on horseback, or near enough, since we, the horse-holders, did not need our horses for any possible engagement; the officers all had two horses each and changed over now and then to use them evenly. Sometimes we strayed off the prescribed route to get some food and drink. The mood had definitely changed all round, for everyone was hoping this campaign would soon be over.

We still had some shock surprises from the French planes, to remind us that the war was not yet over, even though Paris was in German hands. From the news on the radio we learned that Hitler wanted to lay down his conditions of surrender, but nothing had yet materialised.

On 18 June, again listening to Hitler's voice, we heard, after some marches had been played to herald it, the announcement: 'Unconditional surrender is demanded.'

Our rests became longer and we even had time to swim in the rivers, the horses as well. We took their saddles off but left on the bridles for better control, and usually mounted our horses starkers since there were no people about, then rode into the river till the horses began to paddle with their forelegs. The very hot weather was back and it was a simply delightful way to cool off. We were swimming in the River Seine, near Saint-Parres-lès-Vaudes, when it happened: two French planes, goodness knows what type, probably fighters, came screaming along the river and kept on firing. We just froze; I know I did. I even dived below the surface, but what good would that do?

We got hit, though I and my horse by some miracle did not. Three horses were hit, but not badly, and no men were hurt. This really shook us up and we could only thank God for this lucky escape. We left the area as quickly as possible, for it was open country with very little cover in the way of trees or other forms of cover and we could not know whether the fighters would return or not, and we licked our wounds a bit further on between some houses. Our casualties were the vet's two horses and the Adjutant's; fortunately, they were only flesh wounds, and there would be no need for replacements, the wounds could be dealt with on the march. It could so easily have been disastrous.

Relentlessly we marched on, stopping at a small place for a few hours' rest, and then resuming our trek. This went on for a few days, day and night. We marched almost thirty kilometres every day; we really could do with some longer rests as the horses were also in need of it.

On 22 June we stopped in the countryside near a small hamlet. Nowhere could we find any French folk any more; they must have all marched south in front of us. The gardens were well stocked with strawberries, and we got hold of some chickens. When I was a saddler's apprentice in the east of Germany I had learned how to kill, pluck and cook them. We were really beginning to enjoy ourselves. Eventually the Colonel got a replacement for his car, so really I had nothing to worry about except my horses and myself. During the last few days I rarely saw the field kitchen—cooking was becoming for me an interesting and very welcome hobby. Only the best was good enough. If I could not find a household kitchen full of wonderful herbs, I just built myself an open fire, with bricks if possible.

At 1.35 in the morning of 25 June we arrived at Villaines-en-Duemois, a friendly little town, but a very long one, stretching some ten kilometres to Montbard, a somewhat larger place.

The good news was that France had given up—ceasefire in other words. We could hardly sleep, we were dog-tired, but so excited that the war in France was over for us; even the horses seemed to smile.

Villaines suited us very well; the people were actually still there. They

Riding out with the CO of his unit, Colonel von Tchudy (left) in 1940
— the Colonel on Nachbar, Kuhnert on Ire.

In Belgium during the German advance, May 1940. Notice that the polish has gone from his boots, and he has a stick grenade thrust into his belt.

(bottom)   As the Germans overran Northern France, the rider troops of cavalry scouts attached to infantry regiments played an important part in maintaining the momentum of the advance. Kuhnert's unit on the move — he is at extreme left.

didn't want war any more. *'La guerre n'est pas bien,'* they kept saying to us. We became quite friendly with a butcher, his wife and their three daughters. I think their name was Ammoit; the daughters were called Louisanne, Charlotte, and Jeanne. The girls reminded me of the fairy story, *Cinderella*; Charlotte, the pretty one, worked all day, while Louisanne and Jeanne tried to make themselves pretty and failed miserably.

Our horses were out to grass and also had a beautiful brook to swim in. And I too had a beautiful swim, but that was after I met Paulette. She was a petite blonde, seventeen years old, who lived only three houses down from where I was in quarters. While most of my compatriots were competing for the favours of the butcher's daughter, I was busy being nice to Paulette's mother—even bringing her tasty dishes from the butcher over the road, so of course we sat down at the table together. Since we were apparently in no hurry, I took my time in taking liberties and impressed Paulette's mama even more by riding by, the next day— mind you, purely by chance—accompanying the CO. He wanted to get to know the terrain better and also had to visit the battalions which were in quarters around Villaines.

'My,' said Paulette's mother in the evening. 'I didn't know you were so high up. And what a pretty picture you two made.' She almost made me blush.

We, the company, didn't have all the day to ourselves; there were plenty of other things to do and there were inspections, of one thing or another, every day; but the nights belonged to us. On Sunday the whole company marched to church, where Colonel von Tchudy spoke a few words in remembrance of our comrades who were no longer with us, and thanked God for our victory.

Paulette liked walking, but not in the village. She was still very shy, I thought, to be seen alone with a German, so we usually walked from the back of mother's house (her mother was a widow, I found out, but it had nothing to do with the war). We got on very well together, the three of us, and had a good many laughs because of our language, or lack of it.

Lieutenant Becker stopped me one day. 'I have a job for you, if you would be so kind.' The 'If you would be so kind' alarmed me—he usually cared very little if I would be kind or not. What he wanted was a cover for his personal saddle, a beautiful hunting one. I might have known it would be something like that. He handed me a green tent sheet and a long zip. 'See what you can do.'

So I set to it and, with the help of Paulette's mother's sewing machine, I soon got the thing finished. As a reward I took the afternoon off, of course with Paulette. We walked the back way, down to the brook. It was blazing hot, no one was about except us and we were half sitting, half lying in the grass full of buttercups, it was just heaven.

'Why don't we go for a swim?' she suddenly asked me.

'All right,' I said, nodding my head in agreement, and then I remembered that I had no swimming trunks; I had never felt so shy before. I made it quite clear to her, but she indicated that there was nobody there but us. Neither was there any cover other than the long grass and the small embankment. 'Oh well,' I thought, 'here goes,' and took off my boots, then my coat, shirt and socks; and, creeping towards the slope of the brook, I turned round to look at her and there she was completely naked, laughing at me, and I was actually blushing. That was too much, I slipped my trousers off and ran towards her, she turned and raced towards the river. I was glad to hit the water for obvious reasons. We had a lovely time and after bathing and splashing and kissing, we were loving each other inexhaustibly and forgot all about time, war and nationality, we just held each other and did not even speak one word.

The next morning the Colonel wanted his horses. Somehow the world around me was looking much friendlier, but now there was the sadness of an imminent goodbye. Maybe I could go back? Why not? We were both young; I could pick up the language, or maybe she could come to Germany?

'Well? Enjoyed your rest?' the Colonel's voice broke into my daydreaming.

'Yes, sir,' I replied.

'What's the matter, my boy?' He always called me 'my boy'. I told him about Paulette, and could not believe my own ears—that I was capable of telling such a thing to the Colonel of the Regiment. Suddenly realising what I was saying, I tried to apologise, but he waved his hand. 'Think nothing of it, my boy, we all went through similar experiences when young,' and he told me how he felt during the First World War, and how he met his wife, and then, casually, 'My wife comes from France, you know.'

My mouth just stayed open and eventually turned into a kind of relieved grin and we both laughed really loud. I remember the ears of the horses twitching round, a pity they could not laugh, or could they? At least, or so I thought, they gave me a curious look.

The time had simply flown by and it was 12 July, and for two weeks we had enjoyed the rest and the hospitality of most of the people in Villaines, and we had also had great fun organising 'show-jumping' and football matches between the different units. I didn't like to say goodbye, I wanted this life to go on for ever. Paulette was very depressed and followed us with a few other French folk to the edge of the village. I had said goodbye the night before to her mother, who was really a great lady. I did write later on once but got no reply, maybe the letter went astray.

We marched in the direction of Dijon, and then, after a few hours' rest, made a full turn, but on to a different road, towards Montbard, and from then on we kept going, only stopping briefly in small villages, without having much contact with the population.

On 17 July 1940 we arrived at Dienville, a small place right on the River Aube, but no sooner had we got our horses to grass, than the order came to march again, it was all very confusing. So, march we did, via Hancourt (now Margerie-Hancourt) to Saint-Quentin-sur-Coole, where we had quite a lively time with the people, who were very nice and helpful. We were all relieved to hear that we were to be transported by train to Denmark, via Germany of course, and at once there was a sea of smiling faces. Most members of our regiment were from the north of Germany, especially Hamburg. If it was true that we were going to Denmark then we would have to go through Hamburg, and there was a chance of a stop there.

At the moment, though, we were still in France, and we marched to Sommesous, where there was a ramp which we needed for loading the horses. It took quite some time before we started to roll. Our train took us through Reims, then crossed into Belgium, and went via Leuven towards the Dutch border. We entered Germany at Dahlhem and continued through Duisberg in the direction of Hanover. Quite often our train had to stop, especially at night because of air raids by British planes. Travelling by train is not that simple when there is livestock to be looked after; carrying water was one of the biggest headaches, each horse wanted a great deal of water, and they also missed the grass they had got used to. Cleaning the wagons was no simple matter either as the horses stood very close together and we had to creep in between them to clean up, making every effort not to excite them too much. In any case, the smell was awful, and sometimes we left the door open, even though that was not allowed except when stationary.

We arrived in Hamburg on 4 August at 11.30 and stayed there for about two hours. Herbert Schutte, who had a wife and small daughter there, was heartbroken because no one was allowed to leave the train, not even for five minutes; he would have loved at least to telephone. The train rolled on through Neumünster, and we crossed into Denmark at Flensburg.

I had never been to Denmark before and I was excited at the prospect. Our destination was a town called Viborg on the mainland of Denmark, a beautiful little town with a lovely lake. Far too tired when we arrived to appreciate it, we got our horses stabled about a quarter of a mile from the large school which was to be our sleeping quarters.

We stayed in Viborg for nearly two months and had a splendid time there. We took advantage to the full of the marvellous riding terrain, and the lake—we often swam in it with our horses, who also enjoyed it, usually after exercising them on the other side of the lake where there was a kind of race course, and several jumps.

One thing which in particular struck me about Denmark was the cleanliness and honesty of most of its townspeople—even though I did have my coat stolen, with my wallet which had all my papers in it, when I left it hanging on the stable door to go swimming with the horse.

Most afternoons I had to take the Colonel's horse Nacky to the infantry barracks on the other side of the town, so as to get Nacky used to our military band. The Colonel was not a bad horseman, but he was not a brilliant one either. Every time we rode in front of the band, his horse shied terribly, especially at the sound of the cymbals. The loud bangs of the bass drum and the noise of the brass instruments also made him very nervous.

It was, to say the least, very embarrassing to our poor Colonel, and I was ordered to rectify this. So I took Nacky to band practice. Within a week, and with a great deal of soothing and persuasion, our Nacky began to get used to all the noise, and to the sight of shiny instruments and colourfully dressed bandsmen. The bandsmen made a great deal of fuss of him, which helped.

The exercise worked wonders, and no one was more pleased than the Colonel. The next time we went marching through the town to the sound of band music, Nacky was practically dancing to it much to the Colonel's delight.

We returned to Germany on 29-30 September and arrived at the troop exercise area at Bergen in Lower Saxony, to the north-east of Hanover.

8

Rotten Eggs

Now that we were back in Germany our hopes were high for ultimate victory. We had defeated the French, the British were back in England, and we had occupied France, Belgium, Holland, Denmark, Norway and Poland. Our hopes were also high for an early dismissal from the army. We soon received our first cold shower when the announcement was made, that we—that is, our regiment, which yet had to be properly formed—were going to Poland. Little did we expect what was in store for us and no one, not even Colonel von Tchudy, knew what was going to happen. No one could see the dark clouds forming in the east.

I was still in charge of the Colonel's horses, though at the moment we were still awaiting their arrival. I was quite confident that from now on everything was going to be fine, peaceful. Maybe only a few weeks in Poland then the war would be at an end. A few of our soldiers were sceptical, some were saying that we would yet have to fight the USA. I myself didn't believe that, and when someone mentioned Soviet Russia, I could only smile. It was too preposterous even to think about, because in my opinion we had no quarrel with either of them.

So confident were we that very soon we would be at home with our families that we even began to look forward to the assignment to Poland. A few weeks would not make all that much difference. Besides, many of us had not been to Poland.

Since we had left all our equipment—even our sabres—and our horses, in Denmark, we felt rather lost. Only the regimental staff and all the other officers of the three battalions, moved to Germany, the remainder stayed in Denmark. The troop exercise area in Bergen, where we were, was an enormous complex, all new barracks, including a magnificent officers' casino. I heard that Hitler nearly had it pulled down as it was too grand for his liking, as well as being too extravagant in the circumstances. I was housed with the officers, and their batmen, of our old regiment. After a few days of orientation I began to like it—after all, I had practically nothing to do since our new horses had not yet arrived. Apparently, the formation of a complete new regiment was in its first stage.

Bergen, situated in Lower Saxony, was only a small town, and since I had nothing to do, I went for drives with the Colonel's driver, Walter Kleber—in the Colonel's Mercedes, of course. Walter was also a corporal and a fine comrade to be with.

The new leader of the new rider troop was to be Sergeant Helm, a large chap. The officer who should have been in charge had not been chosen as yet. Lieutenant Becker, at present the regiment's Ordnance Officer, had been our troop leader in France but it would not be him; he told me so himself when he enquired about the new stables.

Sergeant Helm asked me, 'Why not come back to the new rider troop?' It would be much better, he said, especially in the way of promotion and he would like to have someone of my experience in machine-guns, etc. After he had asked me several times I told him that I was earnestly thinking about it because I was getting quite soft with not much to do except cleaning the equipment.

Many troops arrived and the barracks were beginning to fill up. It was lovely to hear all the old marching songs again. It was almost like old times in Lüneburg.

At the beginning of March we eventually got the new horses. First to arrive were the Colonel's and the Adjutant's, and eventually the stables were filled with the horses for the newly formed rider troop, about forty in all.

Sergeant Helm approached me again, urging me to make up my mind. I'm afraid I declined. One reason was that Captain Rothansel, who had joined us from an Austrian infantry regiment in Denmark as Adjutant to the Colonel, wanted me to give him some riding lessons. He had had very little riding experience. The other reason for declining Sergeant Helm's offer was that the Colonel had put me in charge of his horses by recommendation of Lieutenant Becker (after the episode at Namur where I lost my horse and many of my companions), and I did not like to betray Lieutenant Becker's trust. I decided once and for all to stay with the Colonel's horses.

The Colonel's new horse was nowhere near as placid or as suitable as Nacky, who had been left in Denmark. Also a dark bay, Albert, a ten-year-old Hanoverian, looked much like Nacky. My new horse was an eight-year-old Trakhener, chestnut in colour and 17 hands high. His name was Siegfried and we took an instant liking to each other. After our first ride on our new horses, the Colonel said to me, indicating Albert, 'My dear boy, I don't believe in whips, but this beast could do with it sometimes.' I quite agreed with him there, but the army did not carry whips except when soldiering.

Once we had our horses, time went much faster and soon it was spring.

Things began to move now, the snow was disappearing—unlike the rumours, there were now so many of them. Colonel von Tchudy told me, on one of what he called our practice rides, that we would most likely be moving out in the direction of Poland, presumably to relieve the occupation troops there. It made sense.

I was very careful not to make too many friends in and around Bergen, for I still thought a lot about Paulette in France. I also had so many girlfriends in other parts of Germany to whom I was obliged to write, to say the least. In Denmark my time was mostly taken up with riding and swimming; only in one or two cases was I more intimately acquainted. As there was not much going on in Bergen in the way of entertainment, I often recollected and reflected upon the good times. I recalled an unfortunate happening in Denmark. As the weather was most of the time brilliant when we were there we had some great times on horseback. The terrain was marvellous and there was also a lake in Viborg, around which was a bridle path, right on the embankment. So we organised a horse race around the lake, the fastest around the lake the winner. When it was my turn, I chose to ride Nacky at first, and towards the end I would take Ire, because he was much faster. So off I went, first at a steady canter, and then I clicked my tongue and gave Nacky more rein; he flattened his ears and thundered along the narrow bridle path through the wooded area, on my left the water, on my right the very steep embankment. And round the corner was near disaster: a woman carrying a basket. We saw each other in the nick of time. She threw away her basket and hurled herself flat on the embankment, and I just missed her. I reined Nacky in and turned round to see if she was all right; she, no doubt thinking I would come for her again, threw her arms up and ran blindly away, screaming at the top of her voice.

A few days later it was announced in the local newspaper that some unscrupulous German soldier had tried to ride down an innocent woman and that HQ in Viborg had offered their regrets and profound apologies, saying everything would be done to find out who the culprit was. Since nobody was hurt we all kept very quiet about it.

Then there was the churchyard affair, where I nearly came to grief. We, that is my girlfriend and I, went for an early evening stroll in the area of the churchyard near the school where our quarters were, and, going further through the churchyard, came upon some marvellous shrubland. We remained in the area for some time and when it became dark we decided to return home. But when we got to the churchyard gate, it was locked. As there was no other way out we had to scale the very high iron fence—it must have been ten or twelve feet high. With shoving and pushing and pulling, we managed in the end. Then she discovered that she had left her keys behind somewhere in the grass. So I had to do it all over again and trying to show off I almost became a eunuch. Dropping down the other side I felt like howling in pain. I only had my lighter with me, but to my relief, after several minutes of searching in the high grass, I found what I was looking for. Then the big climb over the fence again. Since then I have never wanted to go for walks in churchyards; at least, I have become a great deal more careful.

By the end of March, we were a complete regiment and we assembled for the first time. Outside the barracks area there was plenty of open terrain. I had not seen so many units together since the days of Nürnberg in 1937 when I was in 3 Squadron of 13th Cavalry Regiment in Lüneburg and we had been selected to march or trot past Hitler and his staff. Eighteen horses in one line to the music of our regimental march, played by no less than thirty bands at once. It was indeed a splendid occasion. Now, here in Bergen in March of '41, we also had our band playing, but this time I was at the Commanding Officer's side and when the troops marched past, the Colonel took the salute. Three battalions and all the special units such as 13 (howitzer) and 14 (anti-tank) Companies.

The following week we had our first exercise; the entire regiment took part and it lasted three days. It was the first time I was out with Siegfried in full kit. I also had Albert on the leading rein, and he carried an enormous contraption on his saddle. It was a cylinder made of leather holding the stereoscope. This instrument looked like a pair of scissors when in use, which gave it its German name of *Scherenfernrohr*, 'scissor-binoculars'. It was used mainly in trenches but also in high grass or shrubland.

We really had to pull ourselves together, for many of us were virtually strangers to one another. As usual there was a blue unit and a red unit; I belonged with the Colonel in the blue unit, and we were defending a certain point which the red unit had to try to take. It all became a bit of a mix-up in the end, most likely the fault of the Reservists. Once, we had to move through some swamp in order to gain a better position. Colonel von Tchudy was on my right and the path was rather narrow. His Albert, again playing up and sidestepping, began to slip almost into the ground. It was covered with heather, but underneath was swamp. The Colonel being a heavy man was no help to the horse, who began thrashing about to gain a foothold. I jumped off my Siegfried and pulled the Colonel clear with all my might, and then steadied Albert by holding his bridle and shouted for the Colonel to get my saddle off quick, so I could have my blanket. Our blankets were very large and strong. I pushed the blanket underneath Albert's forehoofs and then we encouraged him to get on to solid ground by whipping his quarters; the Colonel pulled from the front, and with a lot of shouting, swearing and sweating, we eventually got him out. Thank God it was only a shallow swamp patch otherwise it would have been impossible. Visibly shaken, the Colonel sat down for a few minutes and lit one of his cigars.

We were all glad when the three days were over, too many events had been crammed into such a short space of time. Still, I had to smile because the Colonel looked like anybody else when covered in mud.

It was 20 April when very suddenly and without warning we got our orders to be ready within twenty-four hours to march to the station in Bergen. Luckily the weather was fine, there were so many things that had to be done—simple things like collecting the washing in town were less simple because there was no transport. Walter, the Colonel's driver, usually took me down, but this time he was very busy himself. Then there were not only the horses to get ready, but also all one's equipment, which had to be loaded almost at once otherwise one had to carry it to the station oneself—some two miles into town.

Several units were already marching, and we in the rider staff got on the move too, loading the horses into the goods wagons, getting food supplies for ourselves and the horses. It was very tiring and by the time the regimental band was playing a farewell tune, we were already looking forward to having a good sleep in the bales of hay in the centre of the wagon.

We got to Warsaw after a long and dreary three days in that slow-rolling train. Eventually it crawled into Praga, the eastern part of the city, and there we stopped to unload. So far we had only seen Poland from the train and only the countryside. It was indeed a big country, and very thinly populated—we had hardly seen anybody, and only then when we stopped briefly to water the horses, when we met a few country folk who seemed very shy.

Now, in the outskirts of Warsaw, we actually spoke to some. There were plenty of young people around, and the first thing I noticed was a small urchin hardly ten or eleven years old, begging for bread while puffing away at a cigarette. I was rather shocked; 'What a nerve,' I thought. In Germany even a woman didn't smoke, at least not openly. The region was laid waste, and the people looked unwashed and generally neglected. I felt rather sad about the whole thing. Why was this happening? I myself would rather be home, and build myself a future in peaceful conditions; instead I was here in a strange country and seeing all this. I found this squalor totally unnecessary, maybe the war would soon be over and then we could get on with something better instead of wasting our lives.

There was no ramp at the station and we had to shift straw bales in front of the wagon doors to create some sort of steps for the horses to get down. It sounds very simple, but you just try to get horses to step down on to bales of hay. Besides, they had been standing on the journey and their legs were rather stiff. We also had to help to get all the rest of the company out quickly because another train carrying a lot of troops was expected very shortly in our place. After unloading, and without hanging about, we marched off in an easterly direction until we were well away from Warsaw and again in the countryside. Roads were non-existent, and we were glad that the weather was dry and sunny; there was, though, a very sharp wind blowing and we had to put our handkerchiefs over the lower part of our faces to keep out the dust.

What made me smile was our band marching with us, not playing, though some carried instruments, looking pretty miserable, not really used to this kind of terrain. We were leading our horses and if you have ever marched leading two horses then you would know that you walk in between them. On rough, sandy terrain it can become a very bumpy affair, being knocked from one side to the other. I soon started to sweat. We also got hungry and thirsty, and sleep too would have been very welcome—since the beginning of the journey we had had very little of it. We stopped well before dark in a large pine wood, really lovely. There were several houses nearby, but they were not for us—one of the villas belonged to a Polish countess, we were told.

The officers seemed to disappear suddenly while we were busy getting water and so on for the horses. It was a beautiful evening, and while we were watering the horses, the field kitchen was now busy for our well being. Even our band got more cheerful after a good meal, and actually gave us a concert later—that is, several pieces suitable for our first camp in Poland. In the end when it was nearly dark a trumpeter disappeared into the wood and played 'Post in the Forest'. It was very moving indeed. Our officers reappeared with some smartly dressed women, presumably the Countess and her friends, to look at our horses.

But where were we going? Nobody seemed to know; I had believed that we were only in Poland to relieve some of our troops, but it became very puzzling as we just kept marching, hardly meeting any people or even villages; it was very sandy terrain and very tiring. After several stops, we eventually stopped at a place called Wolomin, in the middle of farmland. There was a large school building and next to it a big house suitable for all the regimental officers and with enough room for all the members of the regimental company. Our quarters were on the outskirts of the town, with the staff officers', in a big empty house in splendid surroundings, with large gardens and some trees.

We had to provide every comfort for the officers, and I remember the first thing I had to do was to put up curtains. So I set off to get the material in town. There were plenty of shops, if such they could be called—it was all very primitive and the people were pretty poor. Nowhere could I buy any curtains or any cloth, but a nice lady said to me, 'Why not put paper curtains up? You don't have to wash them and they only need pinning.'

'A very good idea,' I said and thanked her. She sold me several rolls of crêpe paper and some drawings pins. The girl was very helpful, and very pretty as well. She only helped out in the shop, she told me. She lived with her mother on the outskirts of Wolomin. Her name was Wanda. I made several visits to the shop for one thing or another, and she invited me for tea on Sunday afternoon. 'Please come,' she said.

After cutting and pinning paper curtains on the windows, we all had a good look at the job and screamed with laughter. There was the blue room, the green room, the yellow room, and so on. Someone remarked that all we now needed was some brown paper for the toilet and bathroom.

At night we had to remove a pin on each side so that the paper could hang down in front of the window. We were all waiting for the officers to arrive, wondering what they would say when the lights were switched on. I remember that Buschmann, the Colonel's batman, prepared a sort of egg nog with 5-star French cognac, just in case the lot of them got mad with their colourful surroundings. Every officer had his own room, and we had put his name on a card on the door. The Colonel had the blue room. Strangely enough, none of the officers said a word, not even in the morning when the light was shining through the colours and it looked pretty weird. A few weeks later, I asked the Colonel how he liked his curtains in Wolomin. 'Oh,' he said, 'all right, a bit loud, otherwise fine. Why?' So I told him why he had the blue room, while the others had the red, the green and so on. We had a good laugh.

The Sunday afternoon tea in Wanda's house was an eye opener for me. Their home was nothing more than a dugout, with earth packed hard on top, where a stove-pipe was sticking out. It was very clean, and they had baked a cake specially. I could have cried; one could taste that it had not been easy to bake a cake without most of the essential ingredients.

The next day I had to go into the countryside for some eggs and I promised myself that I would take some for Wanda; maybe I would find some other foodstuff for them as well. Her mother was very delicate, which was not surprising in the circumstances. So, armed with a basket, I saddled Nineveh, the horse assigned to Lieutenant Becker, who had asked me to exercise her as much as possible. She was a beautiful chestnut mare, very frisky, but lovely to ride. Come to think of it, in those days I must have been very naive to take such a risk—we were advised always to go in pairs. In any case, I enjoyed riding through the countryside, and eventually I came to a fairly large farmstead. To my surprise there were a number of horse carriages in the yard, and many people, all in festive dress, and a great deal of laughter and music. Well, I thought, that is definitely some luck. I was made very welcome as I dismounted by a pretty young woman who handed me a slice of bread and sprinkled some salt on it. This much I had learned already—that it meant 'Please come in, you are welcome'; it was a christening, in Poland a great occasion. All the friends and relations were present, sitting at makeshift tables in the barn. I felt like an intruder, but I needn't have worried. The food was plentiful and there was also beer, wine and the country's excellent vodka. First you eat one slice of very dark home-baked bread with a hard-boiled egg and then wash it down with vodka. I was invited to see the baby, a girl, and wish her all the best in life. I wonder where she is now, how sad to be born into such a cruel world of war and destruction.

After several drinks I was also very merry like the rest; suddenly I remembered the horse I had left in the yard, but she too was being taken care of and someone had provided some hay which she was chewing happily; they had even taken the bit out of her mouth to make it easier.

We were really letting our hair down in the way of merry-making, I remember I slipped out to take my belt off with my gun and hid it somewhere, just in case. Now I really could take part in the dancing, mostly folk dances, and I had a marvellous time. The music was provided by a violin, a harmonica and a balalaika. I even played a little on the balalaika myself to everybody's delight, for I could play the mandolin and they are very similar instruments. I had no idea what time it was, it was very dark when I got on my horse eventually and was carried home. I went back the next day for the eggs and to say thank you properly.

I saw Wanda several times and I made sure that I always had something in the way of food to take with me. They really had no life at all, just an existence and not a very nice one either. Language problems were very few; in fact I got on rather well and I must say most of the people were very helpful in understanding sign language.

The weather had improved, and we were as warm as one could expect at the beginning of May. All nature was in the process of expressing itself in fresh green and colourful displays. I could not help thinking of the time a year ago—how quickly the year had flown by—and I still had a painful sadness when I remembered all the friends and comrades we had lost so tragically the last May. What now for us? Riding around with the Colonel to inspect a battalion, I wanted but didn't have the nerve to ask him what our destination was going to be (I also kept quiet about the christening party I went to—he would most likely have given me a ticking off).

Uncertainty still remained when we got our marching orders. Nobody seemed to know where we were going or what for. Buschmann, the Colonel's batman, our two-legged newspaper, as we called him, could not help either. Off we went, this time away from what were called the main roads and into real, thickly forested countryside, and there was plenty of it. Several times we stayed overnight in the middle of the forest, as long as there was water. It was rather pleasant, except maybe for the lack of grass for the horses.

Mordy was a small town similar to Wolomin but with an estate house with stables and plenty of room for officers and staff. In front of the estate house was a large lawn surrounded by flower beds, and there were plenty of outhouses for the motorpool and field kitchen, etc. Again it was in farm country, with plenty of good terrain for some really good gallops.

In the morning the Colonel and his staff officers attended a flag-hoisting ceremony. I found it rather childish and it reminded me of my young days when I was in the boy scouts. I still have a small photograph of it taken by Buschmann.

The civilian community was a mixed lot of farmers, tradesmen, and also a Jewish circle, made up mainly of rabbis or elders. We could not help but notice them because they were dressed in their traditional dress of kaftan and cap with the funny sidepieces embroidered on the ends. If I remember rightly most of the tradesmen were also Jewish. Now and then we wandered off into the small town when we had time to spare, to get extras in the way of food and so on. Eggs were always a very welcome commodity but not always easy to get hold of. Somehow I got wind of how to obtain a few at a price. The place was a small upstairs room, occupied by one of the Jewish elders who had in his hands practically all the strings of all the rare and difficult things obtainable. Money was simply not good enough for eggs, he croaked, maybe some spirits, or tobacco perhaps. I settled for tobacco—one packet of Brinkman cigarette tobacco for one dozen eggs was agreed on, and the exchange made the next morning in his upstairs room. Highly satisfied with my bargain and already anticipating my enormous omelette, I set off home hurriedly and invited Walter, the Colonel's driver, and Buschmann to join me. Buschmann was important as he had not only a large frying pan, but also the fat for frying. Everything was set for our banquet of omelette.

The frying pan was hot, the fat sizzled, and we set off, smashing eggs. We'd broken about six before we realised that the blasted things were foul, and just howled with rage—not only from the realisation that we had no meal forthcoming but also because the eggs stank to high heaven.

I wanted to storm straight down to the confounded old man and smash the eggs down his throat; Walter said let's all go together, Buschmann agreed, and then I thought better of it. What would it look like, three German soldiers walking down the road with a frying pan full of rotten eggs, seeking an ageing Jew? Maybe he didn't know the eggs were rotten himself—after all, he had himself got them from someone else. Let's think of something better, I said, and maybe something to get our own back. So we all racked our brains; in the end I myself got the idea, when I was with the horses, to exchange tobacco with solid horse manure. I took the tobacco out of another packet, put dried manure in its place and neatly resealed the packet. Satisfied with my work of art, I went back the next day to my Jewish friend and, smiling broadly, I told him how we had all enjoyed his eggs and could he again be so kind and oblige with another dozen for a packet of tobacco.

'Surely, my son,' he said as if he really meant it. I rather liked him in fact and felt just a little bit guilty when he returned from the adjoining room with the eggs in a makeshift paper bag. I thrust the tobacco packet in his hands and, thanking him for his enormous kindness, I hurried down the stairs hoping that the blessed eggs were fresh this time. They were, luckily—if the things had been bad again, goodness only knows what I would have done.

Gina was one of the girls who had been temporarily engaged by the regiment to clean the officers' quarters in their Polish house. She was a very pleasant girl, but one could see that she was very poor, like most of the people in this area. I got talking to her on the rather splendid staircase leading to the many rooms upstairs. She was living with her mother (like Wanda in Wolomin) about four kilometres out of town, and every morning she walked all the way here and back again in the afternoon. 'I can give you a lift home,' I said, for I always exercised Siegfried in the afternoon in case the Colonel wanted to ride in the morning.

'Thank you,' she said. 'But how?'

'Oh, just walk to the top of the town and I will collect you there. All right?'

It was not very simple—Siegfried was a seventeen-hander, and there she was, pretty as a picture and barefoot as well, far below on the ground. I decided to pull her up, remaining in the saddle, rather than try to push her. Siegfried stood like a rock, and eventually she was sitting astride in front of me. I'm sure it could not have been very comfortable but she never said a word. She was eighteen or nineteen and, like most of the Polish girls she was big busted and slim in the waist; she even blushed when I put my arms around her to hold the reins properly. Laughing, giggling and joking we proceeded at a walk right across the open fields and then I saw them, a lieutenant and a corporal of 14 Company. No good turning now, I thought. The rule in encounters of this kind with officers was that I had to report my name, where I came from and where I was going. So I smartly reported as my position allowed it, emphasising that the girl was Colonel von Tchudy's cleaning lady whom I'd been ordered to take home. 'Carry on, corporal,' said the lieutenant, grinning all over his young face while the corporal at his side winked as if to say, 'You lucky dog'. I only hoped that the lieutenant would not enquire too much into the so-called order.

Captain Rothansel, to whom I'd given some riding lessons in Bergen, had asked me to give him some more. He never *told* me, he always asked in a very pleasant manner. There was a large oval lawn in front of the estate house near the stables, which I thought would be the place for it, and he agreed. There was just one thing we forgot—the motorpool which was in the corner near the entrance: since they had no idea about riding and not much to do at the time, they all stood around watching what was going on. Captain

Rothansel's horse Mars, an eight-year-old bay gelding, was marvellous to ride and very safe, even for a beginner like him. The captain was very eager to learn more, and we got on just fine. Except on one particular afternoon.

Captain Rothansel had started cantering around the oval, which had in its centre a flowerbed, when suddenly one of the fellows in the motorpool startled Mars by revving up an engine, and Mars took off. Poor Captain Rothansel, he just did not know what to do. He went round and round the oval in front of the house, and soon all the officers were standing at their windows, some leaning out shouting advice, which the Captain did not hear in any case. I had given up shouting and to avoid a nasty accident stayed well in the centre, hoping that he would fall off on soft ground when the crunch came. If I had only told him what to do in such a case it would have been all right, but he did all the wrong things. I suppose every beginner would have done what he did, leaning forward and pulling on the reins, not realising that by doing so, the horse only pulls more and will always be the winner in the end. If he had just sat back and held his hands still, continuing to ride in a circle but decreasing the radius, the horse would eventually have stopped with no problems at all. Captain Rothansel grew tired, realising that he was fighting a losing battle, and, seeing everybody shouting and waving, steered Mars towards the outbuilding opposite the motorpool. Mars, startled into reality by seeing a solid brick wall in front of him, slowed down and stopped. Captain Rothansel, who had lost his stirrups, came off like a shot, but landed on his feet thank goodness; his shoulders were sagging forward and his cap was down on his neck and, I could have sworn, his knees were knocking. Poor Captain Rothansel, I really felt sorry for him—but also for the fellow who had started it off by revving the engine. After swearing like a trooper at me (who had to catch Mars), Captain Rothansel strode straight to the motorpool. Well, someone had to take the blame, never the rider. I bet he had his leg pulled that evening by his fellow officers.

It was now the middle of June and with the temperature in the 70s or 80s. Troop exercises took place practically every day in our area. More often than ever Colonel von Tchudy would ride with me to visit the battalions in his sector. I asked him one morning what he thought was going to happen and was it really true, as some rumours indicated, that we were about to invade Russia?

'My dear boy,' he said in his usual manner, 'I don't know any more than you. I have a letter in my office only to be opened, in front of all the officers concerned, when I get a telephone call. Then I will know what to do and what is going to happen. Let's hope it's nothing stupid—we don't want another conflict.' So there it was and I reckoned something serious must be in the air. Why all this fuss—sealed letter, mysterious telephone call—otherwise? I had in my time with the Colonel learned one thing—to keep my mouth shut on such matters. No one would hear anything from me and blow it up out of proportion.

We left shortly afterwards in the direction of the River Bug, which in those days was the border of Russia and Poland. We stopped at a small village called Nova Gorniga; like so many of the Polish villages we'd stopped at, it was made up of poor country houses stretching some three to four miles along either side of a dirt road.

'Don't settle in too much, we are only staying for a few days,' we were told. It was all very confusing. I had not been able to ask the Colonel what was happening as I had not seen him in the last few days. He had gone by staff car to several command posts, and in a hurry at that, I learned from Walter his chauffeur. But that is all I could learn—Walter told me that he actually was a bit scared of the Colonel and would never dare to ask any questions like I did.

9

Into Russia

On 20 June 1941 we marched into an area of dense forest, only about four kilometres from the River Bug. Any comfort for man and horse was completely absent; in fact I had to ride a long way to get the horses watered and that was at least three times a day. The conviction grew within me that we were poised to go over the river and therefore over the border into Russia. Most of my comrades to whom I spoke about the situation, however, still did not think that we were going to attack Russia; that we were on the threshold of a new campaign and a frightfully uncertain future was inconceivable to us.

We were wrong. Even I, who had known deep down that it was going to happen and hoped like everyone else to get back home, was shocked on the morning of 21 June 1941. At exactly 3.15 a.m., in the faint first light of day I was on my way to water the horses at the river when the whole area exploded. All hell was let loose and I prayed for the strength to hold my two horses. The noise and sight were indescribable, the earth seemed to tremble, all the batteries came alive out of the darkness of the pine trees. Flames shot towards the border followed by the explosion of the shells on the other side. All around us were what appeared to be great sheets of lightning, torn through by flames while thunder crashed and boomed. The barrage kept on and on, no one could hear anything else and orders had to be given by hand signal. We were ordered to march towards the river, where special units had already erected a pontoon bridge, over which, although we could not hear them, we could see our tanks rumbling. For an hour and a half the firing continued, and then we could hear the Russian planes attacking our invading troops; many of them got shot down by our fighters. Regimental Sergeant-Major Hamann told me to get over the river under my own steam, in other words, I was to get the horses across, but not over the pontoon bridge as there was simply no room for the animals; in any case I believe the horses would have panicked with the tremendous swaying of the bridge—it was a fast-flowing river.

So I took my heart in my hands and, still shocked, rode Siegfried, leading Albert on my right, along the river, frantically looking for an easy way over.

Shells were now flying across from the opposite direction as well, and smoke was filling my nostrils. In fact, I prayed. This was really getting frightening, how on earth could I manage? When we practised river crossings in Germany I had only one horse to think of, but here I was with two and I didn't even know if they liked water. Besides, the whole situation—the shellfire and plane attacks and nearby exploding bombs—had upset them both, not to speak about myself. We moved along the riverside for some time before I made up my mind and thought I'd found a comparatively safe spot, though I constantly scanned the other side of the river for movement. The narrowest part was some 100 to 150 metres across. The procedure began with the triangular tent sheets, of which I had two, having two horses. Into each tent sheet, spread out on the ground, I tightly packed saddle blanket, saddle, saddlebags and two days' supply of oats; into mine—Siegfried's—I added my clothing. Having padded out each bundle with handfuls of the grass that was growing all around, I tied each up with a tent cord—some 5 metres in length—placing my helmet and carbine on the top of my bundle so as to keep them as far out of the water as possible as we crossed the river.

Now came the more difficult part. I decided to go in between the two horses to the water's edge. I fastened the tent cords to my belt, making sure I had enough slack, and with Albert's reins slung on my left arm, I grabbed Siegfried's mane with my left hand and pulled myself up with my right hand on his withers. It wasn't easy but I managed. Off we went. At first both horses resisted, but eventually they walked quite calmly into the river, only snorting now and then in apprehension. Deeper and deeper we went, and I had a dreadful job staying on Siegfried because of the two bundles I had at my waist—if he had not had a long mane to hold onto I don't think I could have managed. Albert was at first on the verge of turning round, and only shouts—and seeing Siegfried being very good—kept him going, till at last we got deep enough and both started to swim. We must have been quite a sight—me with no clothes on, completely vulnerable... not much of an invading force, I couldn't help thinking. All three of us were now swimming, the horses with their heads flat on the water's surface, treading with their forelegs—for myself, the only thing I had to be careful of was not to be hit accidentally by their sharp front hoofs. With my left hand on Albert's cheek and my right on Siegfried's, we were paddling along nicely, but I had overlooked one thing: the strong current and the fast flow of the river. We made some headway, though only slowly, but at the same time we were being pulled at an enormous speed downstream. What a target I must have made.

Now that I had got the two animals more or less settled, as long as I gave them constant encouragement, I had time to grasp the terrible situation I was in. What if there were Russians on the other side, or if the embankment was too difficult to get up? Then another thought struck me: what if I or they get too tired and can't go any further? Since the night before I had had nothing to eat or drink, and I was beginning to feel the strain. The very fright of it must have given me strength, and after a while we came round the bend making headway all the time. The bend slowed the river's flow and we almost felt safe because of the calmness of the river. We got into shallow water and waded ashore only to find ourselves among some dead cattle, and if a horse hates anything at all that is it. Now I really got worried and, weak from the swimming, had a frightful time trying to keep them under control. But I managed to pull the two bundles ashore and then persuade both horses to walk to some bushes along the embankment, where I fastened them and calmed them down. I then walked back to get my bundles and, exhausted and relieved, I just sat down and let the horses graze. What next? I thought. I estimated the drift had been at least three or four miles. So my next task was to get going and find my unit as fast as possible.

Looking out for our divisional insignia, a blue square with a horizontal white line, I set off once more with the horses. Even better if I spotted the number 432 in one corner of the blue square, as that would be my regiment. The heat was now unbearable and the scenery did not improve it. There were plenty of signs of destruction, not only to the buildings but also to animals. There was air activity, not always fighters or bombers but also transport planes, which came very low indeed. At first I took cover every time I heard one, until I could tell by the sound of the engine if it was one of ours or a Russian aeroplane. I marched south-east at first to get in line with the advance route I had been told of by Sergeant Hamann. The terrain was mixed, but so far I hadn't seen any people though I had seen burnt-down houses. I always felt safer in the wooded area and began to hurry a bit, trotting now and then. I was still very apprehensive, not quite knowing where I was or where I was going. At last in the afternoon I sighted some movement in front and, to my relief, heard German voices.

I had had the good fortune to stumble on one of the artillery batteries from our division. They told me to hurry up if I wanted to catch up with my unit as they had marched very fast indeed. 'The Russians are on the run,' they said, 'and we will have a job to keep up with them.' Well, it was good news in one way, but the horses and I needed some rest. Feeling a great deal safer now, I at last relaxed and looked around for a suitable place to water and feed the horses. For myself I was not too worried—I simply scrounged something to eat from the artillery. Then I took my horses off the route into a farming area, where, to my surprise, an anti-aircraft unit had taken position and was already very much at home. They intended to stay for quite some time to protect the supply line to the front. I stopped there for nearly two hours, not too worried about catching up, as I knew that my unit would have to stop at some point and if I was late, well it was not my fault; I had not exactly taken a pleasure ride. I wondered how the others got over the river with their horses. Later I found out that they had been directed to a second bridge, and then a third one—a much larger and safer one that could take all supply vehicles. It could have taken the horses, too.

I caught up with my unit just before it got dark. Sergeant Hamann had been worried and he actually smiled at me after I told him the story. 'I've got a job for you, but better wait till first light, we cannot afford any slip-ups there,' he said.

The job was to go back along the main route and find the field kitchen, the cook and his two helpers, and their driver. Goodness only knows where they'd got lost.

'Get them at all cost. We need the food, etc.'

'Why didn't you send one of the horse holders?' I asked.

'You must be kidding,' he said. 'What do they know about anything? If I sent one or two of them we would then have to go and look for them. No, Kuhnert, you are the one. After all, you were trained for it, right?'

So there it was, not too difficult apparently but I had to ride against streams of traffic, and, as I found out, this was not simple at all.

I decided to leave early, if only to get away from this miserable hungry lot—I found all through the war that a hungry soldier is a dangerous one as well as being miserable. After a few hours' sleep I got ready, entrusting Albert to Sergeant Hamann, and trotted off on my good old Siegfried. I really liked him; I could talk with him, and he was marvellous going forward. The conversation went like this: 'Sorry, old boy, I'd rather sleep a bit longer but you see how it is, besides we are a great deal safer a bit further back.' I could have sworn he turned his head and gave a wink.

The real trouble started when the dirt road everybody used to march east had me moving against the stream, and when the road got narrow there was no room left for me and Siegfried. I came near to being shot by some, especially those in a hurry. Maps of the terrain were practically non-existent so I did not dare to stray off the road.

I found the kitchen about fifteen miles behind. By this time I was fed up; the dust, churned up by all the heavy vehicles, was terrible and, in spite of having my hanky over my mouth and nose, I was gasping for breath. And there they were sitting pretty next to a pond, having a rest with mugs of tea in their hands.

'Whereabouts is the regiment?' the cook asked me. 'I have a lovely kettle of lentil soup for them.'

'Fifteen miles ahead, and marching,' I said. 'So you had better get a move on, otherwise they will shoot you because they really are starving. What happened to you anyway?' Apparently the hold-up had been on the bridge, they explained, where more important traffic had priority over a lousy kitchen. At first they were furious but later resigned themselves to the situation—after all, they had the food and drink, so why worry? We set off right away after I had had a mug of tea. It looked as though it was going to be another very hot day.

I had to be careful not to take the wrong route, for many units had branched off in different directions. There were no roads as such in the west, only field tracks established by tanks and all the other traffic. If anyone wanted to go further south or north they just went across the grassland or fields, as there was usually nothing to stop them. I went strictly by compass, occasionally checking the divisional insignia on the vehicles going east. In the mid-afternoon I went ahead several miles to find a shady place where we could all have a good rest. Waiting for the others to catch up with me I sat down under a tree, leaning against its trunk, and fell asleep. I woke up with my eyelids burning, and I could not open my eyes properly. Then I realised what had happened—I had fallen asleep in the shade, but it had soon gone and the blazing sun had burnt my eyelids. The kitchens arrived just about then and the cook put some ointment from his first aid kit on my eyelids to cool them down and eventually I could move them again.

Disaster struck when Lorenz the driver said something about lentil soup. Since we were all hungry, the cook opened the lid of the kitchen kettle, which was tightly fastened with special screw-clips so nothing could spill when the kitchen was moving. He shouted in dismay, swearing to blue heaven: the precious lentil soup had started to ferment—with the heat in the sealed container and the movement, it was now beginning to bubble and smelling sour.

'What now?' said the cook, who had hoped to redeem himself with the soup. It was a total failure, and not only had we lost a lot of time, but we now had to find more, and also water to wash the large kettle out thoroughly.

It took us two days to catch up with the regiment. They had already given up on us, thinking we were lost, and looked at us indifferently. I made my report to Sergeant Hamann, who, thank God, saw sense when I explained all our difficulties to him. 'Get some rest if you can, but don't stray; we are being deployed soon,' he said.

The Russians, about twenty-two divisions, were desperate to get out of a massive encirclement near Bialystok. Air battles were going on all around us. The rider troop was busily combing the terrain for shot-down or bailed-out Russian pilots. We already had some prisoners of war, most of them stragglers from the retreating Russian forces, looking very bedraggled indeed. What struck me about their appearance was their haircut—their heads were completely shaven. Now I understood why, when we had been called up and had our hair cut very short, we, as new recruits, had been called 'Russians'!

Our route was in the direction of Baranovichi. It was a long way off, and I was ordered to take part in a reconnaissance mission with a squad of Staff Sergeant Helm's rider troop. Sergeant Helm just would not give up trying to get me in his outfit. As Colonel von Tchudy rode most of the time in his staff car instead of on his horse, the sergeant thought I should be made use of as I was one of the former rider troop and was trained in scouting.

'Nice to have you with me, Max,' he said. Rather familiar, this first name business, I thought, but nice. We were again in the fighting line and, as always, all the formalities of rank and so on were dropped. There were ten men, one sergeant and one corporal—twelve of us altogether. Sergeant Helm briefed us. 'Nothing too dangerous,' he said. 'But keep your wits about you. What the HQ want to know is how much distance there is between our infantry points and the Russian rear guard.'

Hmm, I thought, quite an order—we were actually being asked to make contact with the enemy in one way or the other; as long as we saw the Russians before they saw us it would be all right, if not it could be deadly.

It was early in the afternoon of 27 June 1941 and we still had this dreadful heat wave. We were going through open country, so we marched *Fliegermarschtiefe*, maintaining good distances between all the men in case we were attacked by planes. Most orders were given by hand signal on such missions, except by night of course, when such precautions were in any case not necessary.

It was our first real mission in Russia. Everybody was, quite naturally, excited, and the countryside was so vast it was absolutely made for horses. 'Keep quiet, just the same,' Sergeant Helm had instructed us before we set off.

I was riding in front of the squad, having instructed Riders Kipp and Westhold to keep their eyes on the rear. The others got orders to watch to the left and right. Most of the time we relied on the compass as there were no roads of any description. The open country seemed endless, but eventually we came to a large valley with several islands of pine trees. The front rider was sent on a 'drawing manoeuvre'; this involved the chosen scout approaching, with extreme caution, an area where the enemy could be concealed—a forest for instance—up to shooting distance, let's say about 300 metres; he would then act as though he had spotted something or someone, stop, turn suddenly and rush back. It may sound simple, but I can assure you it was not, for no one likes to be shot at. On this occasion nothing happened; if any Russians had been hiding there, they would most likely have opened fire and we would therefore have fulfilled our mission. The next step, to make sure, was to send out a bait, which meant virtually a human sacrifice. The bait was Rider Brodle, a little fellow, very eager. He was told to encircle the first cluster of trees while the rest of us pulled further apart from each other to approach broadways, so as to present very little target, and, if fired on, to be able to retreat quickly. Rider Brodle came out the other side as instructed and nothing happened, so we proceeded as before. Then we heard plane noises approaching from our right. At once we stopped and remained absolutely still. It was one of our own transport planes, a Junkers Ju52. He came very slowly and very low to avoid any Russian fighters, and neared one of the other clusters of trees. He was fired on. Since he had no armament he did the only thing left to him, which was to turn away. Fortunately he was not hit, at least not to our knowledge, but we knew now where the Russians were and Sergeant Helm could send back a despatch rider to HQ with a report of contact, giving the exact location with a sketch on the provided despatch form. This time, since I was the only corporal, it was my turn and as it was very nearly dark Sergeant Helm marked two crosses on the despatch form, meaning that I was to canter and trot, half and half, to deliver the despatch.

I arrived at HQ, pleased to have got through our first mission and expecting to deliver the message to the Colonel or maybe Lieutenant Becker, to a scene of pandemonium. I was told that a large shell had hit the HQ tent where the Colonel and regimental staff were. The Colonel and Captain Rothansel had been hit and had been taken away with Lieutenant Klinger, also of our regimental staff. Corporal Pflog was the only one killed, but the Colonel and Captain Rothansel were not too good. Lieutenant Becker was now in command, Captain Mauve by his side, when I delivered my despatch. 'Thank you, Kuhnert,' he said. 'You have heard, I guess. Ghastly business. We have to do some reorganising all round now. Thank goodness we are not directly engaged—that leaves us a little breathing space. I still can't believe it. Only the fourth day. Blast it all!' It was indeed a sad business. Staff Sergeant Helm said to me, 'Well, Max, it looks as if you could come to my outfit after all.'

'I don't mind now,' I said. What else was there for me to do? Colonel von Tchudy was gone, so I was out of a job, one might say.

However, Lieutenant Becker had plans for me.

10

A Swim in the Beresina

A new unit was to be formed, with five scouts, responsible only to regimental HQ and used mainly for despatches. The regimental rider troop was also to be used, if need be, by all three battalions of the Regiment. To make sure HQ had all the information needed, scouts were to be employed at all times.

I was to be in charge and was therefore promoted sergeant forthwith. Promotion on the battlefield could be immediate and without all the ceremony there is, for instance, in between campaigns and in peacetime.

'Blast you,' said Sergeant Helm as he congratulated me.

From now on I was Sergeant Kuhnert, with an outfit of five qualified or fully trained scouts. These were to come from Sergeant Helm's troop. One, Rider Falk, had been Captain Rothansel's horse holder, like myself from our infantry rider troop. He was a splendid fellow. Then there were Riders Krones, Godecke and Sandelmann, and one corporal by the name of Krizock, a real character. All of them were responsible men, though whether I could really rely on any of them in an emergency I would just have to find out.

Lieutenant Becker called me to his tent the next morning. I had never seen a man usually so devil-may-care as broken in spirit. I was surprised, for I had not expected it of him, but he really had cared for Colonel von Tchudy.

Captain Lorenzen from the 3rd Battalion and Major Stolz of the 1st, were there in the afternoon. Captain Schutte of the 3rd Battalion arrived later. He always seemed to be late, ever since I had known him. I liked him, and yet I was cautious of him. Later on, when I got to know him better, I found out a great many things about him, mostly in his favour.

For the time being, Lieutenant Becker, because he was the Ordnance Officer, was to remain in command until a suitable replacement for Colonel von Tchudy arrived from Divisional HQ. There were other officers, but they probably did not have enough inside knowledge of the Regiment.

As for myself, I had a great deal of organising to do. A completely new life in respect of responsibility was before me. Many details I did not know had existed came before me, and there were new problems to tackle, such as grading the ability of horses for certain missions. Also, I had to get to know the men I was from now on to command; now, instead of being told what to do I had to give the orders, and had to do so in such a way as to gain their confidence and trust. Corporal Krizock was a great help to me as he knew them all pretty well; though in any case the others were very co-operative and eager to make a success of our very own unit, the Regimental Scout Squad.

I handed my trusted carbine in and received a Schmeisser machine-pistol instead. I also carried from now on a pair of field-glasses, marvellous to use, though I could foresee a certain discomfort around my neck. All the equipment, like gas masks, gun and binoculars, amounted to quite a weight, especially when trotting for prolonged periods.

Our regiment was now heading towards Baranovichi, and advancing by motor transport became more and more difficult because of the sandy terrain. For the first time, I was called into HQ to get a briefing on what my small unit's job was going to be.

Keeping in contact not only with the enemy, but with our own troops— that is the nearby divisions—was beginning to get more and more difficult (one has to remember that there were no walkie-talkies in those days) and our main job was to maintain communications with our neighbouring divisions to the left and right.

I knew that my brother Willy's division was on our right and whenever I saw a yellow triangle my pulse went a bit faster, hoping for an encounter with him, however brief it would be. I also had the older fear which I experienced back in France; there were so many crosses on the roadside.

Flies, heat and, of course, utter exhaustion from marching in sandy terrain for miles and miles really got us down. So far, though, we had no problems with water for horse or man, and food supplies were coming through; the only thing in short supply was sleep. Our horses lost weight through the lack of proper rest; consequently, their saddles, no longer fitting well, caused a great many sores or pressure points. I healed Siegfried's pressure points by putting a piece of turf on each of the lumps, keeping it in place with a surcingle for a few hours and, hey presto, the bump would disappear. Apparently the cool soil had all the required qualities to draw out the heat and heal at the same time. Marvellous!

Lieutenant Becker, always the horseman, was very sympathetic and the six of us had a day's extra rest—well, the horses did; we led them.

We saw several Russian tanks standing near us, the first time I had the chance to take a really good look at them. I was told they were T34s; they were grey in colour, rather crude, and on one side was written in very large black letters 'To Berlin' in German. Only one or two had been knocked out by our armour, the rest must have given up, because there was not one scratch on them.

One day, as always looking for water, after what seemed like an eternity, we saw in the distance the large level-beam of a well. These beams were usually about 40 feet long and fairly hefty, and hinged onto a larger post in the middle, somewhat resembling a pair of scales. On one end was a rope with a bucket, hanging directly over the well which could easily be lowered into the water, and then raised full of water.

Full of anticipation we rushed to the well and lowered the bucket, thinking already of a lovely drink and a cool wash-down. But what a disappointment. When we got the water up it was useless to us because the Russians had put chlorine into the well and it was undrinkable. Our disappointment bordered on despair, our oasis had become a mirage. The lukewarm tea in our field bottles had long been finished, and only the field kitchen had water left. But that was not for us or our horses. By the time we came to the next village water was all we could think of. Villages in Russia are up to about six or seven miles long. The houses—of the block type, with handmade shingles— lined either side of the road. With water on our minds it was all too easy to overlook all caution and, I must say, we did rather take a gamble looking for water instead of the enemy. In this case we were fortunate because there were still people in the village. The well was intact—what a luxury, and also, after taking it so much for granted, a revelation of how precious water is.

It was already July, and thrusting further eastwards, we again met enemy resistance. Shells were pumping in our direction, and the activity of tank traffic increased. In the air we spotted some dog fights. I was told to get the horses ready for a scouting mission. Since there were no reliable maps at hand, the compass was essential. We were to comb the area to our left, bending slightly north-east, in the direction of Minsk. I was to send hourly reports on the terrain and enemy contact, but no fighting.

Minsk itself, we heard, had already been taken by our tanks, but since everything was so very vast, there were bound to be many Russians troops around this area. I had four to five hours of scouting to do, keeping in mind that our regiment was marching in the same direction. The rider troop, with Sergeant Helm, was already engaged by all three battalions. We also had to watch out for our neighbour on the left. My orders were to withdraw immediately if the enemy were sighted and give the exact position.

The horses had already been watered and we had filled our water bottles since we were to avoid any villages, if there were any, on our route.

I sent Falk out in front, Sandelmann stayed with me, Krizock was at the rear with Krones and Godecke. The countryside was very hilly and the forest, with every valley looking like the next, stretched ahead endlessly. The heat seemed endless, too. My poor Siegfried was really feeling it on that day. I heard the big horse grunting several times as he bounced along.

We kept our routes dead straight to the given compass number, only swerving to avoid difficult terrain so as not to tire the horses unnecessarily. Falk stopped many times and everyone kept very quiet. It was one of the best regions where trees had been cut and created a kind of dirt road. It must have been used by troops, for all the signs were there—equipment strewn all over the place. So far, however, we had had no contact with the enemy. Maybe he was watching us. While thinking along those lines, I signalled to Falk to turn sharp right and straighten up again. If anyone was about, we could draw them out this way. In the end I sent Falk back, with instructions to be careful. How relieved Falk was. I'll never forget his grateful look, it had been his first real scouting mission out front.

Since it was only too apparent that we must make contact sooner or later, I now sent Corporal Krizock, more experienced and therefore more reliable, out front. On our left, the forest became thinner, almost like in Germany, and it was now possible to ride into the trees without too much difficulty—up to now the woods had been practically jungle, and very hard to penetrate, especially on horseback. I wished then that I still had my sabre with me, but of course we had left our sabres in Denmark. And my right thigh was becoming sore from carrying my Schmeisser handy for firing just in case.

I did not like this situation at all and went up front to consult Krizock; he too was very apprehensive because it was too quiet for our liking. We halted and decided to change direction again. Nothing happened. I rather liked the wood when it was dense as we only had the front and rear to watch, but here in the open forest it was almost eerie, and a shiver came down my spine despite the heat. We were relieved when we eventually saw some light shining through the trees. As we drew near, Krizock stopped, suddenly very excited, and coming next to me, almost shouting, but in a whisper, gesticulating with his arms, and pointing, he told me what he had seen. I signalled to the others to spread, and advanced with Krizock to the forest edge, from where I could see, through my field-glasses, what must have been the rear guard of the Russians. What a sight. Their uniforms looked almost black and they were on horseback. There were more of them to my left. Their horses I noticed were nothing like ours; only small ponies. We watched them for several minutes, skimming the area around us to make sure there were no stragglers, and then we turned back. I filled out the despatch form giving the location as accurately as possible, and sent Godecke on his way.

It was not possible to follow them without being seen as there was open ground in front of us. So we dismounted and kept our eyes and ears open. We waited for about half an hour and then moved on very slowly. We were in a very vulnerable position, with the wood behind and the open country in front. Somehow I was glad when we approached the forest again; yet I knew the Russians had disappeared into it. Oh, blast it all, I thought. What was I going to do now? Following straight on would be foolish as the Russians could be waiting there for us and pick us off as if we were in a shooting gallery. I decided to swerve to the right, circling slowly, and arrived at the end of the wood the Russians were in. There I halted, keeping absolutely still and silent, for sound can carry for miles especially in a wood. We all listened hard for any sound, but heard nothing, and proceeded along the forest in single file. Apparently the Russians had not seen us. Now we were in a very good position and, sending Sandelmann with another despatch, Krizock and I dismounted to wait for the regiment to catch up, still keeping very quiet in case there were stragglers about.

We had fulfilled our first mission successfully. Lieutenant Becker told me himself, giving me a wink, when they came along later on and the infantry patrol took over to keep out in front. When we eventually halted for a prolonged rest, I just felt tears running down my cheeks for no apparent reason. Now I know it was the relief of the enormous tension.

I was pleased when we marched on again, for our horses needed water very badly, villages were hard to find—almost non-existent—and one had to be lucky to stumble onto a brook or a pond. Every time we had such luck it was almost like a holiday.

One pitch-dark night we halted in the middle of a forest. 'No fire allowed, no smoking, and keep quiet' was the order. 'Can we take saddles off?' asked Sandelmann. 'I'm not sure. But as long as you have everything ready when required, it should be all right,' I said. For me taking my saddle off was too risky as I might be called any time, for our battalions ahead were still engaged with the enemy. I simply loosened Siegfried's girth and, slipping the reins over my arms, I bedded myself in the ground which was covered thickly with pine needles. Sleeping was no problem in those days; I could sleep at any time, anywhere and practically in any position. So after a few minutes I was well away. How long I had been sleeping I had no idea, I only know that I dreamt I was walking through fire, and woke up to find that I'd gone to sleep on an ant-hill. The beastly creatures covered me completely from head to foot and I was in agony. At first I was helpless and then I ripped all my clothing off—which was not very easy, considering that I had to take off riding boots, etc. Luckily there was water nearby and I soon began to cool down after a good splash, and then shook the ants off my clothing. Just the same, I did not like my blotchy face in daylight.

Russia is usually thought of as a cold wintry country, but in the summer it can almost be tropical. You haven't got the mountain ranges, like in other European countries, but you have plenty of forest and very beautiful valleys. We were then in the middle sector of Russia; later, when we moved further south, we discovered the fertile country or, as it's known in Russia, the nation's larder or breadbasket. Quite often I thought about it, especially when on scouting missions. What marvellous country to live in, if only mankind could see their foolishness and instead of tearing things down, destroying, killing and burning, concentrated on building up and living in peace and harmony. Many times when I spoke to ordinary Russian people in my broken, phrasebook-assisted Russian I found, just as I had in France, that nobody wanted war. Neither did we as ordinary soldiers. We were only concerned with one thing and that was survival—having somewhere to sleep, having food and water, and getting home in one piece if possible. What really made us mad was that none of us could do anything about it—as soldiers we just obeyed and did what we were trained for. What the ten thousand at the top decided was not for us to question, and I was never interested in any politics anyway; I felt that I really did not know enough about it to air my opinions, and many of the others were of the same mind. It wouldn't have done any good. So we just plodded along and did our utmost to stay alive.

Our regiment turned completely round, and instead of marching north-east to Minsk, we went south-east towards Bobruysk. So far I had had no casualties in my six-man outfit, only a few mishaps and some lameness among the horses. My Siegfried was really shaping up well for the job—if only, I wished, he were not quite so big; mounting in a hurry with all the paraphernalia became very difficult, especially in sandy soil.

We had a new Commanding Officer, also a colonel, sent by the division to replace Colonel von Tchudy, who, we were sad to hear, had died of his wounds (Captain Rothansel was still in the hospital as far as we knew). The new colonel was not the fatherly type, as von Tchudy had been, but a much younger man and something of a new broom.

'You there, Sergeant,' he addressed me the first time we met. 'Come over here and listen carefully. I don't want any slip-ups, only one hundred per cent will do. Understand?' Well... I thought. Such talk got my hackles up right away. Anyway, I had to report to Lieutenant Becker, and he explained the situation to me.

All three battalions were to be engaged, overlapping each other in turn, and also keeping in touch with our neighbouring divisions. In other words, it was a clear-cut frontal attack on Bobruysk, not, as usual, an encirclement. The reason for the frontal attack was the River Beresina; fairly wide, with very high terrain on the other side, the river provided an ideal location for the Russians to spray the oncoming enemy from. That meant us.

Lieutenant Becker told me to help out as much as possible as Sergeant Helm's troop was engaged with all men, keeping in touch not only with the enemy, but also with the other advancing units. I therefore went to Sergeant Helm to get my instructions from him. Communication by field telephone and in some cases by radio—through morse code, of course—was quite efficient but direct or personal contact was appreciated, and that is where we, with our horses, came in.

Now we had the river to reckon with and a big one at that. How we could manage that I had no idea until our dive bombers, our Stukas, arrived. Every time I saw them deliver their loads I felt sorry for the other side; as they dived they switched a very loud siren on, and, howling, dropped their bombs exactly on target. In this case the target was the heavy artillery batteries of the Russians on the other side of the River Beresina. They took a dreadful hammering, and when our bombers stopped, our artillery took over till more Stukas arrived. That might sound very simple but it took about two days to build up enough forces to secure a bridgehead. Once that was established our Pioneer Corps (sappers) built makeshift bridges to get across. We, the riders, had plenty of work to do riding to and fro, and, besides getting exhausted from the lack of food, drink and sleep, we had to put up with a great deal of fire from the other side and did rather appreciate the woodlands for their better cover—after all, on horseback one presents a larger target.

Our two divisions took Bobruysk on 23 July. There were casualties on both sides, and a great many Russians became prisoners of war.

We, of the regimental staff, marched into Bobruysk on 25 July. I can still remember the heat of the mid-morning—our horses just wanted to go for a swim, but of course this was not allowed, until perhaps later on, if we should stop there. Well, we all shouted hooray because we were told that we had six days' rest while a rear division overlapped us. I wrote in my diary, 'We are now, after many days of bitter fighting in Bobruysk, actually having a swim in the Beresina.'

Of course, a few days' rest did not mean lazing about all the time, far from it. There were, first of all, the horses to be inspected and shod. Seeing to all the saddlery was a chore long overdue, and then there were our own needs, like washing and mending, to be seen to. But what is that after all the hardships of peril? Bobruysk had a small harbour for steamers and some were still standing there, or should I say they were moved there? It seemed a lovely spot for doing one's washing and having a swim at the same time. 'Let's have a swim first and then we'll see to the rest,' we agreed so, absolutely starkers, we climbed on to the steamer nearest to us and dived straight in. What a delight! Till we heard the screams and laughter when we came to the surface, for we were not the only ones to have gone there to do our washing: a whole group of women had had the same idea. Well, who would have expected to find women still about? But there they were, and we had to swim round to the other side of the steamer. We could hear them giggling and shouting for a long time. Would they have done our washing for us, if we asked them nicely?

Our new colonel, von Gratz, had altogether different ideas of how to run his regimental business and I had noticed already the results of friction he had caused among his fellow officers. The infantry rider troops, up to now commanded by Staff Sergeant Helm, and very successfully too, had been taken over by a young lieutenant, no doubt applied for by Colonel von Gratz, and I had a funny feeling the Colonel had it in for me as well. I just kept out of his way as well as I could and was very careful in my appearance, as well as that of my men.

The young lieutenant was definitely not a horseman. He had only been through a riding course when he was a *Junker*, or cadet. The first time he spoke to me was when I was sharing a joke with Staff Sergeant Helm, or Erich, as I called him now that I had been promoted.

'Please let me in on it,' he said. 'I am Lieutenant Weigart.' So we told him the joke about the parrot, and since he was only about twenty and very green in what might be called 'soldiers' jokes' he actually blushed, and we could not help but roar with laughter, not about the joke but about him.

So we became friendly with him, which helped to ease the situation all round; even the other three squad sergeants joined us and we all felt much better now that the ice had been broken. We all felt we needed to be strong, if only to keep up with the Colonel's demands. He had all sorts of things in mind to improve, as he put it, the efficiency of that 'lot on horseback'. This remark did not in any way improve relations and definitely did not improve efficiency. It was just as well that we got on our way again, as our six-day 'holiday' was beginning to turn sour because of the Colonel's tantrums. We marched south along the east side of the River Beresina. It was still very hot and so far we had had no rain at all; this, combined with all the shellfire, caused a great many forest fires.

Our destination was Gomel', though this was only the plan. On the way we were to meet stiff resistance, and also have to make our way through the treacherous Rekidnov swamps, which occupied the whole area in between. The main objective was to go as fast as possible south—perhaps our division was needed to strengthen or at least to help out with some encirclement. Relentlessly we marched on, and now we, the 'lot on horseback' really came into our own. Not only had we to scout to find the enemy, but we also had to look for a comparatively safe route for all vehicles, including tanks. You can imagine what it would be like for a heavy vehicle to get caught in a swamp. It was not just a matter of riding ahead now, but of riding ahead of the infantry point, with their scouts on foot. We, on horseback, had such advantages as having four rather than two legs, and of being able to see further; on the other hand we could also be seen more easily, and we presented a larger target. There were scout cars, but in a swampy area they were hardly a first choice.

This was no small order for us and I could see right away that we would have to work hand-in-hand with Lieutenant Weigert's troop. Since the Lieutenant had no experience whatsoever I suggested that he might follow me.

'That would hardly be fair,' Sergeant Helm said. 'It would sap his confidence, or at least hurt his pride. Why not take two of each of the squad of my rider troop and him. It would look much better.' My five members, including Corporal Krizock, would go along with Erich Helm to the Battalion.

'Well... all right, then,' I said, not really agreeing, but seeing the sense. After all, I hardly knew his men, and having such a greenhorn to drag along on an important mission like this went strictly against the grain. However, just for the sake of peace, I agreed and went to Lieutenant Becker to be briefed.

Confounded bloody war, I thought. I really was worried. We parted and set off on our respective routes. The maps were not much help at all; the compass was most important now.

There were eight of us. I didn't even know the names of Erich's boys, so I just pointed to a young corporal to take the first stretch as front scout. Then I followed with Lieutenant Weigart, at a distance but so that we could still see one another, as we usually did in the daytime, and the rest did exactly the same behind us.

Lieutenant Weigert was like a kid, asking question after question, and really took my concentration away, for I had to keep a very watchful eye on the front scout for any signal. In the end I asked him to keep quiet and told him that I would tell him in my own way, if necessary, what was required and when. After all, this was not a training exercise, but in deadly earnest. At most of the forest corners or any bends or groups of houses, I cantered ahead to join the front scout whose name, I learnt, was Ebert. We called it observation halt; I always consulted the Lieutenant first, out of courtesy, blast it. Several times Ebert used the drawing manoeuvre described earlier. After one hour's march nothing had happened, and I again called a halt. I exchanged Ebert with a rider from the rear, by the name of Henkel, a shortish blond chap, a bit scared. It was his first time at the front, and it was showing.

'Well,' I said, 'you have got something to look forward to,' but then I briefed him by telling him exactly what to do. One person was learning fast, and that was Lieutenant Weigart.

It was a highly organised operation. Everyone was connected with the essential units, such as anti-tank guns, two of them from 14 Company. Our men in the rear were in touch by sight with the infantry scouts and they in turn with their company commander. The only difficulties were the flanks.

Max Kuhnert after his return from Russia, probably taken in 1943.
The diagonal ribbon on his chest is for the Russian Front Winter
Campaign, 1941-2; on his left breast pocket is a wound badge.

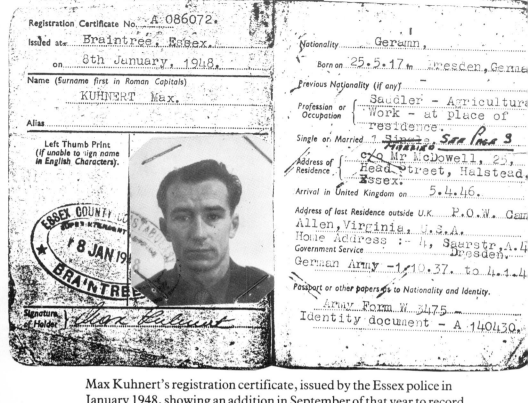

Max Kuhnert's registration certificate, issued by the Essex police in January 1948, showing an addition in September of that year to record his marriage to his employer's daughter. By now he was living with his wife's family in Halstead and working at his original trade of saddler – he returned to his home city of Dresden only once after the war.

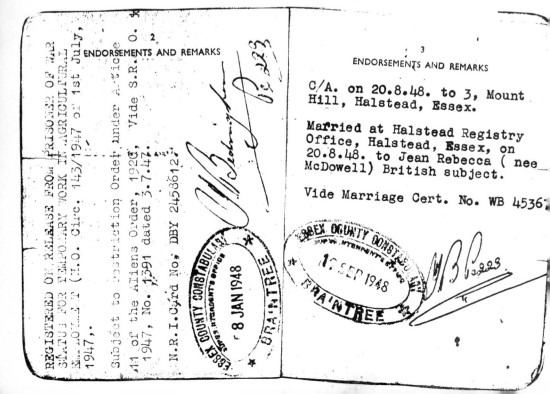

The terrain was changing constantly, and many times we were unable to keep exactly to the strait and narrow, so to speak, as the compass told us.

Our orders were to stop only when absolutely necessary, and a complete halt for a rest or for the night could be made only when it was ordered from the rear, and then only if it was a safe position, whatever that meant.

We were getting rather tired after two or three hours on the march under constant tension. Plenty of wooded countryside was in front of us, but so far we had had no contact with anyone—we hadn't even spotted a plane from either side. The countryside was beginning to turn swampy; we could see, here and there, greener patches of grass with smaller patches of reeds in between. I pointed them out to Lieutenant Weigert and suggested that we send a man back to report it to the company commander behind us.

Henkel, out front, had done very well so far, until we heard rifle and machine-gun fire out front, to our right, a long way away yet, at which he came galloping back.

'Go back,' I shouted, 'and keep going; they have nothing to do with us, but be very observant,' but then I changed my mind. 'Would you mind if I went myself to the front, and you take over here, Lieutenant?'

'No, not at all,' he answered, his voice very throaty. So off I went, hoping that the time lost, about three or four minutes, had not changed anything out front. I felt a great deal better now, not having to rely on someone else. Siegfried also seemed much more alert and his ears were telling me everything, twitching and turning at the slightest sound. The firing had stopped and I approached smaller squarish pieces of woodland, mostly pines and very dense at that. As I stopped for a moment to skim the edges of them with the glasses, I thought I saw something, but I was not sure at first; only when I scanned the area again could I see quite clearly movements among some pines, while the other trees were quite still and there was no wind about. I signalled back to the others to stop and went on till I was in rifle range. Observing the flank where there were also some pine patches, I signalled for an observer to be sent to the left and scout the small woods, and then galloped back to the comparative safety of the trees. Lieutenant Weigert had already gone. But I had not asked him to go, but to send someone. He had left with Ebert and Henkel to explore the woods, trotting, if you please, as if we were on Lüneburg Heath, right across the plain, virtually holding hands with each other. Well, there they go, I thought, mad with myself for having allowed such a stupid thing. What if the Russians were just waiting for them in those woods? After all, I had observed movements out front, and shooting had been going on on the right, so why shouldn't there be any on the left?

I decided to go after them, telling the others to stop and spread. I circled first to the left to try to get a better look around the wooded edges, but could see no one and eventually went straight for the opening between the two forest islands. No sooner had I reached the first corner, than I saw them, about two hundred metres away, still together as if they were inspecting the birds. I knew I had told them to look up into the tree tops from time to time, but this was ridiculous. I observed that they had ridden along the edge of the wood, which was all right, and then had turned in the middle, towards the nice green grass, in the tell-tale reeds. Too late for me to do anything though—fire was spitting at them from the right; instead of riding into the wood on the right, they panicked and turned, galloping like mad, straight into the green that I knew was swamp. They all went down and the only screams I could hear were from their horses. I froze completely, not believing what I saw. There was nothing I could do. I just stood there until they had practically disappeared. I realised that the Russians had not seen me yet because they were concentrating on those poor devils. Oh, how I hated myself.

I galloped along the edge and raced back till I was in touch with the first infantry scout. I told him what had happened and turned to signal to my men, the remainder of them, calling them in, still shaking at the knees. I dismounted then and tried very hard to control myself and not to scream.

Colonel von Gratz called me to his tent, or rather he was waiting for me outside it. What was I going to tell him? Here we go, I thought, I am really for it. Major Mauve and Lieutenant Becker were also there, with several young officers.

'Well, all right, Kuhnert, let's hear all about it. We haven't got much time. By the way, we are all very sorry. Bloody bad luck.'

I told him everything and he said in a whisper, 'I should have known better.... He was too damn young, with no sense, and the other two just lads as well. All so unnecessary. What a waste....

'We've got to get them out, you know,' he went on.

'It won't be easy,' I answered. It wouldn't be easy even to get near the place, and I had no idea how deep they would have sunk into the swamp.

'Have a cognac,' he said. 'You could do with it.'

From that moment on I looked upon Colonel von Gratz in a somewhat different light.

I mentioned to the Colonel the immense difficulty of correct signals in the mosquito-infested swamp. Maybe Lieutenant Weigert had misunderstood my signal, because many a time we had lifted our arms to slap at the beastly insects. Our horses also had suffered terribly and we had tried to wave the mosquitoes away. All the time we had to concentrate on the job. The tension involved had not made things very easy.

Of course, Lieutenant Weigert had never had any proper training required for this type of manoeuvre, such as signals on horseback etc. He might not have realised that three riders in a bunch made an easy target for the enemy. I was still trying to find the right reason—why he took two chaps instead of staying where he was and sending just one, a well-trained man at that. Maybe he was trying to prove himself, as so many young officers did, and now he had paid with his life; not many got away with it. I missed Riders Ebert and Henkel, too; two fine soldiers, they had sacrificed their lives for nothing. Erich Helm came to see me the next afternoon and told me not to get too upset about them; it was not my fault, he said, and he knew how I felt.

My boys had returned by now and Krizock said to me, 'I'm glad to be back, Sergeant.'

Now that we had enemy contact again (though most of the time we had a job keeping up with the retreating Russians), it became a bit easier for us riders, for the moment anyway. Only now and then was one of my men needed to take a despatch to the divisional or Battalion HQ, so we still had time to see to ourselves and the horses. Rest, however, was in short supply.

The heatwave was still on and the mosquitoes were everywhere, it was quite shocking. It became impossible for us to continue normally. Our horses felt those mosquitoes even more than us. Their soft parts were absolutely covered with the creatures. The horses started to go berserk and wanted to roll to get rid of them. I put some wagon grease on Siegfried's tummy, thick enough for the mosquitoes not to get through. Eventually we ran out of grease and only branches and constant whipping prevented near-disaster.

We neared and passed Gomel', a fair-sized town, which posed no problem. There was no resistance offered; we all thought this would come in or around Chernigov or even on the River Dnieper. Mind you, our left flank division had a large enough battle to fight but we were more or less out of it.

11

In the Ukraine: Old Timers

It was now the end of August and we had been marching for five to six days without a proper break. I got an order to accompany Staff Veterinary Surgeon Pohl to go around the battalions for horse inspection.

Dr Pohl, as we called him, an elderly chap—about sixty—was a very jolly, big, well-set man, with a boisterous old-fashioned voice. I told Krizock to keep an eye on things in my absence. I did not know exactly how long I would be away, most likely several days.

So off we went, after I had worked out where it would be fairly safe. This man was no soldier at all—he was just put in uniform, or maybe even volunteered, and I had the impression that he looked at the war as a great adventure. My hair stood on end many a time because of the way he trusted people. Whenever we pulled into a village or a farmstead he would chatter away to the Magdas and pat little Malinkis on the head. Then, more often than not, he would invite himself into their houses and ask for refreshment, discussing matters of food and the cooking of it, just as if we were tourists from a strange country. I really had to be on my toes, as I was responsible for his safety. The Colonel had said to me in confidence, 'Watch the old goat, Kuhnert, we don't want to lose him.'

Every time we went to one of the units he inspected not only the horses, but the meat which was in the hands of the respective cooks. He insisted on abstaining from pork, should there be any about. He pointed out that it was very dangerous because of trichinae. He showed me the parasite worm under the microscope that he carried around, and explained how dangerous the trichina and its larvae could be if consumed. 'Eat chicken or fowl if you need some supplement,' he said, 'and cook everything well, including boiling the water.' We all had been injected against all sorts of diseases, but it was good advice and I, for one, was very careful.

Dr Pohl loved the Russian honey, and I had to smile when he came out of a house with a great chunk of bread, dripping with honey.

'Here get this into you,' he said, handing me the bread. He had clearly been enjoying some—I could see honey in his beard. A bearded soldier in the German Army was practically unheard of because of the gas mask, but

he had said, 'Not for me. I will keep my beautiful beard or quit the Army.'
So there it was, maybe he was the only bearded soldier in our army.

As for the horses he was inspecting, there was no problem whatsoever.
Food and water were plentiful at the moment.

I had returned to the regimental HQ, where all sorts of rumours were flying
about. We called rumours 'latrine news' or gossip. Sometimes there was some
truth in them, but most of the time I preferred to get the facts from HQ.
The current rumour was that a large encirclement was in progress around
Kiev, the capital of the Ukraine, since air activity had increased and we
were urged to march faster. This meant less rest for everyone, including our
horses. I thanked my lucky stars that I was not much engaged at the moment
in the way of scouting, or had I spoken too soon?   It became very apparent
that we were entering the Ukraine, the most fertile part of Russia, and I
admired the vast alternating plantations of tea, cucumbers, and French
beans, some as large as five to six square miles. There were also tomatoes
and tobacco fields. The tobacco in the fields was of course green; large-leaved
plants standing five to six feet high.

I had spoken too soon. We were sent on a scouting mission. Trying to
ride through a tobacco field on such a mission was murder in more ways
than one. First of all, the Russians could be hiding in there, as we used to
hide in long grass as children, and secondly, as the horses ploughed their
way through, crushing the leaves, the fumes and juices were released, which,
despite the kerchief covering your face, intoxicated you and also stained you
brown from top to bottom. The nicotine was so strong it found its way right
through our saddlebags; when I took my white drill suit out later on, it was
white with large brown patches. Riding in a field of this kind was additionally
feared by any horseman because the horse did not like it at all and tried to
get out, which of course made the job of scouting even more difficult.

We thought ourselves fairly safe in the tobacco fields, but were attacked
by two Russian fighter planes very early in the morning. It was only by
scattering very quickly that we escaped punishment. How we got away I
really do not know. Maybe the Russians were not quite sure if we were
Germans or Russians—there were Russian cavalry about, which was why
we had been sent on this scouting mission.

There seemed to be a great many villages about, and the inhabitants were
actually friendly. (Many of the villages had the names of German cities; there
was a Leipzig and a Dresden: apparently the inhabitants had emigrated
during or following the First World War, and had taken Russian nationality.)
Some offered bread and salt to the advancing German troops. Nobody had
offered me any yet, but I did meet some folk and was ever so pleased to be
able to try out my little red book of Russian phrases.

'Russki soldati?' I asked them, and they eventually chorused back, 'Nyet.'

'Skolko kilomyetra?' I wanted to know how far away there might be Russian soldiers. They pointed south, indicating a long while ago by pointing to the sun and then where the sun had been when the soldiers had been in their village. We stopped for the night in this rather large village and felt so safe there that after our regiment had arrived with all its hangers-on (the essential supply units) early the next morning, we actually stayed on another day and night to give ourselves and the horses a good rest, allowing our battalions to overtake us. With plenty of food and water about we had time to get to know the ordinary Ukrainians, but it was spoiled by the message we received that Russian tanks were counter-attacking in our area, and everybody was on edge again instead of enjoying themselves.

I again got orders to report to Staff Sergeant Helm at once.

'Hello, Erich. What's going on?' I asked.

'Oh, nothing unusual, only Fourteen Company want to know where the tanks are so they can get a better position.'

'Charming,' I said. 'What can we do about those blasted tanks? I don't like being a shooting gallery on horseback, do you?' He just shrugged and then we made our plans how best to go about it.

'Be very careful,' he said. 'The beggars are green and when they stop you can hardly see them.'

'What are they?' I asked.

'T34s.' (Thirty-four tonnes in weight.) 'But there are also 60-tonners about. Their fire power is pretty hefty. Machine-guns in the front, besides their cannons.'

I was already worried. I did not fancy being confronted with such a thing when on horseback. Ridiculous, I thought, how can anyone expect us to be so foolish? Yet because of its foolishness it might work, and it was not all open fields.

If you have ever been in a tank you will know you cannot see very much at all. Which is why there is seldom one tank only, usually three. What I had to do was to take my five men, after being shown my sector on one of the rough maps, and just be sensible—and most of all listen, and watch the ears of the horses, their behaviour and tension. My experience was that whenever I was riding alone in a vast area my horse would tread very carefully, almost as if he had been asked to do so, and tell me if he had seen or heard anything.

So off we went, it was almost routine, only this time it meant scouting for tanks. I felt like a little David, armed with a sling and looking for Goliath.

I had Sandelmann with me; Falk was in front; Krizock, Krones and Godecke at the rear. Everybody had his own direction to observe, as always. 'Keep your eyes and ears open,' I said. 'Don't worry. There might not even be any of those beastly things about.'

There was plenty of air activity, and quite often we had to freeze so as not to be easily spotted. All our horses were of a sensible colour—that is to say, chestnut or even bay, but not black or grey.

We approached the first village after only twenty minutes or so. The trouble with those Russian villages was that one could only see one house at first and the rest followed like a string of pearls. Falk did his drawing manoeuvre, the rest of us all on tenterhooks. Nothing happened, and that was always the most awful moment, as we could never be sure whether there really was no one there at all, or whether they had seen us and were waiting quietly. Falk continued, expecting at any moment some grey monster of a T34 to start up its engine behind one of the houses. The horses, though, were very relaxed which was a good sign. One might have to give the horses confidence, but believe me they gave us plenty of it in those moments.

I asked Falk to trot on, knowing now how long those villages could be, and signalled to everyone to keep their eyes on the doors of the houses. Half-way through the village I signalled a halt. There I dismounted and, while Sandelmann covered me, I went straight into the nearest house. I saw nobody at first, but then I heard noises behind the enormous fireplace where everybody usually slept during the night, and there seemed to be some movement below the floorboards at my feet. I shouted to whoever it was to come out, and there they were heeding my invitation. All women and children, no men at all, so I asked them, after directing them into one corner of the room, where the head of the household was hiding. Almost all at once they started to wail and I just could not make out what it was all about. But it eventually became clear that the Russian soldiers had taken all the men, young and old, with them. Apparently the soldiers had been a cavalry brigade and, in need of help to look after their horses, they took all men. They just dragged them along. This had happened three days ago. I asked the women if they had seen any tanks. This took a little longer to explain, even with the help of my little red book. 'No tanks around,' I was assured by their now more friendly faces. Then I asked how many kilometres it was to the next village, and they promptly told me all about the whole area, not just about villages but routes, valleys and rivers. Very helpful, I thought and made plenty of notes.

As a last favour I asked in my phrasebook Russian for some eggs, but they did not seem to understand. After I had managed to describe eggs they all laughed and explained that in Ukraine eggs are called something like 'yaikas'. I never seemed to have much luck with eggs. However, they found me a couple and told me that further down the village there were more chickens and therefore more eggs. I said goodbye and set off, relieved that there were no tanks and no Russian soldiers about.

Outside I called the others together and explained the situation, and then sent Godecke back to 14 Company. I had another twelve kilometres to go before I could call a complete halt and my mission would at last be completed.

We went through two more villages with the same result and were very pleased. Then, unexpectedly, we heard heavy gunfire to our right where there was one of Erich Helm's squad; it could only be two or three miles away. That changed everything. We also heard the dreaded churning of motors, and it was coming towards us, too. The last village was only half a mile behind, so I decided we should canter back and take cover there and at the same time catch our breath and see what would develop. Would the tanks be coming in our direction exactly? In any case, I sent Krizock back with a message and a brief sketch of the layout.

If the T34s did come our way, then I would most definitely choose to ride back; after all, we were only four men now. Also, 14 Company with their anti-tank cannon would soon halt the little advance of the Russians, especially as they could go faster than T34s. We could almost be sure—not quite but we were hopeful—of a slice of our armoured division, who were also heading towards Kiev.

It was now late afternoon, and we were still waiting and listening. The shooting had died down but it seemed to flare up again now and then on our right. We had dismounted and had even got some water for our horses. The people had completely disappeared, goodness only knows where to.

Suddenly there was the sound of churning engines again. 'Mount up,' I shouted, 'and get going.' I did not take any chances, hoping that our 14th would be on the scene any moment now. We rode to the other side of the village. To our surprise the 14th was already there; we hadn't heard them because we were too involved with the other side of the village. They had a marvellous position and we were sure they would pick off any of the tanks coming in behind us. It gave me a kind of cold, creepy feeling, having to look around, not sure how fast those things could travel.

'You cut it a bit fine,' I was told when I made my report to Captain Lauber. 'Those T34s can travel very fast and shoot even faster. Get under cover further back—the horses might not like the noise from the guns.'

We were only too pleased to go, at least another couple of miles. I only hoped that the Russian peasants, wherever they had vanished to, didn't tell the Russian tank commander where we were or then the surprise would be lost and they could really make trouble, even for our trusted 14 Company. As it happened, however, the T34s did not approach us; they must have turned back—maybe some of the civilians had given the game away, and the Russian tanks had decided that here discretion would be the better part of valour.

We found out, by chance, where Russian civilians always disappeared to in such dangerous situations. Sandelmann, my scout, had been snooping around a garden while I had been talking to Captain Lauber of the 14th, and had come upon a strange mound of soil. Next to it was a hollow with a hatch. Everything nicely overgrown with weeds and grass. He lifted the hatch, quite a solid affair, and peeping down the hole, saw a pair of ladders. Slamming the lid back, he ran up to us and explained briefly what he had found, and so it came about that we discovered the ideal bunker, not only for the family but also for all their treasured possessions, contained in two or three big, wooden chests of drawers, wonderfully decorated with a lid and a lock. There were also plenty of wooden barrels filled with pickled tomatoes, gherkins and liquid butter. There were also bedclothes there. The mystery of the disappearing Russians had been solved.

Apparently those bunkers were not only used in war time for safety shelters but also in normal times for storing food and other items. The bunkers were used for warmth in the winter and coolness in summer. I had learned a valuable lesson: if Russian civilians could hide in those bunkers so could the soldiers. I would most definitely keep this in mind in the future.

Sometimes when we were passing through villages, the people would stand at their doorways, grinning, and their teeth, lips and tongues were all blue, which gave them a ghastly appearance. This was caused by chewing sunflower seeds—practically everybody had a sunflower head in one hand and with the other was throwing the seeds one by one into their mouth, spitting the inedible parts out before tossing in another one. They did this so fast and it was so fascinating to watch, that we also tried it when we had a chance. Our dear Dr Pohl told us that sunflower seeds were indeed very nutritious, as long as we did not overdo it, as the acid in the kernels was very strong, hence the blue mouths.

The situation could change very fast, one minute it was almost a pleasure to ride through the Russian countryside, especially when the weather was nice, and then it was back to reality with a bang.

For several days, we had been marching through very fertile Ukrainian countryside. Food for men and horses was plentiful. I even had a young cockerel plucked and ready for cooking, having chased the little fellow through gardens of mixed vegetables for almost half an hour. I was eagerly looking forward to roasting him... and then I got the order to report at once to HQ.

'Oh, go to hell!' I yelled in great disappointment, for my mouth had been watering in anticipation of my little roasted meal, with all the trimmings, like potatoes, beans and cucumbers. Determined not to give it up, I stuffed the fellow into my saddlebag and rode off hoping for only a little delay in my meal.

For almost three days I was on a despatch mission, to our division and regiment and back, and all on my own too! Not a chance to make a fire, or to cook the cockerel—and by the time I got back the thing was stinking to high heaven. My Siegfried was also worn out, and all in all, I was fed up to the teeth.

The ring around Kiev was closing fast, but this only made the Russian forces in and around Kiev all the more determined to throw everything into the battle. At first they tried to break through towards a town called Nezhin, north-east of Kiev, and that meant exactly in our direction. First all their planes, then their tanks—not only T34s but also 60-tonners, huge green monsters, but much slower than the T34s. Luckily for us, we were behind our armoured division, and only strays of the Russian armour got through to us. We had one battery of anti-aircraft guns, but most of the time they were shooting at Russian tanks with their powerful 88mm guns. The Russians were simply no match for them. The problem was that the batteries were not always in the right place and our 14 Company could not, with its smaller cannons, always pierce the Russian armour. We were then in a fine pickle, and with Russian artillery also pumping their shells in our direction, I wished myself many miles away. We were utterly helpless in those situations. Warfare against tanks we had hardly practised because it was not our job on horseback. The best we could do was to get out of the way, seeking cover in the wooded areas, and hope for the best.

However, a defensive position had to be established and so we pulled the horses from most units into the woods and left them with a skeleton staff so that the rest could all find a good position from which to fight.

Our Stukas eventually joined in, to our great relief, but only after we had withstood the desperate onslaught of the Russian forces for twenty-four hours. We were simply exhausted and also had many casualties, not only in the way of men, but horses as well. I was again very fortunate and had not lost a single man or horse from my small outfit, but how dear it had cost our neighbouring reconnaissance unit. Some of them were on horseback, some on motorbikes and sidecars, others in small scout cars. (The cavalry units were equipped with such mixed squadrons, as was our regiment in Lüneburg before we were split up.)

On my way to my horse I could not avoid seeing the truckful of young corpses. It was just ghastly, and those were only a few from our immediate area. Blood was literally running down the side from the floorboards of the trucks, and the driver was, despite the heat, white as a sheet. Shells were still flying about, but we were ordered to get ready to march, not for retreat, but en route to Kiev. So it looked as if the Russian counter-attack had been stopped, but at what cost? We marched on, leading our horses, looking constantly to the skies for attackers and wondering how long this senseless slaughter could go on. Maybe it was the short moment of hope that it would soon be over at least at Kiev or were we really becoming *alte Haudegen*, battle-hardened old timers?

We saw so many corpses lying there at the roadside. And pieces of bodies, some of them scorched or charred from the heat of guns or exploding shells.

Pain, hunger and thirst took second place now, with the ice-cold breath of death brushing our cheeks and sending shivers down our spines. The dream of glory diminished as survival became the only thing that mattered. One could actually become jealous of others who got wounded, not badly mind you, but just enough to get them home or away from this place of slaughter, stench and utter destruction.

The punching of bullets into flesh, the screams, however short, of agony from man and beast. Truckfuls of young corpses—'cannon-fodder' our mothers used to say when young men were called up or mustered and jubilantly displayed their flowers in their button holes indicating they were A1 for service, what a laugh! We had all changed our minds a long time ago, but it was too late to turn back, and where could one turn to in any case?

What day or even what time it was did not matter any more, and when we stopped at last in a small dell in between woods we just sprawled next to the horses face up to the sky, grateful to be alive and in one piece. Then we looked around after catching our breath, to find some water somewhere. Around the corner we saw a large 60-tonner Russian tank. The turret was open but just the same we walked cautiously around to the other side, and there was a dreadful sight, the result of a direct hit. The flames had burned all the clothes off the driver's body and his companion's—and then we saw the woman, also burned, hanging half-way out of the small side door. Already the heat had turned them practically black. The stench was unbearable.

I had had enough and ran back to my group. The Russians had apparently been so confident of their breakthrough that one had taken his wife or sweetheart into the large tank.

Since we had no food supply of any sort except vegetables we had to resort to our iron rations. These were only to be touched if we had had no food for at least three days, so we were well qualified. Our iron rations consisted of a small tin of beef or pork meat and a small linen bag with little hard biscuits tasting of aniseed. There were plenty of iron rations to be had because of all the casualties. I opened my tin with my bayonet and was taking my first mouthful from the bayonet's point when I suddenly got a breath of the tank. It was only about thirty feet away and a sickening stench not only hit my nostrils but went straight to my stomach. I threw the tin away and tried to be sick. Maybe I was simply too tired and the last few days, for me as for many others, had been just too much. We had been in battle for twelve days; it was enough for anybody. Even so, for years to come whenever I tried to eat or wanted to eat tinned pork I just couldn't.

It was nearly the end of September now, and Kiev had fallen. After counting the losses in men, horses and equipment we realised that we in our rider unit had to change our arrangements. The regimental rider troop had lost not only men but also horses and had shrunk to a mere two squads that were usable. Erich Helm explained to me, with tears in his eyes, what had happened.

'Mind you,' he said, 'our losses are nothing like the poor devils of the battalions.' Replacements were out of the question at the moment. The heaviest losses were those of the 2nd Battalion and the reconnaissance unit on our right flank. Many motorcycles with sidecars were standing or lying on the primitive track and there were bodies everywhere. Columns of Russian prisoners of war moved slowly and painfully westwards, also a sorry sight. Field ambulances tried to get by to take urgent cases to main field-dressing stations. Our own field-dressing kit had long been used up and we were promised we'd get new ones come our next rest period.

We marched towards Nezhin but had to cross over the River Desna first. Our horses were actually quite fresh as we had been under cover for some time in the dense woods when we were under fire. Now we could ride them again and I for one was pleased to be carried instead of having to walk. Not for one moment did I envy our poor foot-slogging infantry tramping through the hot and sandy soil.

About half a mile on the other side of the River Desna was a large factory complex, an aircraft factory we heard. I was ordered to ride there with my men and make sure that no stray Russians were hiding in there or anywhere near.

So off we went and dismounted on the outskirts of the complex. We combed virtually every inch of the outhouses and stores and then advanced slowly towards the large hangar. Most of the roofs were shattered and many steel contraptions were strewn all over the place. Krizock and Sandelmann came round from the back of the large hangar, indicating to me that all was clear there. Falk and Godecke were passing the hangar to comb the sides. At that point, I stumbled stupidly over some debris and as I was holding my Schmeisser in front of me, I stretched my arms out front so as not to damage it. I fell headlong to the floor, and my face hit something round and jelly like. I cried out in horror. It was the decaying face of a Russian corpse. Trying to wipe it off, all I did was to smear the stuff all over my face. Spitting first, I was then sick, while the others looked round for water—there was no water anywhere. But we all had something in our field bottles and they were all absolutely splendid, splashing their precious tea and coffee over my face. Krones still had a first-aid kit and washed the dreadful grime off my face with bandages and cotton wool. This must have been one of my worst experiences of the war. Later I rode back to the river bank, stripped completely, not caring a hoot about anything or anybody, and had a bath. I washed my underwear and shirt at the same time, and concealed myself below the arch of a had-been bridge to wait for them to dry. Then Siegfried swam out towards the middle of the stream and I had to swim after him. It just had not been my day.

Early in the afternoon, I got ready to catch up with my unit. Looking around, I could not avoid seeing some shocking pictures all along the advance road, in this case it was the retreat of many thousands of Russians soldiers. The columns seemed not to end. Many of the poor fellows were wounded and limping. All were in tatters, their faces in utter despair. I thought, if I was in such a nasty position what would I do? Why not run away? There was plenty of food in the countryside and they were in their own country. But maybe they had had enough of the war and felt lucky to be alive. We still had to face many more battles and our position was not exactly hopeful; the further we went into Russia, the more difficult it became to get supplies and the summer was gone. Already the nights were getting longer and cooler.

On my way to my unit I noticed many implements, mostly weapons, lying about, abandoned by the Russians. Their machine-guns were on little wheels. I had been trained on machine-guns and I didn't think much of them; I just could not figure having to pull a gun behind me especially in this sandy terrain. Their machine-pistols were different from ours too—they had, for instance, a drum below the shaft, containing 30 rounds. I didn't think that was too bad, but then again I didn't fancy carrying one of those around my neck. Their bayonets were much longer than ours and thinner too: nasty little things, I thought, hoping not to have to encounter them in earnest one day. I was especially interested in their saddles since it had been a cavalry brigade. They looked like ordinary cart saddles; nearly all of them were bloodstained. The Russian horses had been turned loose; the ones I could see still wandering about were very poorly, and their saddle sores were full of flies. One could hear them cry in agony, especially at night. The sound they made was just like the crying of a baby, poor creatures. I felt like making the rounds and putting them out of their misery.

I finally caught up with my unit, just before Nezhin. Everybody was in a good mood, as we had been promised a few days' rest. Even Colonel Gratz, despite the heavy losses we had had, was pleased to see me. He had heard about my face-to-face encounter, and actually cracked a joke about it: 'I heard you found a soft spot in the Russian.' I didn't find it funny, for the very thought made me sick—and I thought I was a hardened soldier!

Nezhin. It was a nice little town; it had not been defended and was still intact—even the people were there except the young men of course. Our band played after the first day of rest. Siegfried and all the other horses got new shoes, and in general all our tack and equipment got a good overhaul. Our cooks really did themselves proud by cooking a splendid meal, we even had a sweet of apple pie and custard. As always I looked after myself and got hold of beans and cucumber—I loved them and still do. One evening when our band was playing a few lively tunes some very attractive girls appeared in their traditional dress, with colourful blouses and skirts and red soft leather boots. They also had a kind of headdress with coloured ribbons. After consultation with the band they danced some of their polkas. It was indeed very refreshing to watch and listen; it almost made one forget the war.

It ended too soon. We had orders to get ready to march early the next day. The route was in the direction of Chernigov, but this time we approached the town from the south-east. I had previously seen Chernigov in the far distance with my field-glasses when we were on our way south towards Kiev.

Chernigov is a very pretty town and quite hilly. Its outstanding feature is the splendid-looking onion-shaped church or cathedral steeples. All decorated in powder blue and gold with chains. We marched through it, stopping only briefly along the River Desna after crossing it for the second time, travelling north-east, still along the Desna towards Starodub and Bryansk. So far we were only keeping up with the units—our battalions and the neighbouring divisions.

It was now nearly the end of September but the weather was still very pleasant, although we had some rainy days and discovered how very muddy the ground could get, especially when it was churned up from tanks and heavy vehicles.

My first assignment after the terrible days of Kiev was a fairly simple one. All I had to do was keep in touch with our battalions, to the left, to the right and ahead.

'Be alert, Kuhnert,' Lieutenant Becker said to me. 'Don't relax too much; there are still some stray Russian soldiers about. And beware of partisans.' Now that was the first time I had heard that word 'partisan'. It meant simply freedom-fighters or resistance from civilians directed by the Russian army, I learnt. The Lieutenant continued, 'Those hoodlums will show no mercy. They might appear very friendly, at first, but then in an unguarded moment, they'll strike.'

Not only would they kill and destroy: they were also after uniforms and documents—'So beware, Kuhnert,' he said, 'and take no chances.'

I could not help thinking about Dr Pohl, our vet, how careless he always was. Maybe he would be a bit more careful after hearing about partisans.

We split up for our assignment; I sent Krones and Godecke to contact the 1st Battalion, Sandelmann and Falk the 2nd, and I went on my own to the

3rd, leaving Krizock behind for possible despatches for the HQ. The order was to return after contact had been made and hand in sketches of their respective positions.

The terrain was pretty up and down, but not too steep and there were still plenty of fields. The corn had been harvested or burnt, but potatoes were plentiful everywhere. I avoided the villages and after several hours of riding I was really glad to see our chaps from the 3rd Battalion. They were all very cheerful—after all, they were only there on guard, so to speak—and I had to hurry to catch up with the Battalion HQ, that is Captain Lorenzen. I was always a bit uneasy with him; he was too much of the old-time officer, and fairly unapproachable. Grumpy old bear, I thought, remembering a talk he gave when we were in Denmark to the regimental staff about morale. When I got to him, however, he was actually very kind and even asked me how I was, which was most unusual.

After I made my report I set off back and really had to hurry or the dark would have overtaken me. The nights were drawing in. Siegfried somehow knew we were going home and stepped out very lively. The sun was very low already, and I did not fancy having to find shelter in the dark. We were making our way through a wooded area of mixed bushes, pines, etc., very sandy underfoot, and all I could hear was the creaking of my equipment, Siegfried snorting now and then, and some distant firing to the north but only by big guns. Then suddenly Siegfried turned his head and cocked his right ear apprehensively to the right. I was startled but kept on looking straight ahead as if nothing was worrying me. After about fifty metres I turned right sharply. I still felt a chill down my spine, for I was convinced that Siegfried had seen some movement in the bushes. Fastening Siegfried to some bushes I took my Schmeisser from my shoulder and advanced very fast but very cautiously in a half-circle towards the spot that had worried Siegfried. Surely, I thought, it must be here, and I crouched down and put my ear to the ground. I heard it then—someone was walking away from me. Lifting myself up, I scanned all the area around me and also the trees, then I heard it again and took heart. I became bolder and advanced towards the noise, then I saw him. A Russian soldier, with no gun in his hand, just a kind of kit bag, apparently looking for me, but in the wrong direction. I jumped and, holding my Schmeisser in front of me, shouted loudly 'Rooky vyerch!' ('Hands up!'). Seeing me only about ten metres away he sank, practically to his knees, and opened his mouth, but nothing came out. His hands then lifted higher and higher.

'Nyet... pazhalsta,' he said at last. Very slowly and cautiously I advanced, my machine-pistol still aimed at him; I could see clearly how frightened he was. I indicated to him to take off his coat. He was not just frightened, he was shaking. Having satisfied myself that he was unarmed, I then took a really good look at him. He didn't look at all like a fierce Russian soldier. In fact, he looked rather homely and was definitely older than average, thirty-five, maybe forty. He seemed to have stopped shaking, having seen that I was not going to shoot him, but he still had a pleading look in his eyes. Indicating to him to put his coat back on, I made my plans as to what to do with the fellow. The sun had nearly gone down, and I was not sure if I could make it to HQ.

Pushing him in front of me I first had a good look at his kit bag. But I did not need to worry—this man was no proper soldier, or at least he was a very bad one.

'Idi,' I said, pointing to where Siegfried was standing. The man was plainly relieved and strode in front of me and kept on going after I had mounted Siegfried. He was not limping or anything; he seemed perfectly all right, but why was he by himself and only with a kit bag? Had he run away from one of the columns of prisoners of war, or was he running away from his own army? I stopped and asked him in my broken Russian if he was alone or if there were more of his kind about.

Pointing to himself, he said 'Petrov. Petrov.'

'Ah,' I said. 'Your name is Peter, and you are the only Russian soldier about... Good. Kharoshee,' I added and waved him on.

By now I was much more relaxed. The poor devil had had enough of the war or didn't like it at all: well, who did? I would soon find out more when Libsky, our interpreter in the HQ, could ask him.

I must say he smelt terrible, like tobacco and leather mixed, also very musty; even Siegfried didn't like the smell—I could tell by his ears. The man's boots were almost non-existent, but he still had his cap and belt.

'What have we got here, then?' someone shouted. In my observation of Petrov I had relaxed too much, and the voice gave me a fright—it was one of our own guards near the HQ.

Of course I didn't let on and behaved as though I had seen him all the time. 'Where are the Colonel's quarters?' I asked, and was directed to Colonel von Gratz's tent. By then a lot of our chaps were about, all wanting to know what had happened and taking a good look at the prisoner.

At first I feared for Petrov's life, for I did not know the Colonel too well on the subject of prisoners. I pointed out the exact circumstances and Libsky did the rest. The facts were that Petrov was a collective farm worker in the Ukraine basin. He had a family, a wife and two children. The army called him up, not as a soldier (although he had had some basic training) but as a baker. This explained his unmilitary manner. He said he had become separated from his unit in the north of Kiev and had tried to find his way to his home village when he was spotted by me, or should I say Siegfried. It was a happy ending for Petrov; he was allowed to stay on with us in the regimental staff as a handyman and got an arm band on his left arm with the letters 'DW' on it for German Armed Forces.

The men I had sent to the 1st and 2nd Battalions also returned, and everything went back to normal, if one could call it so.

Starodub, a smallish town about fifty kilometres from Bryansk, was our next stop. The rumour got around that there was a brewery there—and where there is a brewery there must be beer. So off went everybody who could, in search of a liquid reward. But our battalions in front had already emptied the vats—all we were left with was the smell.

12

The Elusive Supply Wagons

We were now marching north-eastwards towards Bryansk, which was being vigorously defended—we had already had several hits from the Russians' heavy artillery, and their air artillery had also increased.

We on horseback were kept busy maintaining contact with all the units, especially as communication by telephone was unreliable as the wires kept coming, or being brought, down, and the terrain, after days of heavy rain, was too muddy for motorcycle despatch riders.

One day we had to mount up very fast to go after a Russian fighter plane that had been hit by one of our anti-aircraft guns and was disappearing from our view. It's amazing what time it took us to get to it—we thought it was practically next door. There were three or four of us; the pilot got out of the plane and, seeing us, ran like the blazes. Then, realising that he could not make it, pulled out his pistol and shot himself several times in the head. He still wasn't dead when we reached him, but I think he died later on.

Sometimes I was on my own for days. I used to stop here and there in the battalions to get a decent meal. I liked the 1st Battalion's kitchen in particular: the cooks were more inventive and generally better, taking as much trouble as necessary. If they had planned to cook chicken, for instance, they would send out as many parties as possible to get as many chickens as possible so that they could make a really good feast.

While on the subject of food, I like also to reflect upon the ingeniousness of our infantry men. They had acquired for themselves cows which they used, not only for milk but actually for churning butter on the way (having poured the cream into containers which they slung over the cows' backs). They'd then sell the butter they didn't keep for themselves to the rest of the troops on the march—or bartering would probably be a better word for it; say, one ounce of tobacco for a pound of home-churned butter.

Sometimes on my journeys back and forth I slept in between potato lines, leaving Siegfried in a sheltered spot with plenty of hay, or whatever was on hand. If there was nothing else, I would walk—even quite a long way—to get him some clover. I kept a bit of old rein in my saddlebag, which I would lay on the ground and on it pile the clover that I had cut laboriously with my bayonet. Then I would tie the two ends of the rein together in a rough knot and sling the bundle over my shoulder to carry it back to Siegfried.

The potato lines were very handy indeed, for not only could I conceal myself and keep safe from shrapnel or splinters, but in the morning I could just pull out the nearest plant and, hey presto, there was my breakfast. Making a fire in the open was no problem—I had learned that in the boy scouts—but frying potatoes without fat was a different story. There is an old soldier's trick, most likely from the First World War. The procedure is as follows: after building a small fire between two bricks or stones over heaps of earth, you cut the potatoes in slices and put them in the lid of the cooking utensil which a soldier always carried with him, which could be used as a frying pan by attaching to it the handle provided. Now, having no fat, you pour cold coffee over the sliced potatoes, and keep on doing this until they are nicely brown and that's it. (Our 'coffee' incidentally, was barley mixed with chicory, of which there was plenty about.) Not much of a breakfast, but I sometimes carried some butter, fat, bacon or even chicken around. Bread was a luxury commodity; supplies did not always catch up with the field units. Which is why we, when we had a few days' rest, busied ourselves baking all sorts of things, if the facilities allowed. And why keeping our stomachs happy was such a preoccupation with us.

One night on the march—yes, we marched at night again now because of plane activity—we received a very welcome invitation to collect some tea with rum from the field kitchen, which was way behind. The night was dreadful, it was pelting down with rain, it was chilly and it was very dark. Our tent sheets could hardly cover us adequately, so the offer of hot tea with rum in it was music to our ears.

It was a total disaster and everlasting shame to our regimental field kitchen staff. Nobody could drink the stuff; not only did it smell evil, but it tasted revolting. Those clots. They had put tobacco instead of tea into the kettle, which was a very large one at that, to hold some 30 to 40 litres. Then they had put sugar in, and the precious rum. For quite some time nobody forgot those agonising minutes of disappointment and anger. What we called those cooks I will leave to your imagination.

The rain just wouldn't stop, it poured and kept on pouring, the mud became a mire, and deeper and deeper.

Several companies were employed to make runners so the vehicles could get along without getting stuck. Saplings and branches were cut down and bound together so that they could be laid together on the surface of the mud and the vehicles could run over them. If we had any horses to spare we were only too glad to offer some to our infantry. Even up in the saddle, however, feet sometimes touched the mud.

It wouldn't have been so bad if, after a long period of marching, a dry shelter awaited us, but no such luck. Sometimes we marched three to four nights without a break. All the barns we came upon had long been destroyed and although we were now allowed in the houses, they were not adequate to accommodate everyone. Trying to find a dry spot anywhere was difficult and making a fire at night was strictly forbidden. So only small fires during the day was the rule—if you had time. My own task became much more difficult, too, especially as we were pushed to the front again and our division was engaged, so that scouting was on the cards again.

Suddenly our task in Russia seemed insurmountable, our supplies got stuck, and so did our heavy artillery, even with their heavy horses. Tanks churned their way laboriously through the mud which affected their manoeuvrability, and used more of their precious fuel than intended. The whole of Russia, so it seemed to us, was one great basin of sticky mud and we were in the middle of it.

We were now passing over the railroad line of Bryansk–Klintsy and many of our soldiers were re-laying the railroad track—the Russian gauge was much wider than ours in Germany—so that our trucks could roll on them and bring in supplies more easily. I felt very sorry for the Pioneer Corps (sappers)—it was definitely no picnic in those conditions.

Our sappers were in large numbers to speed up the narrowing of the railroad track. The very big danger for them was being attacked by partisans since most of them were concentrating on the job and therefore could easily be taken by surprise. They also had the problem of their relaid track being blown by saboteurs miles behind them.

The mud was of course the largest obstacle for everyone, most of all for our poor horses. Not only had they to carry us, but they had no proper rest or food. Everything was sticky and wet, there was nowhere to shelter. The conditions were impossible for man and beast. Yet we had to carry on, pushed by our troops from the rear. Tempers were high because everybody was starving and dead tired besides being soaked to the skin; and the Russian artillery kept pumping shells in our direction, which of course did not help our morale. The terrain was hilly, some of it quite steep, and we were in the middle of a mixed forest. So trying to find a proper route between the trees and up and down the hills was an experience I shall never forget. Our artillery, which was horse-drawn, was having great difficulties; the heavy horses did their utmost to pull the heavy guns through the soft ground up the hills, with all the obstacles like trees and roots, and one could hear for miles the shouts of encouragement and of despair especially when some got stuck or even slipped backwards. Poor horses, I could not help putting myself in their places.

Quite often we were attacked by Russian planes and we also had problems with their heavy artillery. Scouting on horseback was almost impossible. Not only were our horses tired from lack of rest and proper care, but the muddy terrain weakened them considerably. We not only lost men and materials, even things like trucks, but most of all we lost a great deal of hope of ever getting out of such a darned mess. This was something new and most demoralising.

Peter, the prisoner I had taken a few weeks earlier, proved very helpful indeed. He seemed to have adopted me as his guardian and protector; quite often, some of our chaps didn't treat him very nicely and I had to step in to make it quite clear to them that Peter was one of us and should be treated with compassion. After all, he could have run away many a time, but he was either too afraid of being shot at or just didn't know what to do. He looked after our horses quite well, proved handy if we needed things explained to us, and if we needed food he would come into farmhouses with us and in most cases got what we wanted or needed.

While we were engaged around Bryansk, I was, despite the dreadful mud, summoned for an assignment. Fearing the worst, I reported to HQ and to my great relief was told to ride back and find Paymaster Ebert and his unit. Our paymaster was not only in charge of finance, but he was also responsible for the supply of food and clothing. It was now the beginning of October and our clothing was getting really thin, but food of course was the most important item, which is why I had to go back. Apparently the food supply wagons had got stuck somewhere, and it was up to me to get them—pronto! Lieutenant Becker looked at me and winked sympathetically, and said, 'Take Captain Schutte's horse, Kuhnert. She has been led all day and is fresh enough.'

I really did appreciate this as my poor Siegfried was beginning to get thin; after all, he was a big, lean Trakehner and they need more food than other species.

Captain Schutte was actually of the 3rd Battalion, but he was at the Regimental HQ at the time because we were about to get our orders to take over from the regiment in front, and a great deal of planning was going on.

I had enough time to get a mug of hot tea and after I had got my bearings from my primitive map and scribbled some compass numbers down, I set off with Mickey Mouse, Captain Schutte's horse. She was a lively little mare, only about 15.3 hands high but pleasant to ride, if one could call it riding in those conditions.

It was night and the problem of darkness was made all the worse by the rain that was still coming down. It had turned much colder during the past few days, and some rain had even turned to sleet. My greatcoat was very heavy from the wet which had seeped through my tent sheet, and the rain trickled down my neck as I no longer had my helmet. It had got crushed in between two horses in the beginning when we entered Russia; I had actually been pleased to get rid of it then, since it became a nuisance dangling on the right on my saddle. Now I could have done with it, if only to keep the rain off.

Mickey Mouse was marvellous and strode along the railway line, where the mud was not too bad because the embankment was quite solid, though I had to keep the reins taut to prevent her from stumbling over the sleepers. From some primitive shelters alongside the track I was cheered on by the sappers who had stopped their work on the track for the night.

Getting used to the darkness, I could see quite clearly after a little while, except when some shell or rocket fire lightened up the sky and then everything was plunged into darkness immediately afterwards. A pity it isn't peacetime, I thought. It was spectacular with all the different colours of the different shells.

On those lonely rides my thoughts were very often at home, wondering what was going on there. We heard very little news from home, only snatches now and then over the wireless. What we heard wasn't always good—the bombing of our towns and cities was well known to us, and many of our first-line soldiers were in despair, especially those who had had bad news of their families in the bombed areas. A soldier was supposed to fight on the front and defend his country, and such demoralising news made our fight here in Russia a mockery. For a long time now I had been waiting for letters from home, but the only one I'd had was from my brother Willy who was at a guess only about 20 kilometres away from me. He was still in the same division as he was in France when we saw each other the last time and I was always looking out for him when I saw yellow triangles. He wrote as usual to cheer me up, but what I could read between the lines told me about his anxiety about me. God knows, I worried about him and the very thought about him getting hurt or even worse gave me a cold shiver down my spine. He told me, as always when he wrote, to take special care because Mother at home was a worrier and she had enough problems without getting it in the neck from us. I pictured myself then, dodging the bullets and splinters, etc., solely in order not to give any more worries to Mum at home. But I knew exactly what Willy was on about, and promised myself to be extra careful and not take any silly risks.

As if I had spoken my thoughts aloud, firing started suddenly on my right which woke me up with a jerk and brought me back to reality. Even Mickey Mouse became excited. The shooting was a long distance away, however—it sounded nearer in the dark—and soon stopped completely.

Eventually I saw houses ahead of me, and was pleased because if I didn't find our supply wagons there, I was at least likely to hear about their whereabouts. I got near and was challenged by a young soldier, who then told me I could find the unit HQ in one of the houses. On my arrival I was approached by another guard, rather bedraggled from the wet, who told me the Captain was inside. I reported to him after introducing myself. He appeared to be quite a jolly chap—maybe he was pleased not to be on the front line; he even asked me when I had eaten last. What a stupid question to ask, I thought to myself. I was always ready to eat in those days.

'Yes,' he said, in answer to my question. 'Captain Ebert and his lot are also in the village.' Declining his kind offer of food I asked to be excused and started off in a hurry to find them, as Colonel von Gratz had pointed out rather severely that the front troops were waiting for supplies in case they had to march into position around Bryansk.

It was pitch dark and it wasn't very easy to find them. All the lights were out everywhere and the houses along the road showed no sign of life. Well, I thought, I'll soon fix that, and when I saw all the transport wagons I went into the house nearest to them, nearly falling flat on my face, for the floor was packed with sleeping fellows. 'Get the hell out of here!' came the shouts. 'What do you think you are doing?' and one or two stronger words were thrown at me. I retaliated by bellowing for Captain Ebert's whereabouts. This seemed to quieten them and someone shouted, 'He is next door with Sergeant Kleiner.'

Captain Ebert was still up, but only just—indeed, half drunk by the looks of it. I suggested that we got going at once on Colonel von Gratz's order, but no such luck with him. He staggered to the other side of the room and shook a figure lying there, snoring his head off, whom I presumed to be Sergeant Kleiner. He was a likeable chap, and he was still sober. 'Have a drink,' the Captain suggested. 'We'll move out first light in the morning. There are always too many things to do and in the dark it would be a fiasco.'

It made sense and seeing the state he was in, I had to agree with him. In any case a few hours wouldn't make all that much difference, and besides, a drink of his best five-star from France was too tempting; I could do with something warm inside me. There was just one thing I had forgotten: I hadn't eaten for quite some time and five-star cognac on an empty stomach was too much even for me. Before I accepted the drink though, I wisely found shelter for Mickey Mouse, and there was plenty of hay about. I then made the most of Captain Ebert's kind offer and by first light all three of us were singing. How I got through the next day God only knows. 'Well done, Kuhnert,' Colonel von Gratz said when we arrived, taking my pale complexion for tiredness—well, he was half right anyway.

The conditions had been difficult enough in the summertime, but now it was sheer murder. The first hard frost came, and what that did to the mud, worse still the churned-up mud, you can imagine. It was almost impossible for horses, and I had to go a long way round to find ground that had not been used before to get to Battalion HQ.

Captain Ebert was another civilian in uniform. He had been a bank manager before the war and he relied a great deal on his sergeant and his corporal and the five or six men who were in charge of the wagons. I had many pleasant encounters with him later on... and free drinks whenever I had the pleasure of looking for him and his unit.

Captain Ebert told me that a whole battalion from a construction unit of older men was on its way to take over from the sappers re-laying the railway line for our supplies, and that winter clothing was high on the agenda as our clothes had worn so thin in the last few months. It was now sleeting regularly, a sign that winter was on the way, so this was welcome news. At the moment we were still waiting for a more definite order to indicate where or when we were to be engaged. We were again surrounded by a great deal of bombing and shellfire. Our battalion was of course in the firing line much more, especially since the order had arrived suddenly to swing south to close a circle around Bryansk.

Where are our winter clothes, then? was the big question when we arrived. The only cheerful thing to look forward to had been the arrival of Captain Ebert's supplies. Cigarettes were also most important to keep up the morale. All those seemingly small things played an enormous part, almost more than ammunition—and to get that was difficult enough. On our right was a whole armoured division, which was very comforting indeed; we only hoped that they didn't get stuck, for then it would be up to those poor fellows on foot again. I did not have to return to the Regiment as everybody was on the march anyway, so I stayed at 1st Battalion HQ, waiting for them to catch up with me. Our artillery batteries once again were having a dreadful time moving; many of them were not motorised but, as I said earlier, drawn by heavy horses and, as I have mentioned, we had had a hard frost and the ground was frozen solid after being churned up by traffic.

We had a lot of despatch riding to do because most of the scout cars could not do the job, or other despatch riders could not get through the mud which was now frozen solid. For the horses it was absolute murder too. There were so many different units involved—anti-aircraft batteries, artillery, both light and heavy, anti-tank companies and also scout car units, the latter being greatly hampered by the conditions. Long-range batteries were already in position and firing. The heavy pounding of their guns made everybody put their fingers in their ears and open their mouths to prevent damage to their eardrums; our poor horses, though, they could not do such a thing. I often wondered if anyone ever thought about them; no wonder they kept on shying, even rearing sometimes.

A new menace from the Russians appeared on the horizon, and it was really nasty. It was a rocket contraption on a truck, capable of firing 40 to 46 rockets in a machine-gun-like fashion and, after firing them, disappearing to a different position very quickly so we were not able to reach and destroy it. Apparently it was a frame on a truck, with rockets resembling organ pipes, which when ignited went off like fireworks. We called it the 'Stalin Organ'. Its calibre must have been about 10.5mm, it was very powerful and did a great deal of damage. We had no defence against it at the time, and we had many casualties from it.

When our regimental company finally caught up with us I got bad news, which shook me badly; I had not expected that anything like this could happen to our small outfit. Krones and Falk had both been cut to pieces by those awful rockets, they must have got the full blast. When I reached the spot about an hour later I found only pitiful remains, and their horses had also been torn apart. They had both been waiting for orders from the Battalion and were dismounted, leaning against the wall of a house, holding the reins of their horses. I was told that one minute they were laughing and joking and the next they just disappeared and the earth erupted around them, even the small block-house was flattened. One could only see their burnt remains.

It was just sickening. I could hardly take in the whole bloody mess, the only thing I could do was to heap them together as best I could. It was one of the grimmest tasks I had to perform during the war. I laid what I could find of them on my tent sheet. There was no sign of their identity discs which should have been around their necks, and probably had been, but there were no necks, only charred remains, a foot, a bone or arm here and there, pieces of their torsos were clinging to the beams of wood, which were still smouldering. I got some sympathetic looks and some chaps helped to gather everything together.

More rockets came a bit further over, but we could hear their distinctive whistle and stayed crouched down for a moment, wondering who might have got it next. Those blasted rockets came from only three to four miles away and how they got away so quickly afterwards was a puzzle to me. For a moment I wanted to get on my horse and find the bastards; at that instant I could not care less about anything else—all I wanted was to wipe those bloody contraptions out. Common sense prevailed; it wouldn't have done any good—as I said, they knew exactly how we felt about them and made a beeline for safety after every salvo they fired.

Erich Helm arrived on the scene just after I had finished digging the hole, and, swearing like a trooper, he gave me a hand. Krones and Falk had come from his troop, and he had known them as recruits in Germany, so he was really cut up about it.

'I'll give you the details about them,' he said, as we could not find their discs and it had begun to get dark in any case. After we had buried them we rode back to our regiment, without uttering another word.

Colonel von Gratz was also upset, for he had learnt to like us. Lieutenant Becker expressed his sympathy and offered to write the report for me; we knew the procedure only too well.

The regimental staff were all huddled together in the only decent block-house in the area. There was no comfort this night for any of us; it was far too small to house so many and, into the bargain, the Russians kept on firing, not those rockets but with the heavy artillery. Every time we heard the whistling of the shells going over the house, we wondered if the next one would not whistle, but hit us.

The Russians put up a good fight for Bryansk and our casualties continued to mount. There were nearly five days of tense fighting before the ring around the town was closed completely.

I felt sorry for the Russians, even when our own soldiers who had been killed were littering the advance route. I was almost certain that Willy, my brother, must have been taking part in those battles around Bryansk, because quite often I saw his division insignia on our right flank and in those days no one was absolutely sure exactly where the front line was. The worst was always the pitiful sight of the wounded; there was very little comfort—medicaments and bandages were getting short in supply. My eyes were everywhere at once, looking for Willy, hoping I would not find him among the wounded. It was simply indescribable, not only to see, but to hear their groans and even worse.

Transportation was just too difficult, and carrying the wounded sometimes did more harm than good, especially when they had internal injuries. We tried very hard to get straw or anything to bed them down on, to protect them from the sleet and the snow. Several tarpaulins were erected to make a first aid tent, but I am afraid that it was in no way sufficient. When, I wondered, like so many others, will this dreadful carnage stop? Most of the wounded and dead were very young, some in their twenties, some not even that. There were some Russians among them, and Peter was a great help. I could not but admire the field doctors; they worked inexhaustibly in atrocious conditions and seemingly without sleep or even rest. We also had endless columns of prisoners of war, cowering together or dragging themselves along in utter helplessness and despair.

There were several women and even children about in the nearby hamlets and they were not helping at all because all they were doing was wailing. In the end, watching this, I felt like wailing myself—what a waste, what stupidity, what cruelty. I only wished that some responsible men from the respective governments could see that; maybe they would think twice before starting such a conflict, where everybody was a loser.

There was no bravado left; mercy and compassion were also missing. How cruel could men get? One could hardly distinguish between a German and a Russian soldier; they all looked filthy, in tatters, with blankets around their shoulders if they were fortunate, or anything that would cover them to keep out the biting, damp, cold, teeth-shattering air of the Russian plains. It was now snowing virtually continuously, the many corpses were being covered by the falling snow as if somebody had put a great white blanket over them. Somebody had started a large fire to give some warmth to the wounded, only to be told to put it out because there were still Russian planes about; they even machine-gunned their own columns of prisoners, and the next day they hit the exact stretch of land where Russians were crawling along; many died, maybe it was to their own salvation.

Eventually we had to assemble, and we marched on in an easterly direction—towards Moscow, we were told. Hadn't Napoleon been in the same position? I asked myself.

My reduced unit's job was to make quarters for the regimental staff etc. We had been overlapped by 434 Regiment, and felt more relaxed now, after licking our wounds. Many men in the battalions were missing, left behind or, if wounded, taken to Germany, if lucky.

It was amazing how quickly I could forget all the gruesome pictures of the last week or so—was I really becoming hardened, I wondered, or was I just numbed by all this? Externally, we did seem hardened—our behaviour and language had definitely deteriorated, and not only was our language foul, but so were we; in fact we stank to high heaven. With no rest, no chance to wash ourselves properly and little sleep, we really must have presented a dreadful sight. Our dress was odd enough, too; I for instance had a Russian fur cap on my head—I felt it kept me from getting my ears frozen—and I also wore a Russian coat, a kind of quilted garment; my own coat was far too thin. Many of my compatriots felt just the same about their coats.

A few days later fate had it in for me as I relaxed and fell asleep near a large fire (one could practically sleep standing up in those days). I dreamt that I was sunbathing, only the sun got too hot and I woke up to discover that my boots were burnt and pressing into my feet as the leather had shrunk. I was really in trouble then. Where could I get another pair of riding boots? I had a job to cut the old ones off my legs, too, and to top it all there was cow dung all around, which was activated by the heat of the fire, and what a stink it made! So here I was in the middle of cow dung, with no boots, and with not a hope in hell of getting another pair. It was not very often that I felt sorry for myself but this was one of those moments when I could have screamed.

113

Erich Helm came to my rescue, suggesting that I get a pair of those felt boots that the Russians were wearing. Well, anything was better than nothing, and Erich's troop got going, looking for a dead Russian with my size feet. By the time they had found a pair to fit and I put them on I really looked like a Russian. What with the fur cap, the coat, and now the boots, who would have thought that I was a German soldier?

My strange appearance somewhat perplexed the Colonel when I met him next, but he gave me a kind of look as if to say, 'Would you tell me the name of your tailor, please.'

He most likely would have liked such an outfit himself, for the winter was now really with us and the snow just kept on drifting and drifting. Sometimes it got so bad one could hardly see where one was going for the icicles forming on and around our eyes. And it was only the beginning of October.

I definitely set the trend in our staff. Soon everybody was looking out for something similar to my outfit to keep themselves warm. There was one setback, though: the large felt boots did not fit into my stirrup irons. I therefore took my stirrups off and rode just in the leathers, which I first lengthened. Today I can safely say that those boots saved many of our soldiers from losing their toes or even their feet through frostbite.

We were now forced to seek shelter in the houses, if there were any. Usually we on horseback went ahead and requisitioned houses for the various units of the regiment staff. Whether people were still in the houses or not made no difference, this was war and the people just had to get out or stay if they liked. Most of them disappeared, most likely into those bunker-like shelters which many had in their gardens, as I mentioned earlier, where they stored some possessions and preserved foods.

We usually slept on the floors in the houses and were exposed to all the trimmings to go with it: the little creepy-crawlies like lice and bed-bugs, all disease carriers. The lice always made their way to the spot that one could not reach easily, either to get rid of them, or just to have a good scratch. In our boots, for instance, which would have meant taking them off, or right in the middle of one's back: very often we would see one of our mates standing against a tree trunk or door post, scraping about to get some relief. The only way we could get rid of them was when we got shelter in a house. Then we really got to work. The first thing we did was to make a fire in the enormous fireplace, which nearly every house had. (Behind the fireplace was the communal bedroom because it was the warmest place, a marvellous breeding place for other bugs.) Having made a fire we would heat up water in a bathlike container made out of tin or sometimes aluminium, which was to be found in every house and was used to do the washing in, the baking, and bathing the baby, if there was one. Then we stripped, had a good wash, put clean underwear on if we had any, emptied the bath and the fireplace, and stuffed all our clothes into the bath, including our boots, and then put the whole lot in the fireplace. The fireplace, which was used for baking, had a large metal shield blocking its front to keep the heat in. This we used to delouse our clothing. Having exposed all our clothes to the heat for a least half an hour, we were reasonably sure, at least for a day or two, of having the pleasure of existing without the blasted lice. I still remember when the first louse in our outfit was discovered—by, of all people, Captain Schutte of the 3rd Battalion. He almost claimed a prize for it. He then shouted to everybody what it looked like. 'See the dark spot in the middle of the transparent body,' he said. 'You have to pinch it hard and crack it, otherwise it will live on.'

During one of our searches for shelter, Corporal Krizock and I entered one house, well maintained compared to the others, and found ourselves confronted by an elderly couple who were actually smiling at us. Very suspiciously I looked around, but my alarm was unfounded, for they both, almost at once, spoke a welcome in German. They were actually Germans or, should I say, leftovers from the First World War emigrants, and were both teachers and well educated. They offered us some tea and explained to us about a marvellous contraption, the samovar, a metal urn with a heating device inside it to boil water for making tea. Heating those tea machines was simple and efficient, and cheap, because only a few small pieces of charcoal were required to boil a large quantity of water at the top of the urn. Some samovars were family heirlooms and were kept beautifully polished; they were usually made of brass.

The elderly couple were pleased to speak to us and practise their German. They also told us that it was nearly a week since the Russians had marched through, and that it was only because they were teachers and village committee members that their house had been spared from being burned down. Their home was very simply furnished like most of those houses, and we learned that to decorate a house the western way was an offence, which is why the peoples' homes were just whitewashed or even left bare. Payment for their services came in the form of food or implements, they told us. Everything was state owned, they said, and explained about collective farming in Russia. Farmworkers were never self-employed and certainly never owned a farm. A farm labourer for instance got paid very little for his labours, and it was mostly in kind—a goat, or so many chickens, or even a pig or cow, or perhaps potatoes. The village burgomaster or mayor was also a commissar and had dictatorial power, but he in turn had to answer to a district commissar for anything going on in his assigned territory. The only thing they could grow for themselves were vegetables and fruit, etc., if they were not too tired after a long day's work. Only old people and children up to a certain age and women with small children were allowed to remain at home, all others had to report for work very early every morning at their respective village assembly place, where there was an iron T-bar hanging to which the commissar would give several bangs to call everybody together to get their day's assignment of labour.

The kindly German couple showed us two photographs of their sons; both were in uniform; there was no choice in the matter. They were dreadfully worried. 'Our boys are not really soldiers,' they kept on saying, 'but they had no choice. We haven't heard anything from them since they left the village—only once when they sent us the photographs with some remarks about fighting for Mother Russia and the glorious regime.' I felt sympathetic towards them—weren't we doing exactly the same?

They offered us all they had in the way of food and even their bedroom, which was again very primitive. We declined, of course—we were already used to sleeping on the floor, and even lying on a dry floor was a luxury by now.

Our route was still north-east according to my compass, and goodness only knows how many miles we marched each day. Several times I had to swerve to the right and establish contact with our neighbour, 434 Regiment. I usually took one or two of my men in case anything should go wrong.

Up until now the Russians had been retreating very fast and we really had a job to keep up with them. In the last few days, however, rumours were coming to our ears that Soviet units had counter-attacked not only by making a stand at certain points but also by landing airborne troops at our rear. Since partisan activity had also increased it became a constant worry to us and we very seldom had a good night's rest, especially as the Russians were actually dropping their airborne troops at night. The snowing and drifting hadn't stopped, water became hard to get hold of and our horses were trying to lick the snow, which made them even more thirsty.

It was now the middle of November. We heard that Captain Ebert's supply unit had again got stuck many miles behind us. Since we also knew that they did not have much of a defence against any possible Russian troops or partisans we had every reason to be worried about them. This time it was not just up to me to get them out: Erich Helm and five of his men came along with me, for which I was very grateful as I did not at all fancy riding all the way and back, possibly 40 kilometres, and in the snow, by myself—besides, I thought, who knows what situation they may be in?

The reason that they were always behind us was that in order to get supplies—which was their job, after all—they had to wait, sometimes for days, for supplies from the rear. On top of that, all sorts of things could delay them, of course: the breakdown of a wagon, illness, trouble from partisans, or being snowed up, who knows; and so that is why we set off to find our old friend Captain Ebert and his unit.

We set off in the morning and made good headway as a kind of road had been established by the traffic of troops. We were hoping that the snow would let up, but no such luck. In any case, snow did in fact work in our favour: because it meant an overcast sky, we could not be spotted from the air except by a very low-flying plane. Also the Russians could not drop parachutes, for which they needed a clear night, so the only thing to worry us was partisans or getting hopelessly lost in this frozen desert. The first stop was in a small hamlet in the afternoon, already occupied by some of our supply units. After enquiring about Captain Ebert's unit, we marched on.

The snow eventually stopped and we could actually see the clouds breaking up, and for the first time in quite a while we even had some sunshine. However, it was no comfort to us. The sun was already quite low and it was blinding, something we had not thought of up until now. Our horses could not cope with it and kept shaking their heads. It was actually painful to the eyes—what I would have given for a pair of snow glasses. Night was drawing in very quickly now, so we stopped to make ourselves as comfortable for the night as possible.

There were no people about at all, neither Russians nor our own troops. The unit in the last village had warned us about partisans in this area. We were told that they operated with the co-operation of the Soviet army, and apparently the Russians dropped not only supplies but men as well to work on splitting our communications. A large gap had developed between the front and our supply units, and the Russians were trying hard to drive a wedge into this gap and very nearly succeeded. We had to be very alert, therefore; luckily we had enough men to be able to post guards so we could each of us get at least a little sleep.

The next morning we had a good look around and found a small pond in the village, and on the pond swam three ducks. The ducks meant food in the middle of winter and in the middle of nowhere, so off we went to get them. But the pond was partially frozen, and they were happily in the middle of it, and we just could not reach them. Shooting them was out of the question as it would have given us away to any partisans in the area. So we got a line across and tried to scoop them off to one side, but as soon as our improvised net got near them they very neatly jumped over it. It was really very frustrating; a bow and arrows, we thought, might have been the answer but where on earth could one get such things here? In the end we gave up, and I could have sworn the blasted things were laughing at us.

So we set off on empty stomachs to find our lost unit. At least if we caught up with them we were assured of some food. The only ones with a good meal inside them were our horses, hay being plentiful at the moment, thank goodness. It had started snowing again but it had also got colder, and we felt the cold more now due to the lack of food.

We found our lost unit eventually. They had stopped because of the rumours about partisan units and since most of them were partly civilians, as we called them, they had decided to stay in a larger village where there was also an anti-aircraft battery of ours. Captain Ebert, as always, kept himself warmed up from the inside and Sergeant Kleiner was no better but then he didn't have much choice. We were by then exhausted, and after a jolly good meal and few strong drinks, we slept for some time before setting off to catch up with our regiment in the morning.

From now on, we had to be doubly careful not to be taken by surprise by any partisans. Those devils could be anywhere and in any situation. They could be posing as peasants or farmers, for example, and then quite coolly cut our throats if we relaxed, or they could attack us with modern weapons, especially at dark. Our transport would be a marvellous prize for them, and I for one was convinced that we were being observed most of the time. Many of our soldiers had been murdered by them, we had been told, including one from our artillery. He had left his unit to go behind a bush, and was attacked by a group of partisans. They didn't kill him, what they did was to scorch out his eyes and leave him lying there screaming in agony. Eventually he was found; goodness knows what happened to him, we never found out.

The strain was enormous and very tiring; we were thankful that we had plenty of food and drink in the wagons to keep us warm. Of course, the alcohol not only kept us warm inside—it also made us very careless and we were even singing in a couldn't-care-less way.

There were several houses still standing and we took quarters in them. Our horses actually had the luxury of proper bedding of straw, of which there was plenty about. We took their saddles off and, for the first time for quite some time now, took out their bits.

They really liked it when we gave them a grooming; we brushed them very hard for they too were covered with all kinds of creepy-crawlies. When I looked at Siegfried without his saddle I really could see how he had suffered. As always, tall chestnuts seem to lose weight much quicker than bays, for instance. So I gave him a double ration of oats—whole, not crushed, as we, or our horses, enjoy nowadays. To my amazement Siegfried did not touch the food. He gave me a kind of sorry look and turned to the hay. I spoke to Erich Helm about it and he said, 'Maybe there is something wrong with his teeth.' 'His teeth?' I said. 'He is only seven or eight—what should be wrong with his teeth? I never feed him any sugar.' Erich explained that geldings grew one or two larger teeth at the back of the mouth, and the only remedy was to file them down as they prevented the other molars from meeting to crunch food like oats.

(top) German officers relaxing during the advance into Russia in the summer of 1941. Kuhnert's CO, Colonel von Tchudy, is at right.

(bottom) Colonel von Tchudy (left) and his adjutant, Rothansel, in Bergen, Lower Saxony, where Kuhnert gave Rothansel some riding lessons.

(top) By February 1942 the German Army had reached the limit of
its advance on Moscow, as stiffening Russian resistance and the notorious
winter weather began to do their work. One of Kuhnert's photographs
of officers and NCOs of his unit conferring in an observation post cut
into the snow; unfortunately, it is no longer possible to identify the
officers. It was at this time that Kuhnert was briefly captured by
Russians.

(bottom) A German machine-gun crew in Russia, with a knocked-out
Russian tank behind them.

'Hmm,' I said, 'but how?' Erich was much more knowledgeable than I in such matters and told me to get a file, a special one: 'The supply wagon should have one. Ask Sergeant Kleiner,' he said.

I was lucky; Sergeant Kleiner had one in his treasured wagon box, under his driving seat on the wagon. The file was altogether different from how I had imagined it. It had a long handle and the actual file was only about six inches long but curved like the front of a ski. How on earth was I going to put this thing in Siegfried's mouth and file his teeth? Again Erich came to my rescue. 'Put the bridle on—without the bit, of course—now, if you pull his upper lip upwards with one hand and at the same time keep the noseband tight so Siegfried can't throw his head upwards, I will try to open his mouth and probe first where the overgrown tooth is.' Sergeant Kleiner came just in time to give a hand because someone had to keep the mouth open so Erich, standing on a box, could file the tooth down to the level of the other molars. There was pandemonium, because naturally Siegfried became apprehensive with Erich rasping away inside his mouth, and who could blame him. A little trickle of blood came out of Siegfried's mouth.

Erich was very pleased with his work when he had finished; it had only been one tooth on the lower left jaw. And Siegfried had really been very good, it was almost as if he knew what was going on, but who likes to go to the dentist?

In the afternoon Siegfried was chewing happily on his oats and I was of course relieved. I had not liked his sunken appearance at all. We celebrated again afterwards but eventually came to our senses and got ready to move, still singing.

We got away with it, and after about a week of struggle against a biting cold wind and drifting snow we caught up with our regiment.

13

All for a Bloody Sleigh

The news that greeted us was not good. The Russian troops in retreating were setting alight all the houses, and nearly all had been burned down so we had very little shelter. Disaster had struck our neighbouring regiment. They had moved into a building late at night, and since it was the only solid building standing, the regimental staff, including all the officers, about thirty, had settled there for the night. Someone lit a fire in the large fireplace, and the whole place blew up. The men had all been laid out in the open when we arrived. The few who were still alive were badly wounded, creeping about in disarray. What a pitiful sight. This was something different from anything I had witnessed before. This was dirty warfare and it still sticks in my mind—all the twisted bodies, the torn limbs, and the bitter cold on top of it all.

Partisans, freedom fighters, resistance... you name it, I would only call them dirty terrorists in any language. The Geneva Convention is just a big laugh. I had thought the same when I was in France and had seen the dum-dum bullets. We did what we could until our first aid unit arrived. Many of them died from their dreadful wounds. I practically swore revenge in my anger and disgust.

I had erected a small tent for myself with the help of a parachute of Russian origin and was brewing a mug of tea between two bricks, when the tent flap opened and a face appeared. 'Come in,' I said. 'It gets blasted cold otherwise.' 'General Hell,' he introduced himself; I had invited in none other than our divisional Commanding Officer. I nearly jumped out of my skin, I was so surprised.

General he was, as I saw by his lapels, gold oak leaves on a red background, but I had to say something. 'Want a cup of tea?' I asked. 'I've only got one mug, if you don't mind.'

'Not at all,' he replied. 'I would be only too pleased.' So that is how it came about that I shared a mug of tea with the General. His eyes were very sad as he told me that he personally knew one or two of the dead. He and his Adjutant, he told me, had come on a Fieseler Stork, a light plane used for reconnaissance flights.

A few years later, in 1944, I met the General again, this time in Flanders, and he reminded me of the 'nice cup of tea' I had given him in my makeshift tent in Russia.

It was now the beginning of December and frost was very much about. I wrote in my diary: 'Will it ever stop snowing? Food for our horses is getting short and when we find any oats, they are almost always burnt and therefore useless.' Perhaps I should explain that oats were stored by the Russians in churches, and since all the churches had been burnt down the oats were also burnt.

Our regiment was now to the north of Tula, a large town famous for its silverware, and only about 150 kilometres from Moscow.

We again had enemy contact and had suffered some large losses through their mortars, which were 12 centimetres—the largest in the world, I was told. The noise they made falling about us was in itself demoralising, and their effect was horrendous.

Our staple food had for some time been potatoes, when we could get hold of them. We made, if we had time, 'puffers'—sort of pancakes, only made with potatoes, which could be filled with onions or carrots. If we did not have any time for frying we just cooked the potatoes any way we could, outdoors or indoors, and put them in our pockets to eat while on the march. Sometimes, for a change, we cooked some apples and made purée.

The snow-drifts became so bad that it was quite a job to stick to our route. Troops in front had indicated where the road was by putting branches in the ground, but we had to watch the horses as they would eat anything of this kind.

We arrived one night in Belolipky, a smallish town, though some eight kilometres long. Our longing turned to anticipation of some shelter and we relaxed, pleased that our dreadful march through the snowdrifts was over at least for the night. We were in for a bitter disappointment.

Not only were most of the houses without roofs, but the Russians were now plastering us with their dreaded 'Stalin Organ'. Nothing else for us to do but hope for the best and keep our heads down; at some point they would run out of ammunition, we thought. Several houses were already burning by now, and we received the order to scatter and get out of the town; it was by no means easy to get over the fields because of the big snowdrifts. We were now being hit and had casualties. It lasted for only thirty minutes but we had sixteen dead and many wounded between us. We didn't get much sleep that night, with the groans of the badly wounded, the helplessness of the whole situation, and the expectation that at any minute the firing would start again.

We were now situated on the River Ugra. I had to report to HQ, where

I was given a strange order: to get a large sleigh. Someone had brought the news that there was a sleigh factory on the other side of the river. The river was frozen solid and there would be no problem getting to the other side. There was only one snag, which was that no one knew if there were any Russians over there or not. 'How the devil did they know there were sleighs over there then?' I asked. The answer was that the civilians had said, so who was I to argue with them? I selected Krizock and Sandelmann to come with me. Lieutenant Becker told me to fill up our water bottles with some vodka, which they had in their wagon—apparently they had got hold of a distillery in town. Marvellous stuff this vodka, it tasted a bit like Schnapps, and looked like it, and was also sometimes made from potatoes. A bit bitter perhaps, but it was bloody good stuff to give you Dutch courage, and we needed plenty of it now—Dutch courage, that is.

I sent Krizock ahead and followed with Sandelmann. We had made ourselves kinds of capes out of Russian parachutes, so we were not completely camouflaged but if we had to abandon our horses we could stand a chance in the snow. I kept on observing the other side of the river with my field-glasses. The river was only about 500 yards wide, our embankment was flat but the other side was very steep, and on the top or near the top of the hill was the wood factory and the sleighs.

Sleighs in my childhood days had meant fun and pleasure, but at that moment my heart was pumping far too fast for my liking. Sandelmann, I could see, was very apprehensive and I was frightened myself, though I tried not to show it. I also felt very uncomfortable; I had a bit of string tied round my head to keep my ears close to my head and a bit of plaster over my nose to stop it freezing, and now it all started to itch.

'Watch your horse's ears,' I said to Krizock. I don't think he even heard me, he was not at all happy with this mission and neither were we. We led our horses to the foot of the embankment and because of the steepness had to snake our way to the top. About half-way up we discovered a kind of dugout which I had completely missed when training my glasses over the area. We could see a trickle of smoke coming out of a kind of pipe. I signalled to Krizock to stop and told Sandelmann to ride, if possible along the river's edge, to the top of the dugout where the smoke was coming from. After I had caught up with Krizock, we continued in the direction of the wood factory, which was to the right of the dugout. 'You keep your eyes on the factory while I watch the dugout and keep in touch with Sandelmann.' Half-way up and still nothing happened, I swerved to the left and went straight towards the smoke. Practically on top of it, I rushed forward with my pistol at the ready, straight to the smoke, desperately trying not to slip and fall. I kicked the door very hard with my foot and jumped aside and shouted 'Idi!' Nothing happened, I shouted once more and this time a faltering voice answered. It was very crackly, the voice of an old man or woman, so I went inside. When Sandelmann and Krizock arrived, I was already in conversation with a very old woman. She was all by herself and kept on giving me a nervous toothless smile; she accepted some of our vodka and, blow me down, offered us some of hers. It was homemade, and looked like milk or milky water. Maybe it was not ready yet, and I had heard that the stuff could even blind you. Anyway, we had plenty in our bottles so I only pretended to drink, though I could not resist a little sip. She also offered us a *papiroska*, a Russian cigarette about five inches long, half of it hollow thin cardboard; it was all right too. She told us all about the sleigh factory when she'd relaxed, and said she was sure there were no Russian soldiers about.

She hadn't seen any soldiers for quite some time and in any case she was too frightened to go out much. Sometimes an old friend from the other side of the river came to visit her and also brought some provisions. I didn't believe a single word, and told Krizock and Sandelmann so. At which Sandelmann shot out but returned to say, 'It's all quiet,' adding, 'The horses are quite relaxed too,' which was reassuring.

We were still nervous though, and left the hut. We circled more to the left, then, knowing that we were being observed by our own fellows from the other side, made straight for the factory. Snaking around trees and smaller outbuildings, we approached the larger barns and to our relief saw the sleighs. Unfortunately, not many of the sleighs were finished—only two. Oh well, I thought, at least we've found them, and we started to push the completed ones down the hill towards the river. I told Sandelmann to stay with our horses and to look for some rope or strong string so that we could pull the sleighs behind us when we reached the river.

When Krizock and I returned to get our horses we couldn't find Sandelmann—only our horses were standing there. 'Oh, well', I said. 'He's most likely in one of the larger buildings.' But even shouting didn't bring any results. We then started to look for him. We found him eventually, and it was not a pretty sight. At first we were not even sure if it was him, for his young face was just a bloody pulp. We both jumped up to scan the area, then we took a closer look at him. They had just smacked a beam of wood into his face and had kept on doing so. It was still lying there and so was the rope—Sandelmann was still clasping it with his right hand. Why, for God's sake? What kind of soldier did that? Or was it a soldier—could it have been partisans? I was in tears with rage and could have easily strangled even the woman, as if it was her who had done this. There were several footprints in the snow but they could have been our own. 'Look carefully everywhere,' I shouted to Krizock, who felt exactly like me. 'Shoot the bastard or anything that moves.'

'Why not burn the blasted place down?' he said.

'Yes, why not,' I said. 'Maybe those callous killers will come round, and then we could get at them. But first let's take Sandelmann to the slope. And the rope.' He was still warm when we carried him and also pretty heavy in this snow. We could have done with a sleigh then but they were already down at the river's edge.

'Let's start the fire now,' Krizock said, 'and then we will probably have a better chance of covering ourselves as we retreat towards home.'

'Good idea,' I said, and so we laid the fire. It was as pretty a firework as anybody could imagine. The wooden buildings and the wood inside were full of resin and exploded when burnt. As we stumbled down the slope we gave a glance to the dugout but there was no movement.

'Let her be,' I said to Krizock, for I could see the grimness in his face, and I could see that, like me, at that moment he had no time for compassion.

'She could have warned us,' he said.

'Yes,' I answered, 'and then what? Maybe all of us would have been slaughtered, who knows? Sandelmann must have disturbed whoever was hiding at the top in one of those sheds when he was looking for the rope.'

We couldn't see anyone running away, there was too much smoke and flames as we dragged Sandelmann on one of the sleighs behind us. I was leading Siegfried who had the empty sleigh in tow, while Krizock had two horses, his own and Sandelmann's, to pull the loaded sleigh. My face was hurting, for my tears had frozen to my cheeks but I was not cold, in fact I was boiling, and boiled over when I reported to Lieutenant Becker, who had come running out having seen the fire and us coming down.

'Calm down, dear boy,' he said. 'Calm down'. How could he say such a thing? I said to myself.

'Shut up yourself!' I shouted. 'All for a bloody sleigh, can't you understand!'

Later, I went and apologised, but he only laid his hand on my shoulder and patted it. He knew how I felt. Krizock disappeared somewhere; he and Sandelmann had been good friends.

It was now the middle of December and we had reached a small village only about 10 kilometres from Aleksin, and we stopped there for the night.

Something was in the wind, one could almost feel it in the bones, as they say. In the morning I had a visitor, Captain Ebert from the supply wagon. He offered his sympathy for Sandelmann and then said, 'Come, Kuhnert, get a horse in front of the sleigh and let's have a ride.' He was just like a child, I could not be angry with him, even if it was his fault indirectly as he was the one who had asked for a sleigh. The sleigh was intended for transport purposes, not for pleasure. I took Orleander, our interpreter's horse. Orleander had been used for driving, but how would he behave in front of a sledge was yet to be found out. 'You had better pack yourself in warmly, it's pretty frosty today,' I said, after getting Orleander harnessed with one of the breast plates, and then we set off. There was no breeching on the harness so if the horse went fast I had no way of stopping him. We went like wild fury, and then we hit a lump of ice or rock beneath the snow, and over we went. I thought it was great fun and after I had helped Captain Ebert to his feet we set off again. This time I tried to be more careful and to keep Orleander calm. Captain Ebert had some cognac in his pocket. To be honest I expected it and it was half the reason that I had complied with his wishes. He also had his hunting rifle with him—just like a blasted civilian, I thought, only thinking of pleasure. What he had in mind of shooting escaped me, so I asked him. 'Foxes or even wolves,' he said.

'You must be kidding,' I said. The only wild animals I had seen so far in Russia was a moose in thick undergrowth in the forest in the autumn and one dead wolf flattened by a tank in the early summer.

'Maybe if we tried in a lonely area where there are also some woods we might be lucky,' he said. No sooner had he said that than there was a creature running up the hill to our left. I think it must have been a fox for it was very close to the ground. I stopped the sledge by jumping off and holding the horse, while our expert hunter got ready with his shotgun. The only and very funny thing was that when he had got his gun ready to shoot, he couldn't lift his arm, for he had too many clothes on, and he was dancing around trying to get his overcoat off and I was standing there roaring my head off. If I had only had a camera at that moment. We tried several other spots, Captain Ebert sitting there next to me in the very cramped sledge shivering with his shotgun at the ready. He had taken his coat off and it had started to snow again. His only consolation was his cognac and when we had finished that we turned for home.

We came to Kaluga and went to the station where there was a train-load of supplies, and nobody about but our regiment unit. The rest of the Battalion had by-passed the town and were chasing some Russian units towards Serpukhov.

Captain Ebert and his men got busy and hastily loaded as much as they could from the train on to their wagons and sledges. We also were allowed to take as much as we dared on our horses and baggage carts, but were told to hurry as the Russians were not too far off and several counter-attacks had been reported.

'Not bloody likely,' we said as we stuffed ourselves with all the goodies we had been starved of for so long. Beside our train was the train with all the Christmas supplies for the middle section of our front in Russia. But the next order we got was to blow up the train and run. The Russians had reached the outskirts of Kaluga and were in armoured strength—we would be no match for them as we didn't have 14 Company or any other tank unit with us. We just ran to the best of our ability, stumbling along the railway line as there were fewer snowdrifts there, in the direction of Serpukhov where we knew our battalions had headed. Riding was impossible because of the gaps between the sleepers, and since there was a kind of embankment we had to stick to the middle of the track.

I will never forget the terrible march of the days that followed. It was 20 December 1941 when we realised for the first time what an uncertain position we were in. First the explosions and crackling of the train wagon with all our dream goodies in it—and we had to leave most of the things we had loaded behind. Our skin was more important than the biscuits, the Christmas parcels, the winter clothing, the cognac and the cigarettes. I had my pockets stuffed with Chokakola, dark chocolate tablets—marvellous for energy—packed in small round cardboard boxes about five inches in diameter.

There had also been pressed oat-and-hay brickettes for our horses. By banging them on the ground they gradually became undone and made a jolly good meal for a horse. Goodness knows, our horses needed it badly. Two of those brickettes were in Siegfried's nosebag, which he carried around his neck. Some men had butter, bread or sardines in their pockets; I too had a loaf under my coat to keep it from freezing.

The regimental staff, that is, the Colonel and his officers, had left already in their scout cars etc. 13 Company was our rear guard, just in case the Russian tanks were to advance along the railway, which was very likely. At least we could see miles ahead on those tracks—they were straight as a die. We kept on going, nearly crazy with exhaustion because it took all our energy to walk, if one could call it that, along the unevenly spaced ups and downs of the sleepers. The horses kept on slipping sideways, knocking us off our feet in doing so, but I don't think we could have done it without them for even I held on to the tail of the horse in front to be pulled along at times. If only I had looked for mittens instead of goodies—frostbite could set in without us even knowing it. There had been several cases of severe frostbite—Corporal Kramer, in Erich Helm's outfit was one unfortunate victim, poor devil. He didn't notice that he had his fly open during a long ride at night. Amputation was the only help he got, and he had only got married just before we left Germany. After that I was always very careful; I put my fingers underneath the horse blanket to keep them warm; and I made sure that I did not expose myself for too long, especially not when doing what nature called for.

This was not too easy for me. For the last few days I had felt a burning in my stomach, which increased as soon as I had something to eat, even dry bread. The urge to squat on the side of the road was always there, but when I did so there was nothing but fluid. I believe I had dysentery. We eventually reached the end of the railroad track and had to turn east. I had problems with mounting the horse, not because I was now weak and Siegfried was so big but because I could not stop leaking. It was just awful. So instead of being carried I had to stumble through the snow, oh how I hated the snow. I started to sweat because of the effort and fatigue, but stopping to rest was too dangerous, not only because of the frost, but also because of the Russians. They had still not been checked and they seemed to move faster than us; we could hear shooting and shouting behind us. The Russians seemed to be gaining on us rapidly; where was our 14 Company with its anti-tank guns, and why didn't we get any help from our air force? The only help we had was 13 Company at our rear and they were running out of ammunition fast. If ever I felt like giving up this was the time. Somehow Siegfried seemed to understand my predicament and did not at all seem to mind pulling me along to keep up with the others.

At last we reached the first post of our 3rd Battalion: most of us were exhausted and in no condition to be of any help to them. The order was to get the barricade across the road and make a stand. I must say our boys of the 3rd Battalion were marvellous. They also had one gun of the anti-aircraft battery at their disposal. Those guns were great and knocked out the Russian T34s just like that. With a calibre of 88mm, they cut through armour like a knife through butter. We already felt better, knowing that we at least had something to fight back with. If only I had felt better with my stomach: I must have looked awful for the others kept making sympathetic remarks to me—and in those circumstances, where everyone is for themselves, one did not expect any sympathy at all. Maybe it was because of Christmas. It was 24 December 1941, and we could hardly have been in a greater mess than we were in at the moment.

We had stopped in a very large village, and our unit had been given the order: 'You must hold this line.' The word was passed on and everybody tried to do his utmost. Snow walls were built with anything that could be used to shovel snow with. I had been chewing my chocolate tablet, hoping to get rid of my dysentery, and during the last few hours it did seem to be getting better. Maybe I was lucky for a change, and just thinking so made me feel better. We had almost a whole battalion in the village, or rather at one end of it. In the middle was the battle zone and at the other end was where the Russians were most likely to break through. We had the 88mm gun, 13 Company with their two howitzers, and the machine-guns of 2 Company of the 3rd Battalion; 14 Company, we heard, had gone ahead with the 2nd Battalion.

Two of us, and our horses, camped out in a house with the rest of the regimental troop. That evening of Christmas Eve we shared our food, what little there was—two tins of sardines, a packet of *Ersatzhönig* (synthetic honey), two loaves of bread, already in bits and pieces, and several potatoes. This was to feed about twenty-six men. We also had two stumps of wax candles so at least we could see something; we could not have a big fire in the grate as there was simply nothing to burn. There were several beams left from the burnt houses or outbuildings but it would have taken a great deal of effort and time to cut them into pieces to get them in the fireplace. So that was how we celebrated Christmas 1941. It was a laugh anyway: we were not really thinking in terms of celebrating the birth of Christ, most of us were only thinking of home and hoping that everybody in his family circle was all right. The celebrations were not to last, anyhow. The sounds of shouting, shooting and running soon got us on our feet. Thank God, we had left our horses saddled, and we had even left their bits in their mouths—once they were out it was very difficult to get them back in because of the severe frost. We had just enough time to get away. The Russians had broken through—there was just too many of them, and in the pitch darkness, with drifting snow and biting wind, it had been too difficult to hold them with the limited weapons we had.

To make things worse I got kicked on my left knee trying to get Siegfried out of the very cramped barn full of horses, and my foot was trodden on at the same time. It was just not my day. Wincing with pain, I hobbled along not even daring to lift my leg towards the stirrups to mount. That is until we heard the churning of the tanks coming along the village centre. The pain suddenly vanished and I mounted, it was like a miracle. We spread to the left and right, and how we managed not to get caught I shall never know. Usually when tanks attacked, infantry was close behind, but in this case there was no infantry, so those tanks must have been the spearhead. Even so, it had given us a fright. The tanks retreated after running around for a bit and by the time we could hear their noise disappearing the first light of Christmas morning was showing.

All day we marched, this time in a northerly direction, leaving Serpukhov on our right. In those days it seemed to be utter confusion most of the time, and it was very difficult to know who was who, who was where, and indeed where was where. Of course, there was our air force as well as the Russian one but they could only operate in clear weather and only in daytime. Reconnaissance planes for the artillery were about, but they always seemed to be somewhere else, never where we were, especially when we needed them most. Maybe I'm being unfair, for Russia is a very large country and I imagine even planes could get lost there.

We began to regain our composure after our days of running. Rumours came to our ears that we were to find winter quarters and stay there till spring, when Hitler would resume the offensive and finish the war. If only we could have believed it, it would have been nice, but at the moment we didn't believe anything any more because since October we had been hearing similar stories. We tried to be optimistic, however, and looked around hopefully every time we came to a village. The food situation had not improved at all, and goodness only knows where the supply wagons had got stuck this time.

'Please don't ask me to find them again,' I prayed silently; I still wasn't really very well. The dysentery had disappeared but my knee was still very sore and my foot, the one that had been trodden on by some horse in the dark, had turned septic. I was getting worried about it; even washing the spot (the skin had been broken) didn't make much difference and the whole area around it was turning an ugly colour. 'Don't let the frost get in,' everybody said. 'See the doctor, maybe he can help.' 'Scrounge some ointment, put on the agony, anything to get him to look at it,' advised Erich. He had seen many limping about, so I went and joined the queue outside the first aid place. I felt a bit of a fraud because most of the other chaps were virtually carrying their heads under their arms.

'Why didn't you come and see me earlier with this?' said the orderly. 'It could get really ugly and you wouldn't be the first to have his foot cut off because of the frost.' I got really frightened then and felt hot all over.

'What can you do?' I asked. 'Haven't you got anything you can put on to stop it spreading?'

'Oh sure,' he said. 'Don't worry too much, it's only one foot—some chaps have lost both.'

Charming, I thought, and was relieved when he looked at me with a twinkle in his eyes. So every day, when there was a chance, I changed the bandage and put plenty of zinc salve on it and since my felt boots were fairly big, I wrapped some cut-up towel around my foot as well before putting the boot on. I was also fortunate enough to get rides on sledges, leading Siegfried, who was pleased to get some rest. Poor Siegfried was such a large horse and needed plenty of food, but there just wasn't any to be found except straw or, if we were lucky, some hay left in a forsaken corner. Sometimes our planes dropped brickettes for the horses, along with supplies for us. The Russians also had aircraft dropping supplies and sometimes we exchanged—by mistake of course, our planes dropping our supplies to the Russians, and the Russians doing the same to us. Of course we always liked our supplies much better; the Russian stuff was very course and crude, their bread was dreadful, very gritty and full of potato. It was horrible to eat but when one is starving one will eat anything. We were always heartbroken when we watched our parachutes drifting and drifting towards the Russians and we again had nothing to eat. Oh well, we could always keep looking for potatoes and if they were not black from the frost we would have 'puffers'.

We marched on, through Stepanovska, Feriskovo, and Lapino.

'It is now 31 December 1941,' I wrote in my diary. 'Food is now non-existent and we are really getting desperate for it.'

Then, like a miracle, our supply wagons came through from the north-west and, as if our prayers had been heard, we got all the important things we didn't have much hope for only the day before. Our horses got oats again, the first for quite some time, and I'm sure Siegfried gave me a thankful grunt when I put his nosebag containing the precious oats round his neck. We even had a shave again, the first for a long time, and a smoke as there was also some tobacco. There was no bread but there was flour, and as in the village we stopped at there were still a few houses and barns intact, though no civilians—they had all fled north from the heavy fighting over the Christmas period—we were able to bake our own. Petrov, our Russian friend, came in handy—he was a baker—and he got busy, with everybody helping him to build the fire up in the enormous grate. To supplement the flour, as we only had a certain amount, we ground some corn ourselves—we got hold of some wheat and two of our fellows sat there each with a coffee mill between their knees, turning the handles to grind the wheat. It took some time, but we changed the mills around as arms got tired.

We heard that Aleksin was in Russian hands again, but that Kaluga had been retaken by our troops. Kaluga had a bitter taste for us—it was where we had to blow the train up, with out precious supplies and parcels in it. Nobody had really believed that this last village would be our winter quarters and sure enough after only three days we moved on again, towards Yuknov, a larger place—a town in fact, with an airport nearby. It was safer for us because there were plenty of our aircraft batteries there to protect our own planes. We marched into the town at night, very tired and looking forward to a rest in safety. Yuknov gave me a kind of warm feeling, especially as there were plenty of cheerful faces of our own fellows who were already at home there. We moved into some garage buildings, very cold and very draughty.

There wasn't anything at all for horses, however, although there was water, thank goodness, but that was the only comfort we had. Where could I find some hay for Siegfried? In the end I found an old couch in one of the outhouses and, having torn it to pieces, I returned to Siegfried with an armful of dusty polster. I suppose it looked like hay to him, and he got to eating it. Back and forth, side to side, he chewed, poor devil. He had been accidentally hit by a tank, and his right hock was bloody. I washed the wound, urinated into it to prevent it turning septic, and, worried that the frost might do some harm, put a large blanket over him.

In the basement of the enormous building were the garages. Below the garages were enormous boilers to keep the building centrally heated, but only one of the stoves was going and everybody was cramped into the small space to keep warm. We scrounged some bread from the troops already there and huddled together on the floor and felt very fortunate indeed. For the first time for what seemed donkey's years we were in a really large, solid, stone building; it would take a very large bomb or several shells to get to us in this sort of catacomb.

My last thoughts that evening were with poor old Siegfried. When we moved on again the next morning I was actually pleased as this was no place for horses. As soon as we got into the countryside I looked for food, not only for us, but for the horses.

14

Captured — Briefly

For many days we marched, always northerly and, as we found out, heading for Vyaz'ma. We stopped for the night in the middle of nowhere. There was virtually no shelter at all, the frost was severe and how I hated the snow. Sometimes our path was just ice and snow churned up by the traffic on it. Our feet were hurting from the constant uneven walking on it. It was impossible to walk properly and I was pleased that my foot had healed nicely. I actually felt fit again, even with the little rest we were getting.

Once when we stopped for the night the entire rider troop congregated in a very large barn, but there was no room for my horse, since everybody was huddled into every corner there was. The only place I could find was a small hut on the roadside, if one could call it a road. The hut must have been used in the summer, maybe for selling cherries or other fruit. It was empty, with a door at the back and at the front a little serving hatch. The problem was how the blazes to get Siegfried into it, a large horse, complete with his saddle and all the rest of his equipment, unsaddling not being permitted just in case we had to move off fast. Since I could not lead him in, I pushed and talked till bit by bit he moved forward, standing diagonally, practically boxed in. At least he was out of the bitterly cold wind and drifting snow, and he had plenty of straw and hay. After this I felt much better.

The next morning and after a most uncomfortable night in the stinking old barn, we got ready to march. In my case it was not so simple—my Siegfried had got himself truly stuck in the little hut and all my pulling on his tail was to no avail. Then I crept in but beat a quick retreat because he became panicky. What was I going to do?

'You will have to break open the side of the hut to get him out, there is no other way,' said Erich Helm.

When I opened up the little serving hatch in front, Siegfried only snorted in my face; then I really got mad, after all, I didn't have all day to get him out.

'Get a blasted axe or something,' I called out. 'I have to get him out and I haven't much time left.' The only place that I could get an axe was 14 Company and they were nearly two miles behind us, as was the field kitchen.

In the end I told Godecke to ride back and see if he could find a decent axe. I was so pleased when Godecke returned with a good-sized axe in his hands. I went to the service hatch and held Siegfried and talked to him to calm him down, whilst Godecke hacked away, until, at last, we had a big enough gap to pull Siegfried through.

A similar thing happened a few days later; this time it was because the door to a very small stable was so narrow that our Siegfried got stuck trying to get in through it. Our horses were simply too large for the stables here.

We were still marching in the direction of Vyaz'ma. Like Erich Helm, I could not simply follow, but had to keep my eyes and ears open to know exactly where we were going, where we were and where we had been, in case I was sent on a despatch or even had to scout. As I have already mentioned, those Russian maps that existed were very primitive and unreliable. Drifting snow or even snowstorms only made matters worse, and also made marching very difficult. In those conditions our horses, each following the one in front, did not mind at all when we held on to their tails to be pulled along. I never rode my horse on those stormy days or nights, unless it was absolutely necessary—for instance, if I had to report to HQ, wherever it was situated, or when going on a mission.

As I was being dragged along, some or most of the time on an empty stomach and parched for a drink, I often used to picture myself sitting at a table of plenty, in warm friendly surroundings and peaceful conditions, and tortured myself by imagining I was drinking a nice cool lager or slurping a hot cup of coffee, whatever suited the situation best. Wading through the high snow, slipping and stumbling, one minute freezing because of the icy winds and the next minute getting sweaty because of the fatigue, pushed our morale very low.

After a night spent mostly being dragged along—we had made some brief stops but there was no shelter, simply some burned-down ruins — we saw a village ahead, as the first light was showing. Very tired and badly in need of some shelter and nourishment, we struggled on, full of hope, only to be once again bitterly disappointed.

The village was on a hill, and we were about half-way up when we received a warning from a despatch rider of the battalion in front, told to take defensive positions at once as Russian tanks in large numbers were coming our way. That was the bad news. The good news was that several of our tanks of our armoured division were also approaching, though from what direction was not very clear. One always got this panicky feeling when one was dog-tired. Find cover, shelter or anything to get out of the way of those monsters was the order. Only anyone who was able to help to withstand momentarily the advance of the tanks was to report at once to the front of the column.

Well, that counted me out for a start, so like the others I started to look for somewhere to get out of the way as ordered, listening all the while for the dreaded churning of tank motors and hoping that ours would be on the scene first.

Despite the tiredness it was amazing how quickly everybody disappeared and how quickly the energy to do so was acquired. I got Siegfried under cover in a nice slopey half-barn and stuck with him. We were overlooking the valley behind us on the left. Siegfried was lucky. I had found some forage for him and he chewed away unperturbed by what was going on around him. I had settled myself almost underneath him and was looking through his legs down the valley when I saw the grey monsters, T34s; I spotted two, three, five, and then there were more and I lost count. They were definitely Russian, the stars on their turrets were painfully obvious. They've missed us, was my first thought; my second thought was, I have to report right away to HQ what I had seen. 'Pass it down the line', I shouted. 'There are Russian tanks on our left rear in large numbers going away from us at the moment.'

Soon everybody was shouting and I wondered what message HQ would eventually receive, so leaving my horse in the charge of Krizock, I stumbled towards the front of the halted column and arrived gasping for air at HQ. Lieutenant Becker was the first to spot me. 'Yes, Kuhnert, what is it?' As if he had more important things to do than listen to me. I said to him, 'There are tanks, Russian tanks, at least six or eight, at our left rear going away from us at the moment.'

'What?' he said. 'I got the message that there are tanks somewhere, otherwise nothing new.'

The whole staff stared at me as if I were the angel of death. 'Are you sure?' Lieutenant Becker went on to ask.

'I wouldn't have come running here through the snow if I wasn't.' No sooner had I said this than everyone could hear the firing, coming from the direction I had reported.

'Take cover, everybody, and tell Fourteen to turn around at once, we have trouble at our rear', the order was shouted.

I ran, if one could call it that, back to Siegfried, fearing that the Russians might have kept on turning left and reached the rear of the column where I had my Siegfried under shelter. The firing was certainly getting more intense and it sounded as if the tanks were coming towards us. The noise really spurred me on, and already picturing disaster, I reached Siegfried. He was still chewing his hay calmly. Krizock excitedly pointed out what was going on down in the valley, only about one mile away.

What a sight and wholly unexpected: a fully fledged tank battle right in front of our eyes. No troops, only tanks. There were at least twice as many

Russian tanks as ours, but ours were heavy tanks and had much better fire power. I watched fascinated through my field-glasses as the two sides tried to outmanoeuvre each other. I was amazed that our tank commander was still in his open turret; I think that if there had been Russian troops about he would not have dared, nevertheless he impressed me very much.

The Russians' T34s were simply no match for our tanks with their 88mm-calibre guns; and it took only a short time (how long exactly was hard to say—the excitement was too much for us) before the Russians scattered; thank goodness not up-hill towards us. Some of the Russian tanks practically blew up, others were motionless, while some with their motors damaged were frantically trying to reach safety.

We stayed on for a few days and despite our tiredness we were full of talk, the main topic of our conversation being the tank battle that we had witnessed.

It was now the end of January and bitterly cold, with about 45-50 degrees of frost, and it always got colder when there was a full moon. Supplies had arrived from Smolensk and I got a letter from my father, and one from my brother Willy. He wrote that he hoped to get leave to get married, and was indeed cheerful in one way, though I could sense that he had his doubts about his going home just to get married when so many of our fellows had families at home, some in bad trouble because of the bombing.

Our winter quarters were in a very nice village called Sakharovo. It had only a few houses left standing, but there were two barns which accommodated not only the horses but also the wagons, etc.

With the supplies had come many Christmas parcels, most of them for the men of the battalions, but many which sadly would never get delivered because the men they were for had been killed or wounded. These were to be distributed among those who had not got any parcels for one reason or another. There were stacks of them, each telling its own story.

I was sitting in the lobby of the regimental HQ, just across from our quarters, one night, making out a report and listening to the wireless. How strange, I thought, as the ten o'clock news from Germany came through, introduced as always, first by a bugler and then the very popular tune of 'Lilli Marlene', here I am sitting literally in the middle of nowhere, in snowed-in Russia, listening to this. I could not help feeling rather sorry for myself then, and also very homesick.

The Colonel walked through at that very moment with Lieutenant Becker. 'Well, Kuhnert,' he said. 'Your horses should get some rest now, we have got our scout cars at last and they will get here tomorrow.' He wasn't the only one glad about it, our poor horses needed the rest very badly. But the next morning I got an order to ride to the 3rd Battalion; it was as if fate were saying, 'If you thought you were going to have a rest, you've got another think coming.'

The idea was for me, since I'd been there before, to collect the Colonel from the 3rd Battalion. He had ordered that I should collect him on horseback, as the scout cars were intended for each battalion to get any urgently needed supply as swiftly as possible to the companies. So I still had to go from HQ to HQ if no one else was available. Unfortunately for me, the telecommunications people were having problems getting a line to the 3rd Battalion.

As miserable as sin, I went to get my horse ready and tell the corporal in charge of the Colonel's horse to prepare the Colonel's horse. Of course it was still Albert, and when both Siegfried and Albert stood together I could not help smiling; they knew each other so well that I could have sworn they had a conversation, probably about the dreadful conditions they had to put up with.

I set off, just like in the old days, leading Albert on my left. I had only about eight or nine miles to go, and I followed the caterpillar tracks of the new scout cars clearly visible in the snow. There was some shooting going on way out front; it must be our mortars, nothing to worry about, I thought, as I walked the horses to save their strength in the deep snow. After about three miles I saw the forest in front of me, a pinewood, but with very large and well spaced trees. I had trotted through it before on the way to the battalion. The snow wasn't so deep in there and it cut the distance quite a bit, especially since I could also trot there, which in the open was not possible because of the constant drifting.

Once more on Siegfried's back, I took Willy's letter out of my despatch case on my belt and had another read. He wrote that he was sheltered at the moment but had little confidence that it would last. He wished me a safe and happy Christmas and a happy new year. He also said, 'We never dreamt of such a mess, did we, Max? If we get together later, we will think and talk about this, won't we?' He had also sent me a snapshot of himself, probably taken in Poland. I heard firing again, mortar fire, coming from the wood I was heading for. I stuffed the letter and the picture of Willy into my coat pocket, beneath the white parachute cape I had made to camouflage myself better. Entering the wood, I looked round for the route I had taken a few days ago and trotted on. Albert snorted and I remember saying to the horses, 'We will soon be there.' I stopped. A group of men had suddenly appeared in front of me.

Believing they were our own soldiers, I shouted, 'What are you doing here?' Then I was pulled off Siegfried hard; they were Russians. It was like a nightmare, I was helpless, I felt as if a great pair of pincers had been applied to squeeze the very life out of me. I don't think I was thinking about anything; I remember that I was petrified and my knees felt like putty. There was a lot of shouting going on. One of the men kept on pushing me while at the same time the others ripped my clothing apart. I also got hit on my right shoulder, and felt a stabbing pain there. A man took my watch, others ripped off my belt with Willy's pistol, and took my despatch case with all my personal things. Protesting only brought laughter from them, and an ugly little fellow grabbed me by my front and held something into my face, it could have been a pistol. Then a voice shouted. A tall man with a bright red star on his fur cap approached us. I smiled in his face, not a defiant smile but a nervous one, and he smiled back. Oh my God, I thought, having at last regained my senses. I frantically tried to speak a bit of Russian to explain, but not a single word came out. I just could not speak. He pointed at my shoulder, most likely indicating that I was some officer or at least some rank, and his smile became a grin.

All the blood drained from my brain and the last thing I remember thinking was, where are the horses? Then it happened as if my prayers had been answered, except that I hadn't prayed at all, I had just stood there, and I was extremely wobbly at that. Very hell was let loose, and everybody dived for cover.

Mortar shells came from the German side, and the Russians were running; so was I, only I was running in the opposite direction. My legs felt like lead, but with superhuman strength I was running and leaping through the high snow, not daring to look back, until I collapsed from utter exhaustion, at the same time wriggling myself into the snow. There I lay very still, trying to stop my panting, not even daring to breathe. After a while I lifted my head, I was alone and for the moment I felt free. The shells were still coming, but further down the wood. I braced myself, not really believing that this had happened to me, and I jumped up and ran again, this time taking more sensible strides. On reaching the open edge of the wood I was confronted by our own soldiers. I heard their voices first, before I could see them, but they at first thought I was a Russian, and it was only because the Russians had ripped some of my clothing off, revealing my German uniform, that I was not attacked a second time.

Then Lieutenant Leither, from the 2nd Battalion, recognised me.

My face was smeared with blood, a result of the beating I had received. Nobody, however, gave me a second look—they all had enough worries of their own, and wading through the snow towards the enemy was, of course, not the time to make a fuss about me. I was sure they did not even believe my story of the dramatic escape. Oh well, I thought, at least I was on my way home, that was surely in my favour; I was, quite simply, pleased to be alive. I reached for a handful of snow and had a good wash. The pain seemed to have increased in my right shoulder—that nasty evil-smelling Russian must have hit me with his rifle butt or something, I said to myself. I scooped up some more snow and stuffed it into my mouth, not really caring if I only got more thirsty—after all, I only had about two or three miles to go. I was getting rather hungry, too. The sun was getting lower and I fixed myself a point to keep straight at it.

I then took stock of myself. Those rats had taken my compass, my watch, and all my private belongings—all the photos and letters, except Willy's which I still had in my coat pocket. But what really hurt me, of course, was that they had taken the pistol Willy had given me in France. My Schmeisser machine-pistol and my binoculars were also gone; my greatcoat had been ripped off me, along with my homemade parachute cape, and several buttons were missing from various other garments.

It was getting colder already, as always in the afternoon, and I was shivering in spite of the arduous walking in the snow. Thank goodness my legs are all right, I thought. There wasn't a soul anywhere—then I saw them, before they saw me, eight or nine figures, all on horseback. Pulling myself into the snow and making myself as white with it as I could, I peered over the heap in front of me, warily observing them coming nearer and nearer. 'They must be our chaps,' I said aloud, 'please let them be ours.' They were. I recognised Erich Helm's big chestnut and Godecke's black mare. They had seen me—they had field-glasses—and Erich cantered towards me, shouting and waving.

'We were looking for you,' he said, clapping my shoulder in delight. I winced but said nothing. 'Where are your horses?' he asked. By this time all the others had arrived and I told them the whole story. I got a lift on Godecke's mare, the strongest of the horses, and slowly we moved towards Regimental HQ. Many things came into my mind on the way. What would happen to Siegfried and Albert? It was my own fault, I thought, how could I be so bloody stupid and dream my way through a wood? Me of all people; was I not always telling my boys to be alert at all times and never take things for granted? It had nearly cost me my life, I only thanked God that He had spared me—that commissar wasn't being friendly when he grinned at me; he probably wanted to interrogate me first, before shooting me. And that poisoned dwarf, I promised myself, if I ever get my hands on him... he had most of my things; the watch wasn't much good anyway, I thought, he probably wouldn't even know how to wind the thing up, he looked a proper primitive.

There was some good news for me after I had reported to Colonel Gratz and Lieutenant Becker, who grinned at me as if to say, 'I'm glad to see you back in one piece': Siegfried was with the 3rd Battalion. He had virtually galloped straight to the HQ, with his stirrup leathers flying and reins tangled up. But there was no sign of Albert, the Colonel's horse. Since we had at last got a telephone connection we asked Hallach, Captain Schutte's horse holder to bring Siegfried over the next day.

'What happened to you?' I asked the Colonel. 'After all, it was you who asked me to come and collect you.'

'Oh', he said. 'We got there, but the Russians had penetrated and Lieutenant Friedrichsen brought me back here. It was then that we were fired on by the Russians—mortar fire from a wooded area, the very one you got stuck in. We'll soon fix you up with all the things you lost. Sorry about your personal items. We are all pleased to have you back in one piece, but you had better get that shoulder of yours seen to.'

The shoulder wasn't broken or anything, but it was badly bruised and blasted painful. What had happened to me really came home to me that evening, when I rolled myself into a blanket, after a hot meal. I suppose the shock of it had to come out some time. It was good to be alive.

All the glamour of my very lucky escape was overshadowed three days later. Lieutenant Becker had gone for a ride in Lieutenant Friedrichsen's scout car—it was just like him, a big kid with a new toy. They most probably had gone through the countryside towards the 3rd Battalion, the same route I had taken only a few days earlier, and it looked as though they had strayed too far and been caught by the Russians. Anyway, they did not return. Erich Helm went out to look for them, and scout cars from the 2nd and 3rd Battalions joined in the search, but with no result. It was hard to believe that Lieutenant Becker of all people was missing. 'He always had the luck of the devil with him,' we said. 'He will surely turn up, you'll see.' But after three days, there was no sign of any of them—Lieutenant Becker, Lieutenant Friedrichsen and his driver were lost.

The Colonel was furious—not only had he lost his Ordnance Officers, but also a driver and a brand-new scout car. 'Everything seems to have gone wrong just lately,' he stormed. 'I haven't even got a horse to go about on.' I winced at that; that, I felt, was overdoing it, but I could understand his letting off steam.

The following day, 15 February 1942, there was a kind of conference of all the officers of the regiment—that is those who could be spared; our battalions and companies were already stretched to the utmost, and, like a chain, only as strong as the weakest link. We knew that there was something in the wind every time all the officers assembled. This time it was only a change in position and that meant marching. Ironically we marched along the same route I had taken to reach the 3rd Battalion only five days before, when I nearly had my chips. Riding my Siegfried alongside Erich Helm I was able to explain the circumstances. I even pointed out the very spot, looking hopefully in the trampled snow—maybe one or two of my personal effects had been dropped by the Russians when everybody had dived for cover and I had run like hell. No such luck of course; in any case, our own soldiers would surely have picked anything up. For a few brief moments I relived that whole dreadful episode and as a final gesture, as if to put it all behind me, I brushed my sleeves. I was still furious with myself for being so bloody stupid.

As I said, our battalions were very stretched, and we had hoped to get some replacements sent on, for we had many losses and holding our position became a strain for everybody. We heard, however, that most replacement troops had already been frost-bitten before even reaching us.

We, without noticing it, had become hardened because we had had the advantage of going slowly into the cold climate whilst the fellows being brought in by plane as near to us as possible, ran straight into the coldest temperatures they'd ever known. Even many Russians had never experienced the 50 or so degrees of frost we sometimes had. Occasionally the temperature rose just a little, but as soon as our hopes for warmer weather got a bit high, it started to freeze again. It was very difficult even to bury our dead, and we had to wait for special commandos to come and blast large holes for mass graves, sometimes twenty or more boys together, just rolled in tent sheets.

I remember with some horror one dreadful experience. It was 16 February, the day after we'd started marching, and our battalions were moving from one village to another, overlapping each other, with some Stuka support, which helped a great deal, though even so we had many losses. That particular afternoon after a village had been taken I combed some houses to find odd useful things, such as newspaper or felt for boot innersoles, anything that could come in handy. There was a great deal of wailing coming from a dugout behind a building, where about eight or ten women and children were huddled together; the sound was spine-chilling. On the doorstep sat an old woman, cuddling and cradling a bundle and weaving back and forth. She was sitting in front of the doorway and in the bitter wind, which I found rather odd. So I went to her, wanting to tell her that I felt like wailing myself. I looked down at the bundle in her arms and I saw that it was a small child and it was asleep; putting one hand on the woman's shoulder first, I touched the child on its forehead, it was icy cold. The child was dead and must have been for some time. The woman didn't even look at me, so I went away towards a kind of small garden shed.

When I eventually managed to open the door latch I had to jump back, as a whole load of dead bodies rolled out. They had been packed in there like sardines in a tin, and they were still warm as I found out when I started trying to put them back. It was impossible to get them back in, and some moved as if they were still alive. Round their necks were their identity tags. All of them were Germans, they had all been killed only that morning or early afternoon. Nearby were several bomb craters and I thought, well, they will all be buried in one of them, the craters are quite deep.

We went on to another village without further casualties, apparently the Russian resistance had been broken that afternoon. Since it was already dark, we just stumbled first into the nearest barn, where we settled the horses, and then into one of the houses. Some of our soldiers were already there in the large front room, warming themselves and even starting to cook, those who had anything to cook. There was a second room but this one was in darkness, not even the usual small oil-lamp with its representation of the Madonna was to be seen; maybe they had run out of oil. Some people had already bedded down on the floor. Erich Helm and I and one or two others found just enough room to huddle in between; all we wanted was warmth and sleep. Still thinking about the events of the day, the dead bodies of soldiers, the small child looking like porcelain, I fell asleep.

Someone was cuddling up very close to me and that someone was not a man. We had long hair all right, but not that long and especially not with a ribbon in it. I closed my eyes very hard and opened them, straining to make out who was cuddling into me. One thing I was already sure of, it was not a Magda, for they never took their headscarves off and besides whoever it was was not evil smelling. I felt hot all over and could not help getting excited; the last time I had been near any woman was in Poland. She rolled over and was face to face with me now and as she opened her eyes I sensed her stiffening and moving away from me, lifting herself on to her elbows. For a moment I thought I had a sailor in front of me because of the blouse she wore. The light came in faintly through the window and dawn was already breaking—my God, she was beautiful, and a thrill came over me when I realised that I had actually slept with her. I got up first, indicating to her to be quiet because everybody was still sleeping. What am I to do now? I wondered—after all, it wasn't my fault and nothing had happened anyway. I left the smaller room and stepping over all the rest, went outside to see if the horses were all right. Wasn't it maddening? The first time for God knows how long a pretty girl cuddled in with me and it had to be in a room full of strange people.

The cold air soon sobered me. Maybe I would find the field kitchen and maybe they would even be busy boiling some water for whatever was on the cards, coffee or even tea. Sometimes we couldn't taste the difference, but as long as it was hot and maybe even sweet...

The horses were not all right as I had hoped—the blighters had strayed off down the road to find better pastures. I had got Siegfried and Erich's horse back in the barn, swearing under my breath because of the inconvenience, when I suddenly came face to face with the girl I had slept with.

Now I could take a proper look at her. She was petite, blue-eyed, with black hair in braids: she did indeed have a sailor blouse on, though now she had a shawl slung over her shoulders. She gave me a lively smile; it actually made me blush and her laughter made me realise that she had seen my cheeks redden, despite my unshaven state. Come to think of it, I must have looked a right neglected so-and-so. Haircuts were not heard of any more and only if we had water and time did we shave. I sat on one of the bundles of straw and took my small box of Chokakola out of my new despatch case on my belt and offered her some. To my amazement, she actually sat beside me, but she had no idea what I offered her, she had never seen chocolate before. I had to eat some myself first, then very slowly she started to chew. We ate the whole box and had a marvellous time trying to make conversation. Her name, she told me, was Lupa and she and her mother were travelling from Georgia to Tula when the war broke out, which was how they had got stuck in this area. They were looking for her father, up till now with no luck, but as he was a silversmith and Tula was the place for silver they had decided to go there.

I had a really good clean-up after this and did my best to smarten myself up for the afternoon, as she had promised to meet me at the same place. I was also hoping that we would be staying for some time at the village, it really could be quite pleasant. In the last few days I had taken a dislike to any Russian and anything to do with Russia. The whole country was just against anything I stood for, and the only thing I had wanted was to get back home, away from this place. Now I had met Lupa, a nice little girl, drawn into a conflict with no idea what it was all about, and I liked her a lot.

I saw Lupa sooner than I expected because she was with her mother in the house we had slept in. She was busy, like everybody else, some kids were screaming their heads off and the place smelt of fresh bread, in fact it was a typical Russian scene. I watched her for some time till she spotted me; she paused a moment, looking me up and down, I hoped approvingly. I had taken my fur cap off, and had also shaved. When I went over to her she nodded towards an older woman and said, 'Magda'; the resemblance was there all right, her mother even gave me a shy smile. It really made my day.

Eventually, the afternoon arrived. But so did bad news for me—we were ordered to march on to a larger village to make quarters for a longer period, on standby. It was good news in one respect but not in the other. Lupa came into the barn all smiles, and what lovely smiles. She had heard that we were moving, and between embraces, I promised to come back by myself in the next day or so, in any case as soon as possible. What is the matter with me, I wondered, have I gone crazy or something? Not a bit of it—I had just fallen for a very pretty girl and I knew that that had to compensate for a lot of hardship. She was not just pretty, she was beautiful and could she kiss...

many times afterwards I wondered where she was and if she was thinking of me.

I did go back to the village, only two days later, without telling anybody—it was only about eight miles away and I knew there were only our troops about, so it wasn't a great risk. Nevertheless, it was irresponsible of me; on the other hand I couldn't very well go to the Colonel and ask him for permission to go and see my girlfriend—he would probably have blown his top. But to my sorrow she was no longer there, and nobody could tell me when and where they had gone.

It was 22 February 1942. We received post and supplies, the first since January. I got a letter from my sister Lotte; it contained news that I'd been dreading: my brother Willy had been killed on 16 January. Not all that long before I had received a letter from him and I had been on top of the world, believing he was all right. Willy's birthday had been on 11 January, and he was twenty-seven years old. Willy complained very seldom about anything but in his letter he admitted that he didn't like the whole situation, especially the ragged front line. Nobody knew where one was, sometimes the Russians were in front and other times at the back, it was jut too nerve-racking. I was shattered and felt numb for several days and then I read Lotte's letter again and again, still hoping it was simply not true. She also wrote that Kurt, my eldest brother, had been called up and was a paymaster in the Afrikakorps. Kurt had always been good with financial matters and was now, after a short training session in Germany, in North Africa.

Well, I thought, at least he is not on the immediate front line and doesn't have to freeze. In the last few days it had turned even colder, with 50-52 degrees of frost. This night I went into the barn, behind our very primitive quarters, where I had stabled Siegfried and Captain Schutte's horse, Mickey Mouse. (Captain Schute had said very insistently that he would be interested in having me as a permanent scout for the 3rd Battalion as our rider troop had shrunk from about thirty to a mere ten. I only had Krizock and Godecke left.) When I approached Siegfried he looked at me as if to say, 'Sorry.' I had told nobody about my brother, maybe I still did not believe it. Putting my arms around his neck, I talked to him as I often did, and for the first time, my tears came, wetting his neck. Who else was there here to talk to? They all had their own problems and worries. Looking through the large holes in the roof I could see the cold moon lighting up the snow-covered scenery; even the beams in the barn were glistening with the frost. Everything was so hopeless, and now that Willy had gone, even more so, it was just meaningless. I had better write a letter home, I thought. My mother and sister were probably waiting for a sign of life from me and were now even more anxious than ever.

The next day I told Captain Schutte about my brother as I accompanied him to the 3rd Battalion HQ. 'I'll get in touch with your brother's company commander,' he said. 'I'll simply telephone. At least I'll try. After all,' he went on, 'we are practically neighbours and since we are a bit more settled it may be possible to get in touch with one of the chaps your brother was with.'

I was transferred the next day but it didn't matter, except that in the battalion position we were much more exposed to fire from the Russians, especially mortars. Most of the personnel I already knew very well. Our position was in a small clearing in the woods, the companies were in dugouts made of snow, very much like igloos, only more makeshift. One of the companies had had a near escape only a few days earlier. They had taken quarters in a village school, in which there were three large cannon-stoves and also coal. As always everybody had been tired and cold; they had lit the stoves and put plenty of coal in, but without making sure that the stove pipes were clear. They had then all lain down on the floor to sleep, filling their lungs with carbon monoxide. Only after about fifteen men were found to have lost consciousness was it realised what had happened. They were dragged out into the snow quickly, and a tragedy was avoided. They all looked very healthy lying in the snow with their red faces.

No sooner had I settled in with the 3rd Battalion than I got my first mission. The mission was on foot. 'Take those two chaps of yours and re-establish contact with the 2nd Battalion; I can get no answer from them, the blasted line must have been broken somewhere,' said Captain Schutte. We—Krizock, Godecke and I—put on our homemade parachute capes (now with three black stripes on the left sleeve to distinguish us from the Russians who also wore white parachute capes) over our coats and after taking our bearings, set off, wading through the very high snow. After an hour or so we entered a wood of tall, well-spaced-out, pines. After my misadventure not so long before I was now always very nervous and the smallest disturbance made me jump. Krizock stopped. We all knew one another well enough by now never to have to speak aloud on missions, and Godecke and I stopped too. Krizock waved me over and showed me several fresh footprints coming from the right. Now it became interesting; if the footprints were Russian, which was almost certainly the case, then we had to be very careful. If I had had more men at my disposal, I would have posted two of them and they would have been waiting for the Russian patrol to return. But our orders were to find our 2nd Battalion. So after making sure that there was no one nearby, we carried on as before, but looking back now and then.

It was my turn to see something now, something moving up and down, close to the ground. Since there were also some smaller pines, looking just like Christmas trees loaded as they were with snow, it was difficult to make out what it was exactly. We were still about a hundred yards away from it and I signalled to Godecke to advance in a half-circle. Still puzzled and getting suspicious we crept forward, till eventually I could make out what it was. Of all things most unexpected, it was a cow, submerged in the snow, with only her head sticking out, hence the weaving motion. Beside the cow, lying in the snow, was an old woman. She was dead, still gripping the leading rope tied to the cow in her hand. The cow was groaning and only just alive, buried up to the neck and firmly embedded in the packed show. It would seem that the cow had sunk into the ditch filled with drift snow and, unable to scramble out, had been threshing about and got deeper and deeper; the snow had then melted with the wretched creature's body heat and turned into ice. We still had severe frost and the old lady must have been exhausted, had fallen asleep herself and had died. That, at any rate, was the conclusion I came to. We decided to leave everything alone until we returned: the cow would definitely be very useful, as we could do with some meat, but shooting it now would have given us away and alarmed everybody in the area. So we continued on our way to find the outposts of the 2nd Battalion. Keeping going was the best policy in those situations, for one gets very hot wading through deep snow and stopping even for a moment could bring on nasty frostbite. We had had many casualties caused that way—if while marching, for instance, men had to take cover, even just for a short while, the damage could be done.

There was still no sign of anyone. If we didn't make any contact soon we could be in real trouble as it got dark very early in the afternoon; we had looked for telephone wires, but without success. We came out of the forest of tall trees to find an apparently endless expanse of small pines in front of us. To make it more difficult they were pretty close together and as we crept through we kept on being showered with snow, and the task of keeping our direction became all the more difficult. Since my encounter with the Russians I no longer had a march compass so we could only get a definite direction by our watches if there was any sun. But the sky was overcast, and heavy snow clouds were promising more of the dreaded stuff. If it started to snow now our own tracks would be filled and we could get hopelessly lost on our return journey. It was my turn to go in front, but from now on we stuck close together, with only about five or six yards in between, crouching and creeping and getting more and more worried. Suddenly I found myself staring into a pair of eyes. I froze, not quite sure what to do next. The fellow staring at me, I noticed, was dressed just as I was—but who was to know? A figure in a white parachute cape half lying in the snow could be Russian or German. After a few anxious moments I lifted my arm to show my stripes. The other did the same. Phew, I thought, that was a close shave, and in relief we shook hands. He was a lieutenant from the 2nd Battalion. Two other men showed up behind him—the three of them had been on their way to make contact with us.

So we all stopped there to have a quiet smoke, and keeping our voices down, we exchanged all our news, good and bad. The bad news was that we were to advance and overlap our neighbouring regiment. The lieutenant didn't like this at all, he said that they had just settled themselves down nicely a few miles back.

The good news was ours—the cow in the snow. We could not just keep it to ourselves, they would like it just as much as we would—but how could we halve a cow? They came back with us to the cow—it was only about two miles. We warned them about the Russian patrol and we all kept our eyes and ears open. The cow was still alive and the lieutenant agreed that shooting it would be foolish and that it would be quite impossible to get it out without any spades, etc.

'Leave it where it is and we'll send a slaughter party first thing in the morning.' The chance of a really good meal would bring plenty of volunteers from both sides, and at the same time the breakage in the telephone lines could be found and repaired. Satisfied with our so-called day's work we set off for 'home' after saying cheerio to the lieutenant and his party, who also went on their way. The snow was really coming down now.

There was bad news for me when I got back to the Battalion HQ. Before we had left on our mission in the morning I had stabled Mickey Mouse with Siegfried across the road in a barn packed with bales of hay. Mickey Mouse was standing there but half leaning to one side, and I could see a large hole on her near-side saddle flap. As I watched in dismay the life ebbed out of her, and very slowly her knees buckled under her. She looked at me as if to say, 'Help me. What is happening?' There was a pool of blood on the off side where the shell had left her body, it must have been one of the 25mm anti-aircraft shells. Soon after that she was gone, and I had to be quick to snatch the saddle of her before she went down on all fours.

When I told Captain Schutte he just shrugged his shoulders. 'Funny', I thought; but then, he never had been much of a horseman and only rode when it was absolutely necessary.

The next morning the whole battalion staff company had to line up in front of Captain Schutte's HQ. Everybody was full of misgivings because every time we had to line up there was some bad news. Well, the news was not exactly bad but it tasted bad. Everybody had to swallow one large spoonful of cod liver oil. When I was a small boy, I remembered, my mother always gave us some of this dreadful-tasting stuff in the winter time. This time it forced some smiles on our faces, because Captain Schutte and his office staff all had to set an example and swallow a spoonful in front of everybody.

We had a consolation afterwards—the field kitchen had a kettle full of splendid bean soup with some meat in it. Goodness only knows where they got the meat from, although I had my suspicions but said nothing. I avoided eating the meat... poor Mickey Mouse.

Just then, when everybody was gathered around the kitchen not only for the soup but also to get some warmth, a familiar sound came to our ears, the whistling of heavy shells. So long as we could hear the whistle we were all right, although apprehensive. But then the whistling stopped and everybody dived headlong into the snow. The precious soup was gone for ever, while, our heads buried in the snow, we waited for the big bang.

It never came, the big shell embedded itself with a hollow thud in the snow only yards away from us, its tail sticking out. We edged cautiously away from the *Blindgänger* (dud shell), swearing blue heaven from the fright while, of course, glad it did not go off.

As we had to move on, we never did get our cow.

15

'Shoot the Prisoners'

March had arrived, but not the spring; it was colder than ever, and water was hard to get hold of. One night I had to sit up and massage Siegfried. He could not pass water and his penis had swollen to an enormous size—so there was I, whistling to him and stroking it to make him pass water. The vet told me that it was water colic and that it only happens when a horse gets no or not enough water to drink. With the severe frost we were having, it could be dangerous, he told me, and advised me to give Siegfried this rather intimate sort of massage. I eventually managed to scrounge a bucket of water, and Siegfried recovered after slurping it all up.

We set off again and came to a village called Rubiskino, a very small place but with most of its houses intact, where we stopped. There were still some civilians left there, and the cottage in which my small unit and some of Erich's troop stayed was occupied by a woman, though she always disappeared at night—to stay with friends, we assumed.

It was our turn to be thirsty now. Our field kitchen had stayed behind and in order to get tea or anything else, a rider had to shoulder an insulated metal container and ride back and forth at least twice a day. I had to ride even further back to find our ever-elusive supply wagons. Goodness only knows how they managed to get lost so easily. My direction was easy enough but the road wasn't; it was pitch dark and only by listening to the overhead wires on the roadside dingling in the bitter cold could I keep my direction. Of course the telephone wires were useless for us and had probably not been used since the war began.

I was extremely fortunate—I reached a small hamlet and found them in the first house; if I had been five minutes or so later they would have left, and most likely, as they told me, in the wrong direction. Captain Ebert as always was pleased to see me; he was also very generous with his cognac, maybe because he needed a small excuse, I suspected, but perhaps I was wrong. I stayed overnight and was very glad to get some rest; the day had been very long for me.

When we arrived back in Rubiskino it was obvious that something was in the air again. We received mortar fire at one-hour intervals, and it got nearer each day. It was rather worrying as we had a wagon full of ammunition, mostly hand grenades, in our yard, and if we only got one hit on the wagon it would have blown us sky high.

The barns where we stabled our horses were only fifty yards away from the house; it was my turn to fetch the soup from the kitchen, and I was preparing to set off. Siegfried was standing at the ready, the saddle was already on him, and I put the container for the soup on the ground and was just putting the bit in his mouth when the familiar sound of oncoming mortars came out of the blue and *wham*! There was no time to take cover, one came down only a few yards away from me, Siegfried was hit in the head, right in between my hands, below his right eye, and also in the left saddle flap. I wasn't touched; only my cape was torn and burnt. Siegfried turned his head towards his saddle, indicating where it hurt most; very slowly his front legs buckled, and he rolled on to his side, his eyes wide open and staring straight at me. He seemed to say, 'So long. I've had enough.'

I was numb. I stood there in utter desperation, looking around for help to get Siegfried back on his feet. I just could not grasp the situation. This could not happen to my Siegfried.

I slapped his neck, it was warm, I expected him to turn around and at least make an effort. He was very still and his eyes lifeless. 'Get up,' I shouted, at last recovering my voice. 'You can't do this to me.' My tears were blinding my eyes—what was I going to do without him?

In all the many months (it had been like a lifetime), he had been my comrade, my protector; he had carried me out of trouble many times; he had listened for me and warned me of any danger. I had always relied upon him in a thousand and one situations. I had cried on his shoulder when I was in despair, and he had even made me laugh at some of his antics. He had never complained when I had nothing to give him, not even water.

To me he had not been 'just a horse', he had been my best friend, a friend in a thousand, full of warmth and understanding.

I remained kneeling beside him, my hand resting on his neck, it was slowly getting colder. Suddenly I felt utterly alone. Several more mortar shells had exploded, I was not in the least interested. What was going on around me was no concern of mine. I was in a nightmare, a dreadful one. 'Why has this happened to you?' I said to him, stroking his ears. At the same time I felt a shiver down my spine as I realised Siegfried was gone.

'Come on, Max,' I heard a voice say, it was a voice from far away. 'We have got to get him out of the yard.' Reality can be so cruel, I had seen many comrades cut to pieces, or heard them scream for a moment before the last gurgle of life left their mouths, and I had felt for them. But here was I holding on to my horse, sobbing inside uncontrollably. At the same time I was fuming with anger and swore revenge if it was possible.

I did not help pull Siegfried out of the yard, but I watched, telling the other boys who had brought another horse to do the pulling, to be careful, as if Siegfried could still be hurt.

I suppose it takes a horseman to understand how I felt at that moment. Slowly I came back to my senses, there was plenty of work to be done, the mortar attack was over and we had to shift all the explosives and ammunition out of the yard— we really had been living dangerously the last few days. It also took my mind off Siegfried, for the time being anyway.

There were no other casualties in our unit but the tension was high. One thing we found out was that the woman who returned every morning to the cottage had been an informer and had been running back and forth. We never saw her again after this attack.

Captain Schutte had had enough, and a conference was arranged; all the responsible officers and also some NCOs arrived the following day. Lieutenant Leitner of the 2nd was there, as was Captain Lorenzen. Since the 1st Battalion was positioned some way away and were not affected by the constant attacks, as the 2nd and 3rd were, they were not represented. I was present, as I had no horse at my disposal although I was still in charge of the despatch and scouting section.

'Get yourself a horse as soon as possible, Kuhnert,' Captain Schutte said. I winced. In any case, it was easier said than done; however, we'd see about it after we got back from whatever that night's mission was to be. The plan was for a very large patrol, consisting of several officers and experienced men, numbering fifty or sixty all told, to surround the Russian unit that had been giving us constant problems with their mortars. Captain Lorenzen was to be in charge. One of the oldest officers in our regiment—about forty-five to fifty at a guess—he was always very solemn, and also very brave.

We were warned of mines in the area; several fields had already been cordoned off with white ribbon, usually paper—looking like a kind of gusset—but not every one could be found, which is why the area was so dreadfully dangerous, especially at night.

'Will you come with us, Kuhnert?' Captain Lorenzen asked.

'Yes, *sir*,' was my reply. I was so surprised and of course greatly honoured—maybe someone had told him of my recent bit of bad luck.

'Right,' he said, leaning over the small table with the oil lamp. 'This is what we'll do.' He pointed out the small villages in the area, and explained the way he thought was best to tackle the task in hand. This took some time and when he finished he straightened up and said, 'What's your opinion?' Looking around at everybody present. This again took some time, everybody had to study the primitive map first and make up his mind in his own time. There were some minor details suggested, but on the whole everybody approved. The plan was to send one party towards the Russian centre as bait, the others were to split up and circle to the left and right, and meet at the back of the Russian unit, like a pair of pincers. We were to retreat to our own thin lines or the outposts of the various companies if anything went wrong. It took some time again to explain the exact locations of our posts so that we could avoid being shot at by our own men. We synchronised watches, a great many good luck wishes were exchanged and we set off into the night. We took as little as possible in the way of equipment—it was bad enough wading through the deep snow without having to carry a lot of heavy, noisy and totally unnecessary paraphernalia. As always in such operations the tension was very high; on top of that, we were starving and had only a mug of tea—or was it coffee?—to warm our insides. One does not eat before any attack in case of internal wounds. Vodka was in short supply and cognac seemed to be limited to the regimental HQ or the paymasters. My last orders before leaving were to Hallach and Kruger, the two despatch riders left over in the 2nd Battalion, and of course my own two men, Krizock and Godecke: they were to make preparations for the next day and to find out where there might be a suitable mount for me.

Captain Lorenzen was, as always, very quiet and very precise in every way, and very stern. Only whispering was allowed, but in any case there was far too much tension for any kind of conversation. The night was very still, no firing anywhere, almost peaceful, and I wished it would start to bang somewhere to break the nerve-racking silence. It was early evening, about 8 p.m., so we had plenty of time—the left-hand and right-hand parties were expected to meet up at the back of the Russians at 10 p.m. The centre party, ten men led by Lieutenant Leitner, was expected to be spotted first, and in fact they were to make some noise to draw attention to themselves—after all, they were the bait. As soon as they got fired on we, the other two parties, would speed up our advance, while they were to retreat, depending on the strength of the Russian forces coming at them. The whole operation was to take place in a five-to-six-square-mile area.

We had now passed our outposts and were already in no man's land. Most of the terrain was tall pine woods but still the snow was very deep, about two feet, and very tiresome to get through. The only sound we could hear at that moment was the crunchy, screechy noise of our boots on the hard frozen snow and our laborious breathing. Captain Lorenzen was in front, and I followed with Sergeant Gebert of the 2nd Battalion. I hoped it wouldn't start to snow, that would have made it so much more difficult. Many times during the war I observed how most operations had depended upon the weather.

Our eyes got used to the darkness and, helped by the light surface of the snow, we could see quite well. Then suddenly the whole sky seemed to light up, followed by two short bangs; the Russians must have seen something suspicious and had fired a flare. It was, as expected, in the centre of our advance. The flare, of the type which has a small parachute attached to it, was drifting very slowly to the ground. A second one and a third one followed and we all went down. We in our section did not want to be discovered, not yet anyhow. After a few minutes we carried on as before, still in single file, but now and then changing the lead to have a new man making tracks in the show—following a ready-made path in the deep snow was less energy-sapping. Our eyes had got used to the dark again after the flare, and we could not only see but also hear machine-gun fire aimed towards our central section. Short-calibre mortar was also involved; one of the newest weapons of the Russians, it was only 25mm, and the actual mortar was a spade handle with two wires as side levers to put the spade into the ground and keep it standing up. The handle was hollow with a firing pin at the bottom. The shells were carried in a belt over the shoulder. It was not too effective except on morale, especially in a wood, because of the threatening noise it made.

It was time for us to speed up and try to get around the Russians and meet the left-hand party, led by Lieutenant Brandt of the 2nd Battalion. We were in all about twenty-five men, armed only with the necessary equipment, consisting of a machine-gun a 34,* well-oiled with glycerine to keep it from freezing, several carbines, and of course the officers and NCOs had machine-pistols as well as P40s.† We also had plenty of hand grenades. We took it in turns to carry the machine-guns and the three metal boxes of ammo, each containing 300 rounds.

Several clusters of small pines appeared in front of us and forced us to split up into two parties; we decided to meet after about half a mile in the centre behind the wood if nothing happened. We reached the taller trees all right, and the snow was not so deep there. Captain Lorenzen was out in front again, followed by myself, and there was a man with the machine-gun just behind me, I could hear his heavy breathing. Sergeant Gebert brought up the rear.

The clouds were breaking up overhead and a very bright moon appeared—we had hoped for complete darkness as being spotted now could be disastrous. It slowed us down a bit, but Captain Lorenzen kept on going and, turning round, said to me, 'See that everybody keeps up, the sooner we get this over with the better.'

By his tone I could make out his feeling; he was just like me whenever I had a job of this kind to do. I would work myself into a temper, mixed with defiance and hatred and vengeance—I had not forgotten that little Russian;

---

* The MG 34 was introduced into the army in 1934, hence the name.
† The P40 was introduced into the army in 1940.

I could still see his face in front of me and smell his foul breath; I only hoped that he was in among this lot we wanted to surprise. I actually began to get heated and had to calm myself down. My God, it was bitter cold, the icy, blistering wind coming down against us was maddening, it cut right through us as if trying to sweep us off the face of the earth. I even tried walking backwards, but that only made things more difficult. It was as if a phenomenal power was pouring frost wave after frost wave just at us; it sapped our energy, it stopped our breathing and laughed at our clothing. How much longer could we go on like this? I turned and took the machine-gun from the man grunting behind me, no doubt he was grateful. Only the face of the Russian dwarf kept me going, especially since the gun's strap hurt the shoulder he had hit. Thank God we were fit, we had to be.

Captain Lorenzen stopped, waited for everybody to catch up, and waved to us to gather round. 'What we now have to do is get the rest of our party, and then the left-hand patrol,' he said. No sooner were his words out than we heard and saw firing out front or to be precise on our right since we had made a large left-hand circle.

'Blasted hell,' Captain Lorenzen shouted. 'Those idiots haven't waited for us and they've attacked the Russians at the back. Or else they've been spotted.' The only thing we could do now was to speed up and close the gap between our two groups. I was relieved of the machine-gun and Captain Lorenzen called me to his side, at the same time giving the word to be handed down to advance in a line, but without firing until told to do so, and to keep going till we actually made contact. I know my heart was pumping fast and not only from the wading through the snow. I was also swearing under my breath because I felt it below my dignity as a rider to be an ordinary foot slogger in the infantry advance. My Siegfried was still on my mind. There was nothing I could do about that now. I made sure that my machine-pistol was warm enough and that I had one spare magazine with 25 rounds in the top of my felt boot. Sergeant Gebert, who now had the machine-gun, said to me, 'The snow is far too high to get this thing into the ground.'

'Well, use it from your hip then,' I said. 'Take a short piece of ammo with you in your pocket and let it roll through, that will work all right—you only have to fire short bursts in any case. But make sure there aren't any of us in front if you do.'

Up till now, our party had not been spotted; we had by now left the wood, having been joined by the others of our units that had peeled away earlier. The firing was now intensifying and several flares went up to light the scene. I thought it was rather stupid of the Russians, for they would only be seen, just like us. There were several small barns in front of us, we could see them now, thanks to the Russian flares; we also saw flames, so something had been hit by our partners on the right.

'Keep low,' Captain Lorenzen shouted. 'Take no chances and only fire when you see something, otherwise keep on going forward.' Now we were suddenly fired at, but it was only rifle fire. Sergeant Gebert gave a burst of machine-gun fire in its direction, and we ran as fast as the snow allowed towards the barns. The fear had gone out of me, I was almost looking forward to meeting the blighters. I was armed this time. My machine-pistol at the ready, and straining my eyes because the flares had gone out, I overtook Captain Lorenzen who seemed to have breathing problems. Machine-gun fire was now coming in our direction, I could almost feel the impact in the snow beside me. I heard a piercing scream coming from Captain Lorenzen's direction and hesitated, but then I kept on going to reach the corner of the first barn. Small mortars were exploding around us now, and I could not help just for a moment thinking of my brother Willy. That is how he met his death; I had received a letter from his machine-gunner No. 1 only a few days before. I kept as low as possible, Sergeant Gebert was on my left and the rest were spread out. Gebert pumped some bursts into the barn. He fired as I had suggested, from the hip, and we safely got to cover, we wanted to catch our breath. I tore one of the hand grenades off my button holes, slung my machine-pistol over my shoulder, and looked round for the barn door. It was wide open so I jumped and slithered towards it; then, pulling the grenade's pin, I threw it right into the middle of the barn. The flames and explosions blinded me for a few seconds, then, ripping my machine-pistol to my hip, I sprayed the inside as much as possible, before diving back to take cover. Everything was very still in there.

'We might as well go on to the next barn and make sure they are not hiding in there', said Gebert. The firing had died down and we could not see a soul. 'The devils must be somewhere in there.' As I moved forward I indicated to the rest to give me cover and waded towards the next barn opening. It was at too sharp an angle to throw a grenade, I kept going along the wall, getting into conflict with some large icicles. The breaking of them gave my position away, for suddenly two figures hurled themselves out of the barn, firing and screaming at the top of their voices. Thank God, I was pressed against the wall and they missed me completely. But I did not miss them. I can still hear it now, they seemed only to inhale loudly, and then crumpled. It was the first time I had shot anyone so near, they were lying at my feet and I could smell the blood. More figures appeared on the side of the barn and I threw myself to the ground. Sergeant Gebert was firing like mad from behind, how he missed me I still don't know but I was safe for the time being.

'Where is Captain Lorenzen?' I asked somebody. No one seemed to know—they all had their own skin to worry about at the moment. I remembered the scream a little while back and realised that something must have happened to him.

'Take over,' I shouted to Sergeant Gebert. 'Just hold the position until I get back. I am worried about the Captain.'

Captain Lorenzen was half-lying half-sitting when I got to him; he was crazed with pain and rocking back and forth.

What a brave man, I thought. 'What's the matter?' I asked, fearing the worst.

'It's my blasted foot,' he said. 'It must have been a mine, one of the wooden types.' Those mines were very effective and would blow anybody's foot off and could not be detected very easily. The moon had appeared again and I could see the blood in the snow besides smelling it. There was no right boot any more, only a bloody mess. He must have lost a lot of blood and I had to stop it. I also had to stop his weaving about because the movement was pumping the very life out of his body. I had only got my small first aid pack in my left top pocket and I pulled it apart to get to the bandage, I asked him where his kit was. He was already getting very weak but he managed to point to his pocket just the same. I started to tie a tourniquet above his knee and he pointed to put it below the knee. I was glad about that actually, for I knew then he still had all his senses and I was sure I could get him to safety. I applied a few dressings to his stump, feeling like a butcher, and then ripped a part of my coat into pieces to wind around the leg to keep the frost out. He was numbed with shock and pain and I felt for him. He was not a light man and carrying him was out of the question so I decided I would try to pull him bit by bit towards where my men were positioned, but in the end I had to give up. He was shaking terribly from the shock, but there was nothing I could do apart from trying to keep him warm. Covering him up with my coat, I ran as fast as I could back to the position to get help.

As I waded through the snow I began to realise that I had to be careful not to get exhausted; as I had no greatcoat on the danger of frostbite was all the greater. There was firing going on not too far off, some stray bullets screamed past my head, and I could also hear shouting. I strained my eyes and ears to find the spot where I had left Gebert with the machine-gun. The scene was lit up, both the barns were ablaze making it more difficult to get near because of the smoke and the ever-changing visibility. One minute it was bright, the next it was plunged into darkness despite the dawn breaking.

I paused for a moment, chilled and uncertain of what was going on before me; I felt very helpless and thinking of poor Captain Lorenzen half a mile back did not help either. Clasping my machine-pistol at the ready I took my heart in my hands and kept on wading towards the burning barn. Some figures appeared in front of me and I lifted my arm up and down several times in the prearranged signal for recognition.

'Is that you, Kuhnert?' I heard Gebert calling. It was like music to my ears. 'Where the blazes have you been?' Two more of our chaps appeared and I told them about Captain Lorenzen.

The shooting had stopped for the moment, one could only hear the crackling of the burning buildings—we also got some very pleasant warm air coming from there.

'We have to get him,' I said. 'Is there anything we could carry him in?'

'What about something from the barn, if one can get near it?' So we managed a kind of makeshift sledge and eventually got Captain Lorenzen back to base. We had to loosen his tourniquet several times on the way, but he was surprisingly cheerful despite his pain and the knowledge that he'd lost his foot.

Lieutenant Leitner and his patrol had taken the Russians completely by surprise—they had most probably not expected three parties and had put up their hands. Before we set off for home, with Captain Lorenzen in tow, we had to destroy the mortars which had given us so much trouble.

As soon as it began to get light, we took stock of ourselves and the prisoners of war. Lieutenant Leitner had taken charge, as Lieutenant Brandt had his right arm in a sling; he had been hit, but only superficially and walked alongside Captain Lorenzen's makeshift sledge. We had several casualties—two killed and six wounded, including Captain Lorenzen; Lieutenant Brandt wasn't counted as wounded. We took eighteen prisoners; there were some badly wounded among the Russians—they were attended to by our men who stayed behind to establish the new defence line and fill the gaps between our company outposts. The weather conditions being what they were, there was no direct communications with the regiment or other units, and therefore we had hardly any medical staff or even medicaments. The worry was how soon we could get the help needed for the badly wounded, especially injections against gangrene. We all felt the biting freezing cold wind cutting through us, especially now, since it had got light; maybe we felt it even more because we were badly in need of nourishment. These conditions raised certain questions regarding the prisoners—for example who was going to look after them when we got back; we hardly had any men to spare to take them to the regiment as it would have meant endangering anybody who was unlucky enough to be chosen for the job. The Russians had no such problems in respect of prisoners: they just shot anyone, especially if he was wounded. We had found a number of our own men, who had even been stripped of their uniforms, and two men had had their eyes gouged out. It still makes me shiver even to think about it, how fortunate I was.

I did look over the prisoners—they looked just as bedraggled as us—but I could not find the dwarfish Russian or any other faces I remembered among them.

When we arrived at the battalion HQ there was some hot soup waiting for us, after we had carried Captain Lorenzen into the house. Captain Schutte had a good look at Captain Lorenzen and then made speedy arrangements to take him to regimental HQ by sledge with one of the remaining horses adding, 'let's hope the creature can pull.'

We only had four horses left, and Hallach's being a grey was chosen—one never knew when there were any Russian patrols about, and a grey could not be seen too easily in the snow.

I asked Krizock if he had had any luck so far in finding a horse for me. 'Well,' he said, 'the only way would be to steal one from the neighbouring regiment.' This, of course, would mean a twelve-mile journey at least, with two horses to get there. 'We might as well try for two horses,' he said, 'whilst we are at it.'

'Give me a couple of hours. Later this afternoon maybe,' I said. 'I need some rest. Besides, I have to get my greatcoat back from Captain Lorenzen.' He had been thickly wrapped up in blankets and was by now well on his way; Kruger and Godecke had gone with him. Before I could settle down in some warm and quiet spot for a nap, I was called to report to Captain Schutte. He wanted to know every detail, especially about Captain Lorenzen, as he had to write a report for the record. He also had something very gruesome and unexpected for us: 'You know the prisoners you brought with you this morning?' he said to me.

'Yes,' I answered. 'What about them?'

'Well,' he said. 'I just can't find any other way out—we have no men to spare—we have got to get rid of them—take them half a mile out from here and shoot them.'

'I can't do that,' I protested. 'I wouldn't know how.'

'What!' he shouted. I could see he had already worked himself into a temper. 'I can't do this myself, so get on with it, damn you,' and he simply ran out of the room.

Eighteen very tired-looking prisoners were wading through the snow in front of me. I am convinced they thought they were being taken to some camp. We were situated in or just on the edge of the wood, the next wood was about two miles away in the direction of the regimental HQ and I could see in the snow the sledge tracks and hoofprints of Captain Lorenzen and his escort.

I was just as tired as they, maybe even more so because I was in a dilemma and only the cold bitter air kept my senses awake. We were really creeping along, but I did not care—this was too much and completely against my grain.

I had a long debate with myself and even when I considered all the things in favour of shooting the lot I concluded that it had to be a decision between telling a whopping great lie and committing cold-blooded murder. I believe that, deep down, I had already made up my mind—anyway, what was wrong with a lie if the lives of eighteen men were at stake? Maybe Captain Schutte was expecting one, he had so clearly washed his hands of the whole thing.

I decided to march them to the wood, it wasn't too far off now. One or two of the prisoners kept on looking around, giving me questioning looks. The majority of them were older men, their greatcoats hanging rather loose on them, of an olive-brownish colour; they hadn't any belts left, and their felt boots were in tatters. I put myself in their place and wondered what they were thinking, and at the same time wished myself many miles away.

When we reached the wood I waved them on, to keep going, and then I changed my mind because I sensed danger in letting them move into trees. Some might make a run for it, and I might be forced to shoot. I shouted to them to stop and indicated with my machine-pistol for them to line up. I then saw the alarm in their faces. One of the older ones ripped his front open, and clutching a cross on a string said in a pleading voice. 'Malenkuye, Magda,' (little children, wife). I could not stand it any more, and waved my hand in the direction of the wood, lowered my machine-pistol and turned to go back. I didn't turn around for some time, but after I'd gone about twenty metres, I looked over my shoulder, and to my relief could see no one about.

On my return, for the first time since I had joined the army I did not make a report, and when I saw Captain Schutte the next day it was about a completely different matter.

This different matter had to do with two horses. Later that day, after I had not exactly obeyed orders, Krizock and I set off at nightfall in the direction of our neighbouring regiment, some twelve miles south-west. Since Kruger was with Captain Lorenzen on the sledge, I borrowed his little mare; she was very stocky, virtually a pony. We approached, enemy fashion, the village where the regiment was quartered, and then once we were in the village went blatantly along the road there until we found out where that regiment's rider troop kept their horses.

We knew that they had been in the village for some time and reckoned that they would have had time to find a large barn for the horses. Sure enough, we found it, and luckily only a few hundred metres from where we had entered the village. We dismounted and I told Krizock to be at the ready for when I would return with, I hoped, some horses. 'In the meantime, keep quiet and get out of the way if anyone approaches,' I said. There were many horses in the barn as I could tell from the warmth and smell. The entrance had a large cloth or tarpaulin pinned across it. I could see a guard walking slowly along the centre of the barn in the dim light provided by a small oil lamp hanging from a central beam. He was walking away from me, his hands buried deep in his pockets, his shoulders hunched, trying to keep warm. I went back just outside the tarpaulin and took a handful of snow, pressed it hard between my hands, making it into a solid ball, and threw it across to the other side of the barn. Peeping inside again I saw the guard walking to the other entrance to investigate the noise. That was my chance and I took it, grabbing the first two horses on my right nearest the entrance—thank goodness, they had only their leading rope fastened by a simple knot, they wore bridles but no bits. I pulled them back and diving between them, head down, lifted the tarpaulin. They both followed without a sound. They were big horses and it took two goes before I got on one. Now I only wanted to get away quickly, and, digging my heels in, I trotted on to the road, where Krizock was waiting. Not a word was spoken until we reached the end of the village and I asked Krizock to canter ahead to lead the way as my horses were a bit sluggish to say the least.

'Well, I'll be blowed,' said Krizock. 'They are marvellous horses;' and I could hardly believe it myself, it had been all too easy.

On our arrival we put the two horses in the barn with the rest till the morning, when I could look for a suitable saddle in daylight. I was naturally becoming excited, anticipating a decent ride again after the small, tired mounts I had had to borrow since my Siegfried had been killed.

My dream was short-lived. Only after a few minutes of putting my new horse (a beautiful bronze mare) through her paces, a squad of riders approached. It was hardly daylight and I sensed trouble right away. As they came nearer I could hear excited voices, and someone shouted, 'There she is!' They were looking at me. Since I was in front of the battalion HQ I had to keep up a front, and I turned to them and asked, 'Are you looking for someone?'

'Not any more—we've found what we came for. You are riding our commanding officer's horse. The Colonel won't be too pleased if he finds out.'

'Finds out what?' I directed my question at the rider in front, a tall fellow and seemingly the leader of the squad.

'I am Sergeant Janke of 434 Regiment Rider Troop. Two of our horses went missing last night. The tracks led here, and you are riding the Colonel's horse.'

'I am Sergeant Kuhnert,' I countered, 'and two horses did come our way—you were fortunate that they ran to us and not to the Russians. If I were you I would make sure that in future they cannot run about.' What a pity, she is a nice mare and just the horse I'd been looking for, I thought.

The door opened at that moment and Captain Schutte stood there waiting for an explanation of the commotion. Sergeant Janke pulled his horse towards the Captain and, introducing himself, dismounted and explained.

Captain Schutte looked at me and waving me to come over, said, 'Well, everything seems to be in order,' then '... Right, Sergeant Kuhnert? Let them have the horse and say no more about it.' Sergeant Janke turned around and said that two horses had been stolen, not just one, the other one belonged to the Adjutant.

'Stolen?' Captain Schutte thundered. 'Who said anything about being *stolen*? Did you, Sergeant?'

'No, sir. Missing, I meant to say.'

'I should think so,' Captain Schutte said and, looking at me, continued, 'You wouldn't do a thing like that, would you, Kuhnert?'

'Oh no, sir. I need a horse all right, but stealing, never.'

'Well, there you are,' said Captain Schutte. 'My regards to your Colonel, Sergeant, and off you go.'

I could not help feeling rather sheepish as I dismounted and took the bit out. I knew that they knew we had pinched their horses, but since they had recovered them, Sergeant Janke would have to invent some cock-and-bull story to tell the Colonel of his regiment of how the horses had gone missing. Besides, he had no proper proof, had he, now?

Captain Schutte gave me a knowing grin after they had left; I think he felt he had rather redeemed himself after his behaviour the day before when he had passed the buck and stormed out of the room. 'See what you can do at the regimental HQ—maybe they can spare you one,' he said. He added, 'By the way, we are entitled to send a dozen men there for a little film show.'

I looked at him puzzled. 'Yes,' he said. 'A unit has come our way to entertain the troops. I only got to hear about it late last night. You can also get your clothing fixed. Oh, and bring the post back if it has not already been collected by Captain Lorenzen's sledge party.'

Regimental HQ was about seven or eight miles away—a long way if one had to wade through deep snow, but there was already a nice track made by the traffic. The sun was shining, blinding us, except of course in the wooded areas, and our party of twelve, including Sergeant Gebert and Corporals Krizock and Hallach set off cheerfully.

'Keep your eyes open for Kruger and Godecke—they should be on their way back, unless they've also been invited to the film show,' I suggested. 'We don't want to be shot at.'

We were telling jokes and on the whole everybody was in a good mood. Maybe it was because of the treat ahead or because for a couple of days we had had no shooting matches with the Russians, not even artillery shells or any strafing by planes. Now I started to get worried, because a longish pause usually meant a kind of build-up, prelude to some offensive, the calm before the storm. Oh, what the hell, I told myself, forget about it for a day, don't spoil it for the others.

It was just like a homecoming when we arrived at the small hamlet where our regimental HQ was situated. The first thing we were after was a decent meal—bad luck for us though, it would take at least a couple of hours we were told. Weisenberger, the cook, had been promoted Sergeant. I could see the newness of his silver ribbons on his collar and shoulder pads. He grinned with genuine pleasure when he shook my hand; I could feel he was pleased to see me.

He also, however, had some bad news for me: Captain Ebert and the supply wagons had been ambushed. They had only found a few bodies, the rest, including horses and wagons, had disappeared. Nobody could identify the bodies properly— all had been mutilated except Sergeant Kleiner's, which was why they knew it had been Captain Ebert's unit.

I said to Sergeant Weisenberger that, in my opinion, the supply wagons had never had proper protection, it had all been too easygoing.

Weisenberger said, 'It's most likely that they ran into some partisans, poor devils.'

'What are you going to do now?' I asked. 'I mean, you haven't had any supplies coming, have you?'

'Oh, that has been seen to,' he said. 'Food is always a priority, especially with the regimental staff.'

Lorenz was about, and so was Petrov, the man I took prisoner in the summer. When he saw me he came to me and asked when I would come back. I told him about my Siegfried; he was absolutely shocked, he had grown very fond of Siegfried too. Captain Lorenzen, I was told, had gone, with an escort, to the main dressing station, and Kruger and Godecke were about to return to our battalion HQ, so I made sure they took the post, etc. back.

In front of a large barn were two vehicles—the film unit, I was told. The show went on all the time, except at night: over and again they showed one big film and the *Wochenschau* (the weekly newsreel), a bit out of date but we did not expect anything else, after all we were an awful long way from home.

In the barn there were some planks to sit on and the cold was kept out with a lot of sacking and blankets, it served also to keep the barn in darkness. The film was *Die Fledermaus*. The music alone was so marvellous, it brought tears to many eyes; it was just like a miracle in the depths of Russia. There we were, linking arms to keep close for warmth and also to steady ourselves because the beams and other implements we were sitting on were not exactly armchairs (though we did not mind at all) and taking it all in.

Half-way through, though, we became alarmed—not only could we all smell smoke, but we all began to choke. That, we discovered, was caused by some idiots practising throwing smoke candles right next door to the film show. Most of the smoke had been sucked into the barn. It took half an hour or so to clear the barn of the smoke and by the time we were asked to go back in the place was like an ice-house.

The swearing was too spicy to mention.

Afterwards, I went to see Colonel von Gratz and told him all about Captain Lorenzen. He wasn't in a very good mood and I decided to forget about what I had wanted to ask him, namely what the chances were of my getting a new horse. I mentioned it to Major Mauve instead and he promised to do his best.

The long-anticipated meal was ready at last. Weisenberger even lent me one of his precious tin plates—knife, fork and spoon were always in our pockets. Nobody knew what we were eating but it tasted delicious. If I had known then what it was I don't think I would have eaten a single bit. I, the renowned horseman and horse-lover, had devoured horse-stew. Everybody enjoyed it, including me.

All too quickly, the day was over. We had been told to be back before nightfall, so, still filled with the marvellous melodies of *Die Fledermaus*, we started for home.

Weisenberger, the cook, thrust a small bundle into my hand, and Petrov told me once more how badly he missed me. At the moment he was employed in a job he had never dreamt of doing. He had to pedal to keep the drill going for the dentist. I just screamed with laughter. I imagined him standing there having to listen all day long to the patients' cries of pain. Well, at least it would keep him warm. Then another figure came towards us, waving frantically and shouting. It was Erich. 'Hello, Max. You weren't thinking of leaving already, without even saying hello to your old buddy, were you?'

'Of course not. I just couldn't find you,' I said. 'Where were you hiding out?'

He and his troops had their quarters at the other end of the village, and he had found out that we were in town, so to speak, from the regimental HQ. He had something special for me. 'Can I have your field bottle, Max, in exchange for mine?' 'Sure,' I said, thinking he just wanted a kind of souvenir, then I realised that Erich wasn't this kind of man.

'It's full of the best vodka, Max. Have a drink on me.'

Bless his heart, I thought, what a splendid comrade; he knew that the life in the battalion wasn't easy.

'Keep your chin up, Max, spring will soon be here, and maybe it will soon be our turn to go on leave.' Well, one could always dream....

My bottle was only half full of lukewarm tea. I put my arm around his shoulder and turning away from everyone, asked him if there was anything in the wind that I ought to know.

'Hmm,' he said, 'there is always something brewing. The only fact I know is that there are several *Sturmgeschütze* [heavy tanks] about, and they wouldn't be getting ready if we were to stay much longer in our present position.'

'I knew it,' I shouted.

'You knew what?'

'Oh, just a feeling,' I said, and explained the very quietness of everything.

'Come to think of it, you're right,' Erich said. 'Let's hope everything goes well. You just look after yourself, and if I get a horse for you, I'll send it over right away.'

'Thanks, Erich, and take it easy also. See you.'

This was my last conversation with Erich. He and his men went out on a scouting mission only two days later and never returned.

I was shattered when I learned about it. Captain Schutte told me himself, saying. 'I know you knew him very well. Poor devils, there's not a chance, after five days, of any of them returning.'

16

Walpurgis Night

On the 8 March 1942, I wrote in my diary: 'The engagement against the Soviet airborne troops is very difficult, one village after another must be taken. We have a tough time with our two remaining horses. Sleep is almost impossible as all the houses left are overcrowded and we, the scout troop, sleep sitting in the snow.'

And on 13 March 1942: 'It has started to snow again and drifting makes everything difficult, the ice particles seem to find their way practically through our clothing and into the eyes, ears and nostrils and it is bitterly cold. When will this damn winter stop?'

Sergeant Gebert had attached himself to our troop. I was very pleased, now I didn't have to worry about every little thing or detail myself.

That morning Corporal Hallach had to report to Battalion HQ, which was situated in a filthy cowshed, draughty and freezing cold. When he got back to me he said, 'I am promoted to sergeant and have to report to 5th Company right away.' His lips were still trembling and I knew he didn't like it one little bit. It meant he had to leave everything behind, except his bundle which he was able to carry, and move into one of the foxholes in the woods. We had a very thin line there, it was almost like a sentence, despite the promotion.

He handed me his horses: I really felt for him. Walther Kruger, his buddy for quite some time, said, 'I also wanted to become a sergeant, but not like this.'

The next day, a brilliant, sunny day, all hell was let loose. We had just been told that it would be the last day for us, and that Regiment 434 would overlap us to give us some rest, when the attack came. I believe everything the Russians could muster they sent over. First we had air attacks, then came rockets from a 'Stalin Organ', after that mortar and artillery fire. I kept on looking up from the snow where I had buried my face and seeing the colours of black, white and red. They were everywhere: black from the explosions, the white of the snow, and red from the spilled blood. It seemed as though I was not really there; at least, I felt like an observer, as I watched so many crumple and then lie still, and heard others screaming. Bullets were exploding all about us. There was no place to run to any more, and in any case, most of us were too exhausted; the only thing I was hoping for was to be killed outright, or wounded in the limbs—mind you, not too badly. Being wounded internally meant the end in any case, as we had no dressing station in our area.

Periodically, someone had to scramble to Battalion HQ and back, to report on positions. It was Wally Kruger's turn and he did very well at first; then he did a stupid thing; instead of creeping low on his return, he waded almost upright for the last twenty metres or so. Someone shouted at him, 'Get your bloody head down!' Then he fell forward. At first I thought he had heeded the warning, then I saw that although he had lifted an arm up, he was making no headway towards us.

'Get him quickly!' I shouted. 'He is hurt.' We had been situated behind some snow heaps and two men dashed out to pull him to safety. Already the tell-tale pink air bubbles were on Kruger's lips.

'Lie very still,' I said. 'Don't move, whatever you do; we'll soon get you into care, don't worry, Wally.'

'Is it bad?' he asked.

'Ssh,' I answered. 'Not if you keep quiet.' But Wally, like most of the lung-shot cases, started to wiggle about, and in the end we had to strap him to the sledge we used to fetch provisions. Richard Eli, a clerk from HQ, volunteered to take him back to the regimental HQ where he was likely to get better help for Wally.

Wally said to me in a whisper, before Eli pulled him through the by now very deep snow, 'I won't become a sergeant now, will I?'

'Don't be daft,' I reassured him. 'You are just going home for a little while, but when you come back, we'll see. All right?' He died on the way to HQ, Private Eli told me the next morning. He just wouldn't lie still and then he convulsed, then it was all over. One little stray bullet, I thought. Wally was married with a baby daughter in Dortmund. Now I would have to tell his young wife. It just wasn't fair.

We had to shovel snow to make way for our heavy tanks, hoping the while that those monsters would not get stuck before they reached us. Before they arrived the Russians counter-attacked, but this time from behind their T34s, and there were plenty of them—we thanked God for our 88mm flak guns. Just the same, the Russians kept on coming, it was almost as if they were being driven forward. We had two machine-guns, which kept on hammering away, but it seemed as if an enormous Hydra was confronting us, screaming their chilling sound of 'Uriagh, Uriagh!', the more we mowed down the more appeared. My hands were actually burning from firing my machine-pistol when they came too near, and then I had no more magazines left, and wouldn't have any till we got some with our next supplies. We threw all our hand grenades and prayed that our machine-guns wouldn't jam. Then Captain Lauber of the 14th appeared from nowhere and shouted to us to draw back to a better position—'I've got my guns at the ready.'

So, one by one, we retreated, feeling safer already, and then our tanks arrived, only three of them, but what a beautiful sight for us.

Counting the cost, I wrote in my diary: 'We have had many casualties, 43 dead and 71 wounded.' It was 26 March 1942. It had been a bitter blow for us, especially as we had already been hard-pressed for men.

Behind our tanks were the first companies of Regiment 434 to overlap us. God knows, we needed the rest badly.

The terrain around us looked like a butcher's shop the next morning. Bodies were everywhere, some with most of their clothing torn off by the blasts, and many limbs were strewn about. It was simply ghastly. As we tried to pick our way between them, the hard frozen bodies clinked like porcelain when accidentally knocked. We had to get away from this terrible scene. In any case, all the buildings had been completely destroyed or burnt down so there was no shelter for us.

The village we moved into, a few miles to the north, provided a place of refuge, where we could lick our wounds. Behind us we could hear explosions but they were nothing to worry about. It was the burial commandos, blasting holes—there were usually ten men to one hole, rolled into a tent sheet, if there were any left. The ground was frozen for about 1½ metres down, so it wasn't very easy to get deep enough, there were just too many to be buried. We huddled together in the only decent barn still standing and with a roof. We also had all our casualties with us, some badly wounded; there wasn't much we could do for them, except to cover them up, keep them warm and wait until eventually the magic figure of a doctor would appear. Doctors were very scarce, and medicine and bandages even more so.

We all looked very grey, at least everybody I saw did and I don't suppose I was an exception, and eyes were becoming very sunken. The whole hopeless mess was too much, nobody even spoke any more, we were too tired and disillusioned.

For two days we holed up in that stinking barn, it was the only shelter. The groaning and whimpering of the wounded was getting unbearable. Only one orderly from the regiment had arrived, he had enough serum for most of the wounded, but the paper bandages soon got soaked and started to freeze. 'My God,' I thought, 'will we ever get out of this?'

It was 29 March 1942. We got the order to move out, but then, just before we got going, a couple of sledges arrived with the supplies we had all been praying for. We stayed on for another day and night, feeling much better after our first hot meal (lentil soup), and I actually had a shave, the first for quite some days. I also had toothache and told the orderly about it.

'Lucky fellow,' he said, and turned towards the wounded; many had died during the night. I felt rather ashamed for a moment . . . well, I had only hoped for some tablets. I know that some men had actually lost teeth, they just broke and fell out, it was because we had no greens to eat and most of the time were living on scraps like bread, horsemeat, or black potatoes.

I had been feeling rather lonely lately, especially when we had a pause in the fighting. Maybe I had more time to think; one by one, all my friends had disappeared, and conversation was impossible. The only men I really knew and trusted were Krizock and Godecke, by now we had known one another for a long time. Sergeant Gebert, who had attached himself to our small unit, was a nice enough fellow, but then again he was an infantry man, we were of the cavalry; and sometimes he seemed too frightened for my liking and very unsure of himself. He had been a clerk in Battalion HQ and had been in charge of writing those awful letters to the relatives in Germany when we had casualties. He was kind enough to arrange the sending of the short letter I had written to Wally Kruger's widow, besides the official one.

On 6 April 1942 we heard the good news that a few of our regiment had actually set off on leave to Germany. One had to be married with six children to be on top of the list—rank didn't play any part—but there were exceptional circumstances, for instance, if one had lost members of the family through bombing.

We marched the following morning, somewhat refreshed, but still full of misgivings. Some of us had had post from home, which had come with the supplies the day before. Burgwedel, a large, black-bearded chap from 1 Company of our battalion, had received a letter with the official police stamp, informing him that his house had disappeared in the bombing raid in Düsseldorf, his wife and two children were no more. I will never forget the man's face, it somehow seemed to alter and age rapidly. His shoulders slumped forward, and then he took a key out of his pocket, turned slowly and threw the key far away. He took a few steps forward and dived headlong into the ground, burying his face in the snow. And Burgwedel's case was by no means an isolated one.

I had a letter from my mother in Dresden. She wrote of Kurt, my eldest brother, now a soldier in the air force. He was now, she told me (as Lotte had written to me) a clerk in the Paymaster's Office of Rommel's Afrikakorps, and was on his way to North Africa. Trust him, I thought (but without rancour), to get an easy position—and in a warm country, too.

I somehow became more aware of the fierce cold as I read this. It was a clear morning and there seemed to be two suns—one was a reflection in the extremely cold atmosphere, I was told. My mother also wrote that my father was a guard or porter in some war production complex. And that my sister,

Lotte, was fretting about her husband Wilhelm—she hadn't heard anything from him for a long time. He also was on the Russian front. At least my mother was cheerful enough, she even said, 'We don't have to worry about being bombed in Dresden, we are too far in the east for their planes.'

Our destination was only a few miles further north towards Vyaz'ma, a small hamlet called Pretishova, where we relieved the 1st Battalion—at least there were some warmed-up quarters for us, nothing posh, but homely in comparison with our big stinking old barn.

We soon settled in, and I even found a shelter for our two remaining horses. Poor creatures, they both looked very poorly, even with the hay we had received lately by parachute. The real problem was still the lack of water though we kept a large bucket full of snow constantly over a fire. Would it ever get a little warmer? Perhaps warm enough so the river would flow again? The River Ugra wasn't too far from us, but it was still frozen solid.

As always when there wasn't much fighting, I was snooping about one day, looking for felt to mend my soles again when I came across some skis. In fact there were a lot of them heaped up in a corner, but some had been broken up for firewood. They had been left behind by a Russian unit who had been surprised and had gone in a hurry. Since the terrain was hilly I slipped a pair on to my enormous felt boots, it wasn't too difficult, the Russians had probably also worn felt boots. There was nothing sophisticated in their skis—they were in fact very primitive indeed—but I had ski'd as a boy and I just could not resist them. I must have looked a proper nana with my makeshift attire, especially the parachute cape, flowing behind me as I whooshed down the hill. Our outposts, two of them, were waving and shouting; I waved back, it was very exhilarating, and for a moment, it was like being on a skiing holiday. When I reached the bottom of the hill, approaching the river, I saw the blasted things, exposed by the ever-present icy wind—mines. It was too late for me to turn or even to stop, I was already in the middle of them, gliding right over the top of them. One wouldn't have thought that in that cold one could get or feel colder, but believe me, an ice-cold shiver hit me right down my spine. Now I knew why the outposts had waved and shouted, they had been warning me.

I kept on gliding in a large half-circle, till I was almost sure I was free of the minefield. Still apprehensive, I kept on looking for exposed mines, but again I had escaped a nasty disaster, and I arrived safely on the other side of the hill at the spot I had started from.

We left Pretishova on 15 April and moved into the forest area about sixteen kilometres further north. We had several attacks from some

Russian ground troops, but our flanks were well protected by our companies who were armed with 88mm anti-aircraft guns because of the T34s of which there seemed to be more about of late.

In our wooded area there were no houses at all, but only two kilometres away we found some remains of a village. So we salvaged all the old beams, timbers and so forth, and shifted them into the wood and began to build some bunkers. This was a new experience for us. Even our two horses were made to work—I used them to pull some beams through the snow.

On the 24th, we were actually able to get some water for the first time, from some small streams. Immediately, however, we were warned not to drink any without boiling it first because there were suspected dead bodies further upstream. It is never without trouble, I thought. Nevertheless, we all felt there was a glimmer of hope—spring had to come some time.

No sooner had we finished, more or less, constructing ourselves a shelter, and a very primitive one at that, I was ordered to go on a scouting mission with Company Sergeant Hamann and Captain Schutte, on foot this time. In any case, Sergeant Hamann had never been on a horse, he told me. The mission was a kind of inspection tour of the Company outposts. I looked forward to seeing Sergeant Hallach again, and scrounged some vodka for his bottle from the cook.

It was strictly march compass work. In some places the snow was chest high, and it was still drifting, especially at night when it was also freezing. We changed around every so often because the front man was a kind of snowplough on legs. When we got into the denser forest the snow wasn't quite so deep, but still the going was very slow. We had passed our battalion's guard some time ago and were now in the terrain where we had to look out for our outposts. Those poor devils were really in the forefront, and no longer had anything between them and the Russian posts. We weren't out because we expected trouble—we simply had to make sure that they were still there. Because the daytime temperature had risen a bit it was no longer necessary to fire the machine-guns now and then to keep them from freezing, and so we could not hear the outposts any more. We really did have to look for them now, and of course they did not know we were looking for them, so we had to be doubly careful, even if we came from the rear.

I must say it was rather nerve-racking, not a sound anywhere.

'Look for tracks,' Captain Schutte said, and turning to me he said even more softly, 'I'm always very scared, I am really a coward, you know.' I just smiled at him—well, what else could I do or say? He hadn't much experience in this sort of thing, otherwise he would have known that everybody is scared in those situations.

We looked closely at every cluster of bushes, first on the ground and then up, and up is where we had our first contact. Up went our left arms twice. It was Hallach who broke the silence. 'Nothing doing around here,' he shouted, grinning from ear to ear; plainly he was pleased to see us. Oh, how I felt for him and his three comrades, huddled in a sort of treehouse.

'How are you?' I said, handing him the field bottle with vodka.

'Bloody awful, and . . . well, I'll be glad to get out of here. Are you here to relieve us?' The silence was embarrassing, even Captain Schutte, I could see, was taken aback by this question.

'Not this time, Ratze,' I said. (Ratze was his nickname).

I told him all the good news first, what there was of it, like the winter clothing had arrived at Regimental HQ and we would soon get ours. Captain Schutte pulled some letters out of his coat. Ratze was still grinning, even after I told him about Wally, his buddy-buddy.

We continued on our way and found another four outposts, much more easily this time, as Hallach had told us where they were.

We were wacked by the time we got home, some home. It was freezing again, and overhead we could hear the Russian observation plane, the 'duty sergeant' we called it, so we knew it must be 2200 hours, as it was always on time.

It was now 30 April 1942. For many days we had again been suffering Russian mortar fire, and only because we were in the woods and pretty well bunkered did we have no more than a few casualties. In the end Captain Schutte had had enough. 'We have got to do something about those blighters, we will not get any peace otherwise.' What a good joke! 'Take as many men as you need and find out how many there are, take a couple of prisoners if possible, we must get some results.' It was me he was speaking to, and for the first time in the whole war I felt frightened, in a different way, if there is such a thing. I just wanted to protest, even plead, with him not to send me, yet in spite of this I heard myself saying, 'I think we'll manage all right, Captain. When do you think is the best time?'

'Well,' he said, 'it's up to you—any time, really.'

It was afternoon, and the shells kept on coming at irregular intervals. How different from the French, they had always been very tidy—one could almost take a walk in between with them—but not so with the Russians; what an untidy lot, I thought.

Seeing the snow clouds overhead, I decided to go at night. There was a fairly large plain to cross to reach the next forest edge; after that it was anyone's guess where the mortar units were hiding. Captain Lorenzen's idea of approaching from the rear was, in my opinion, still the best. 'That is all very well,' Captain Schutte replied when I said this, 'but we haven't got the men, Kuhnert.'

We set off at nightfall, I took only Krizock and Godecke, knowing that I could rely on them. Sergeant Gebert approached me saying, 'Look, Max, I haven't been on a scout yet, will you take me?'

This took me by surprise. 'Of course, Waldemar,' I answered and had to stop myself smiling (in German this is a dainty name) as I thought to myself, how appropriate—it was the first time I had spoken his name.

'I'll be all right,' he said, and I detected slight apprehension in his voice.

'Take only an MP and nothing else?' Godecke had his trusted Mauser, Krizock also, like myself, a machine-pistol, and there were several assorted hand grenades for everybody. The most important items were our parachute capes.

I then said, 'Whatever happens, we must not be seen, especially when we cross the plain. It is only about three hundred metres across; we have to keep very low and creep, no rushing—any sudden movement could give us away. I don't know if they are on the forest edge or on the other side of it.'

The snow had melted in the daytime, so we had about two foot of snow and one foot of ice-water underneath, it was awful, it soaked through our boots in no time. 'What a lousy mission,' I thought, lift your boot out, plunge the other one in, and heave to pull the other one out, every time you do so it gives a plop. . . I was in front to start off with, and when we came near to the plain, Sergeant Gebert—or Waldemar—took over. I whispered, in between the plops, 'Keep straight, with the edge on the right. When we are there we can swerve to the left and then comb the wood.'

Krizock was next to take the lead, and I told him the same.

'All right, Max, we'll make it all right.' What a splendid man Krizock was, very brave, intelligent and reliable. If anyone should be a sergeant he was the one I would choose. We were about half-way across and Godecke was about to take over as the human snowplough, when the skies lit up, followed by a crack—it was a flare, and it was now slowly floating to the ground. Everything was like daylight. Instead of whispering I shouted, 'Keep still!'

Another one, another and another, the cracks came, always between, we were sitting ducks. I said, 'We have to turn back, but only if we get fired on'. The word 'fire' was hardly out of my mouth, when we got it.

'Get back quickly and keep low, we must get out of their firing range.' The bullets were ripping into the snow and it was only a matter of time before they must hit us. More flares lit up the sky, my heart sank and fear crept into my very soul. 'Run, damn you!' I shouted, as mortar shells exploded nearby.

Gebert screamed, 'I've been hit, Max.'

'Come on just the same.'

'I can't, Max. Don't leave me.'

Krizock and Godecke were already getting near the forest edge where we had set out from.

I stared at the scene in horror. Was this possible? There wasn't even a sound from Gebert, just a gurgle. I turned to Waldemar.

'Come on, you can make it.' And he walked, I never knew how, but he did. I was in a hurry to get to Krizock and Godecke. What a mess. They were practically lying on top of each other, and I could see they had been badly torn apart. I had reached the forest edge and turning towards Gebert, was confronted with an almighty flash. My right arm came up automatically in front of my face. It felt as though I had touched some electric live wire, nothing more, except the warm trickle of blood down my sleeve.

'Come on, Waldemar, we are nearly there.' There was another flash and this time I heard a terrible scream. I still remember realising that it was Walpurgis Night, the eve of May Day, the night the witches danced on the top of the Brocken mountain in Germany.

Captain Schutte was walking up and down, saying to me, 'Kuhnert you did your best so stop blaming yourself. You too could have been killed—by the way, how is your arm? It looks pretty torn and bloody.' When I got my coat off it started to hurt for the first time, up until now I had other things on my mind. The wound was on my right upper arm; if I hadn't lifted it to protect my face, I would also be lying out there. I felt very tired suddenly. One of the staff kept on dabbing the blood off, it wasn't a very big wound but it hurt as if somebody was twisting my muscle. They had also cut my sleeve length-wise so it could be worn over the bandage. After eating something, I got a new bandage and then slumped on to my bunk. I woke up several times during the night feeling very dry in the mouth. I knew I had a high temperature.

17

'Do Not Kill Your Neighbours' Chickens'

The next morning, 1 May 1942, Captain Schutte was standing in front of me, saying, 'Get your stuff, Kuhnert, Eil will accompany you to regimental HQ.' (Eil was the only messenger left in our battalion HQ.) 'You are in no condition to go by yourself.' Apparently I still had a high temperature and had been talking in my sleep. Also, my upper arm had swollen to an enormous size and was very tender. I just shook hands with Captain Schutte, slung my few belongings over my left shoulder and followed Eil who was already in front. My boots were still very wet and I was glad that it had turned considerably milder.

On our arrival at Regimental HQ I reported as best I could to Colonel von Gratz, explaining the happenings. He had already heard by telephone, and, smiling at me, he said, 'Well, congratulations, Kuhnert. Let's hope your arm doesn't turn nasty or you could be the envy of us all'.

I could not help thinking how low morale had sunk—if everybody was thinking along those lines, we might as well have stayed at home. Maybe that would have been best.

Petrov was very concerned and insisted on taking me the following morning to the main dressing station, about fifteen miles south-west. A pony and sledge had been provided, that was about all I could remember; I was still delirious, with a very high temperature. I had been given an injection of something, but maybe it was taking longer than expected to get through into the bloodstream.

Clutching my left hand with my right one, because it had become really painful, I slumped in the sledge. I was still not completely aware of what was really going on, but after a few miles and several stretches of walking beside the sledge because of bad terrain, I felt my head was clearing. Petrov was looking at me very anxiously, and when he saw me smiling at him, his face lit up. I could understand his concern, we were still in an area where one could expect a surprise from the Russians, sometimes some fighters would appear from nowhere, and, in the open as we were at the moment, it could get nasty. Petrov was unarmed—even if we had trusted him completely, it just was not on to issue him with any kind of firearm—so the only weapon we had was my P38 on my belt, everything else I had left behind, such as binoculars, compass and my trusty machine-pistol.

I still couldn't believe it—I was actually going homewards; but my arm worried me very much, I had seen too many of our chaps go to sleep and never wake up after gangrene had set in, with no one to help properly. However, we arrived safely at the main dressing station, a largish barn in a small village. The barn had been partitioned off to create a sort of operating theatre, with, behind a large tarpaulin, a ward next to it.

At this point, Petrov came to me to say goodbye. He held both my hands, and then he put his arm around my shoulders, said something in Russian and turned away. I knew that there were tears in his eyes; what would become of him? I wondered.

Everybody was bedded down on straw, unless you had some excuse to stand up. Since there had been a lull in the arrival of casualties, it was my turn right away to be seen by the field doctor in charge. After the orderly had taken my bandage off, the doctor felt my upper arm which was still very swollen; I think he was probing for bits of schrapnel. I could have kicked him, it was agony.

'Take off the ring on your right hand,' he then said. 'When did you have your last meal?'

'What has that got to do with it?' I said.

'We've got to take the arm off, otherwise you might not survive.'

I jumped two metres back and without thinking shouted, 'You are not taking my arm off!'

In disbelief this man, in his bloodstained clothing, just growled at me. It sounded much like 'Get out' or 'Get lost'. So I left, a very shaken man.

Staggering through all the patients lying on the barn floor in rows, I found a place next to an elderly chap, and we started chatting.

'What's up?' he asked.

'Oh, they want to take my arm off and I'm having none of it. What is life without my right arm?'

'What are you going to do now?' he said.

'The only thing you can do is get the swelling down,' a voice next to me said. He was a small chap, an orderly with the rank of corporal. He sat down next to me and very kindly explained the obnoxious menace of the head surgeon. 'He upsets everybody, don't take any notice of him, he is a real butcher, he just likes cutting off limbs.' Nudging me, he pointed to the elderly chap next to me and whispered in my ears, 'He cut off his legs.' Shocked, I looked down to detect the missing legs, and said to the orderly, 'He told me only a minute ago that his feet were itching.'

'That does happen when you lose limbs,' the orderly explained. 'It's the nerves, you know.'

'What do you think I can do to get the swelling down?'

'Put snow on it and keep doing it, it's the only way.'

Across from where I was lying there was a very young fellow, his legs were pulled up and so were his arms, all bandaged, of course, but just the same they were roped up to the rafters—there were no ceilings in those barns. Another chap was holding a lighted cigarette, and now and then put it to the young fellow's lips. I couldn't believe my ears—they were actually laughing and joking; I felt like I was in a very strange dream.

Later on, after I had seen many similar kinds of cases, I found that the most severe cases, especially amputations, were always very cheerful, while minor injuries brought a great many groans and exaggerations to my notice. Maybe I was very fortunate with just my arm. I did what the orderly suggested and after a couple of days the swelling had gone down considerably.

On 3 May, we, the wounded, were told to get ready for a journey to Alexanndrovkoye, about 45 kilometres south-west from our dressing station. We stayed on until the 9th.

I had the chance to write to my mother, to let her know on the very first line that I was perfectly all right. My writing was pretty bad as it was the first time I had written with my left hand. My right arm had been propped up to keep it still, and doing even the simplest thing with just my left arm was an absolutely ridiculous performance. For instance, the everyday functions became a nightmare—combing my hair, shaving, going to the toilet or even eating. The blond, young fellow, the one with all his limbs strapped up high, told us all about his encounter with the Russians, when several others were inspecting a broken telephone wire. They had the telephone wire, which was lying along the ground, and were probing for broken points, when, from the opposite direction, some other Germans approached—or so they thought: they were in fact Russians in German uniform. The Russians opened fire right away, from the hip, with sub-machine-guns. Our young friend and his comrades were hit and as they lay on the ground in the deep snow were sprayed with more fire. All of them died, except our young chap. He had had about forty hits, but all of them in his limbs, none internal. Sightings of Russians in German uniform had been reported all along the front—this was why so many of our comrades who had been killed had by the time we found them been stripped. It was incredible luck for the blond Bavarian.

When we arrived in Alexanndrovkoye we all hoped that the war on the Russian front would be over for us, at least for the time being. However, we were only a few miles west of the Russian front line, despite our journey south-west—the front line was indeed very crooked—and we were buzzed by Russian planes several times during our stay at this very large dressing station. The station was housed in an enormous barn, with several outhouses attached to it. The bunks were filled with straw, which was alive with bugs. I was particularly unlucky and had to bed down right next to the surgery.

There was a battle going on, not too far from us—apparently the Russians were trying hard to break through—and many desperate cases came in or, should I say, were carried in. The screaming, groaning and even whimpering from grown-up men made me feel guilty with just my arm sticking out front on a wire support. One chap was lying on the ground on straw which was wet from being trodden on too much. He had been dragged from the surgery—there were not enough helpers about—with his head bandaged all over, his face completely covered with only his mouth and nose free. He was lying very still among the others, most of whom had already had treatment and were lying with resigned faces, possibly under sedation. Then suddenly he convulsed and gave a gurgled cry, was violently sick and then lay still. I went to him to see if I could do anything. He was dead.

One of my problems was lice—the beastly things had got inside my bandage. I found a stick and poked with it to get at least some relief by disturbing them. I also had problems getting my braces back on after I had been to one of the latrines. The latrines were highly dangerous and one had to be almost an acrobat to survive a session on those contraptions. They consisted of a large ditch with two crossbars one at each end, in the centre was a hefty beam, lengthwise, and another beam further to the front to put your legs on: just imagine a chap sitting on the centre beam with his pants down—he had to lean well forward because if one overbalanced backwards there was no return. The ditch was quite deep and, as you may imagine, not very inviting either.

The food was terrible here, it had been much better at the last place and there it had been bad enough.

The next day a wagon train was established, made up from sledges and some wagons, and everybody who could get on it was indeed happy. I think everybody who was wounded wanted to get away from this place of death, pain and suffering. There were several heaps of dead bodies back at the surgery. Two chaps, with resigned faces, were dragging one body after another, in very slow motion, to some place of rest.

The journey—about 95 kilometres—to Roslavl', a larger town with train connections, I will never forget. I still thank God many times that I was able to walk and even capable of helping others. When we were slogging along the road, which was only serviceable on one side, we had to stand aside many a time, for more important traffic from the opposite direction. We also got buzzed by Russian fighter planes again.

We made it eventually and were attended for the very first time by some German, female nurses. It had taken us nearly ten days.

After we had stripped, our clothing was put into a cleansing chamber, we had showers and were sprayed with some powder, DDT I believe. With scarcely a pause, we were loaded on to trains to Warsaw, but stopped at Siedice, a location outside Warsaw. There there was a large field hospital with all the necessary equipment. The food here was excellent, and after being deloused, we got real beds, and I felt I was in heaven as I rolled myself carefully on to my left side to fall into a deep sleep.

The next morning was just an unbelievable wonderland, there was even music, and female nurses were running about smiling. Everything was clean and light. I had an X-ray on my arm and was told that four bits of schrapnel, the size of rugged cherry stones, had lodged in my upper arm muscle and if I gave them a chance they should capsulate themselves and if I was careful I should have no problems. We cannot take them out, I was told, as that would mean cutting into the muscle, which would result in a limp arm. Well, I thought, I've got my souvenir from Russia for good, let's make the best of it.

During my second night in my nice clean bed—the bed I had dreamed of so many times, especially when sleeping, or trying to, in the snow—I took stock of the situation, counting the cost. I was alive, but I had lost all my friends, especially my dear brother, Willy. The pain, suffering, heartbreaks, and loss of loved ones, men and horses. I had seen cruelties and destruction and my health was deteriorating, our mental outlook was low.

Those in authority had realised this, which is why we, those about to return to Germany, were each handed a leaflet. On this leaflet were pointed out the rules of civilisation and how to abide by them. 'Do not chase and kill your neighbours' chickens,' the leaflet told us for instance, or 'Stop swearing the way you have got used to doing in Russia'; and there were many more similar injunctions.

At first it seemed very funny, but on reflection it was a sad state of affairs. The more I thought about it the more I began to understand what mankind was doing to itself. Taking all the other happenings into account, I came to the conclusion that this war was lost already, no matter which side one was on. I could not accept or believe that one could blame one person or even one nation, there were too many involved. The truth would surely be known many years after the war, if we are still here. God help us.

Before I fell asleep, I heard laughter from some of the male nurses, followed by the shrieks of some female ones. How could they understand? They had not seen anything yet. It was only a few hundred miles further east that the war in its cruellest form was being fought. But here in the hospital was warmth and security and plenty of food, in comparison.

I had aged in the last twelve months or so, not just time-wise but in understanding. I realised that men, for the sake of power, were willing to have millions slaughtered: the lives of other people meant nothing to them, as long as they themselves were safe, as long as they had their own way. Suffering was for the poor, the stupid ones who trusted and believed their leaders, the ones who believed in decency, the ones who sacrificed their health or even laid down their lives for their comrades.

With those thoughts, I must have fallen asleep.

I was beginning to enjoy life in the hospital. I thanked God that I was wounded only slightly, it was the wound that every soldier on the front prayed for. How long we had to wait before we got to Germany depended on the number of wounded coming in from the front. When there were enough to fill up a train, then we could move on. In the meantime, there were film shows and other entertainments, mostly in the evenings. I wrote several letters to my family in Dresden and friends in Germany. I got on very well writing with my left hand, as my right one was still in a wire cage. Shaving was no problem now since a pretty little nurse had volunteered to do it for me every day; during my last days she also insisted on feeding me, even though I assured her that I could manage with my left hand. 'You'll only make a mess of it,' she said. I suppose that in some respects she was quite right. Cleanliness had to be acquired again, after all the months of animal existence. I got the hang of doing all the other usual things, and only now and then did I have to ask the orderly to give me a hand—especially with fiddly actions like buttoning my braces up.

It was 25 May and my birthday—on the front such things as birthdays and any other celebrations had been completely forgotton; after all, one was never sure if one would see the next day, not to mention the following year. I remembered my last birthday, we were then in Poland, in Mordy, to be exact, the day poor Captain Rothansel nearly came to grief, riding the horse, Mars, or trying to anyway. There he was, hanging on for dear life, while all his fellow officers were leaning out of the windows of the mansion, shouting advice, which he did not hear.

I had no longing for another year like the last ones. I wanted only to forget them, and of course I never shall.

The big day at last arrived, the day we were told to get our few belongings together and be ready to leave the station. Everything I owned I could carry with my left hand quite easily. It consisted only of my despatch case, the one I usually carried on my belt, my P38 and my toilet utensils, the ones I had been given in the hospital. We all had large labels on our chests, with individual medical records written on them; as usual there were many stretcher cases among us. In general, everybody was impatient to set off for Germany. Last of all, everybody got an enormous paper bag with a couple of days' food ration.

Our destination, we were told, was Haguenau, in West Germany (Alsace). For two days and nights we travelled right across Germany, stopping only to get water for the steam engine.

The further we got into Germany the more we could see evidence of bombing, especially in some city areas. I still remember that as we approached Cologne, everybody pointed out that the cathedral was still intact. We arrived at our destination, Niederbronn, on the evening of 29 May 1942 and I for one was extremely glad to be able to stretch my legs, after sitting so long in the very hard uncomfortable train compartments. We had also had very little sleep. The hospital we stayed in for the next few days was marvellous, everybody there was just great, and I felt almost as if I was in dreamland. I also felt a bit guilty—there wasn't really much wrong with me, only my right arm, and that was nothing compared with all the much more severe cases. Treatment started right away; when it was my turn the wire cage was taken off, and to my relief I was allowed to walk about with my arm just in a sling.

Life was beginning for me again, Russia was a long way behind; giving time not only for my arm but also for my mind to heal. Everything would be well, new friends would emerge; leave would be on the cards and no doubt I would tackle all the problems coming my way. But here began another chapter of my life. At the moment I was more than thankful to be in one piece, and was hopeful of a better future.

EPILOGUE

Max Kuhnert was taken prisoner by American troops in Normandy in September 1944, some three months after the Allied invasion of Hitler's 'Fortress Europe'. From there he was transported to the USA, thence through the states of Texas and Oklahoma, and finally to the POW camp at Allen, Virginia, which, after the horrors of war, he came to regard as more of a holiday camp than a prison.

On 5 April 1946, after two years in America, he was sent to England, fetching up at the High Garrett POW camp near Braintree in Essex. Prisoners from that camp were employed in agricultural work, but as Max's trade was that of saddler he was sent to work for Mr E. McDowell, the local saddler in Halstead, the next town on from Braintree.

Romance blossomed between Max and McDowell's daughter, Jean, and on 20 August 1948 they were married. He settled well in Halstead, and Jean bore him three sons, Don, Chris, and Robin. He remained in Mr McDowell's employ until 1966, when he opened his own saddlery business in the town.

Max came to like England greatly, and looked upon it as his home. His family had little knowledge of the traumatic life he had lived before the age of twenty-eight—until, that is, he wrote this book. He returned only once to his home city of Dresden, in 1967, to visit his mother and his sister, Charlotte; he found that the bombing and subsequent rebuilding had changed the city almost beyond recognition. During that same period he also visited his brother Kurt, who had served in the Afrikakorps during the war and who was by then living in Stuttgart with his family.

Max died in Colchester Hospital on 26 June 1990, after a short illness. With him died his personal record of the events between June 1942 and September 1944. All we know of what happened after the point at which this narrative ends is that, after a short leave, he soon returned to the battle lines of Denmark, Belgium and France (where he was wounded twice more), until he was captured by the Americans.

Max Kuhnert's family knew him as a great husband and father, a man who never became cynical or bitter, and who had a fine sense of humour and an ability to live life to the full.

The Family Kuhnert
November 1992